The Insanity of Gambling 2 – Consequences

Christopher Raddings

Contents

Acknowledgements

Chapter highlights

Introduction

Chapters 1 - 13

Acknowledgements

For my Mum Betty. Forever in my heart.

Thank you Karl, Elizabeth and Debbie for whom your help, wisdom and talents helped me to tell the story.
For my close family, Bernard, Debbie, Lisa, Shaun and John.
Thank you to the weekenders and the groovy gang, true friends.

The Insanity of gambling 2: Consequences - chapter highlights

Chapter 1: Early memories/career considerations
Chapter 2: Gambling versus working for a living/driving
Chapter 3: Training for a new path/nothing as it seems
Chapter 4: 1995/Meeting the legend Choc-Ice-John/flashback
Chapter 5: The Flashback continues
Chapter 6: Back to 1995/Lottery/gambling explosion
Chapter 7: The good times/the FOBT/sad time and inheritance
Chapter 8: A day out in Scarborough to remember/aftermath
Chapter 9: Another trip to the east coast/the posse
Chapter 10: 2006/Pharmacy/new hope/reality check
Chapter 11: End of the line/redemption/a cry for help
Chapter 12: Going too far/calling in favours/worse than a loan shark
Chapter 13: Up to the modern day/fate of the characters/Choc-Ice-Johns encore

Christopher Rodey
6/7/2020

INTRODUCTION

You know my story from 'The Insanity of Gambling' and how the years I spent as a punter started with the best of intentions, and a determination to progress into a professional gambler, losing in the early months was only seen as learning my trade.

I was quick to discover that my temperament wasn't right for this game, but I refused to give up on my dreams, often getting myself and others into tight situations, leaning on my family, transcending into stealing, lying and a whole host of problems that occurred as I believed I could mend what was the highlight to my problems, me.

All visions of my future were of success, in which I'd have vast wealth and the dreams that go with this, I'd see myself with a cottage in the country, a flash car that I roam around in, as well as a collection in my garage of other vintage vehicles, not to mention my six-feet blonde model girlfriend and holidays in the sun several times during the year when the racing was unsettled.

I'd be donning smart clothes and my wallet would have a permanent bulge with a section for cards, which would contain the highest American Express Visa with a five-figure credit limit, behind this would be my membership of the best restaurants and wine tasting clubs, above all it was about being my own boss and not having to be your average production worker or 9 to 5 slave.

While this is not your average person's way of thinking, most want the opportunity to work and build these things for themselves, and along the way, maybe getting married, buying a house, bringing up a family and investing for the future, paying into pension schemes for early retirement, and having it all later.

While that wasn't my direct view it did appeal to me because the one thing I craved was normality, but at 17 years old I was of the thinking that I could buy 'normal'.

While I didn't like the idea of working, this was a realistic backup, even though I left school with no qualifications, I still felt the world was at my feet, and I knew the opportunity was there to work hard to gain the skills I needed and to forge a career in the workplace of my choosing, as earning a living was real and a guarantee.

What transpired as I reached the last year of being a teenager, was two possible paths in front of me, working for a living or becoming a professional gambler, I knew what I wanted, but if that didn't work then I made sure I had a backup and an emotional tug of war ensured because if I couldn't have one, I would have the other.

Chapter one begins with some more of my early memories of gambling, to get us back into the mindset for you to come with me on the journey once again, then we explore, as already promised, the early wrestling between the two realities of work versus professional gambling, and how fragile the line is, as one reality fails, the fantasy of the other becomes more appealing.

You will see why certain types of employment appealed to me, and what happened after I took the measures to get there. I'm sure there will be a laugh or two here at my exploits, but don't get too comfortable, as the main part of the story then follows, time to fasten our seat belts as we meet an old friend.

As we reach the third chapter, the main 'protagonist' takes over for the majority of the rest of the story, and a new account of another gambler, one with a journey that began similar to mine, but with a different outlook, one that fully succumbs to the beast with no other desires beyond the addiction itself, and without wanting to go down any other path, as we re-Introduce Choc-Ice-John, but this time we get to know the whole shocking story.

John is my senior by ten years, almost to the day, we are a week from sharing a birthday, maybe there is something more significant about time zones and star signs, indeed this could almost be the gambling version of Mario Puzas's The Godfather part 2.
You've been down the insanity of gambling with my exploits, now Choc-Ice-John will take you down the same road, again we will have a few chuckles along the way but this is seriously disturbing stuff so be warned as we go to the next level!

CHAPTER ONE

"When I grow up I want to be an Arthur," I said to my best friend Darren during the hot summer of 1981, as always, I was bunking off school and hanging around Hull's East Park to avoid being detected by anyone who would see me and then tell my Mum that I wasn't where I should be,
"you mean an author?" replied Darren,
"no, I mean an Arthur, just like Dudley Moore," of course, I was referring to the film of the same name that was playing at the local ABC cinema, which was the story of a lovable layabout that had shed loads of money and all the time in the world to enjoy it.

This may have been humour based and an attempt to make my friend laugh, but something was appealing about that movie.

Two years later, I left school, or should I say, I didn't have to truant any more, but I felt a million years (and pounds) away from having the lifestyle of 'Arthur', I didn't even have a clue what I wanted to do, but I knew where I wanted to be.

At this point, the thought of work, even in the future, scared me, but only partly for the reason you would think, sure, I dreamed about having a life of leisure, who doesn't? but I felt the intimidation and bullying I received as I approached my teenage years in full-time education would eventually transpire into the workplace, only not the same, more subtle.

I didn't expect to come home from an adult work environment with bruises on my shins where I had been kicked, or a fat lip where I had been sucker-punched, or hungry because someone had snatched my sandwiches from my hand and thrown them into a puddle, I ruled all that out, instead I imagined a more evolved way of the same result, so, my future was in my thoughts.

I did have some friends at school, and they had clear insights to what they wanted to do, they focused on what was a normal career route and even though I had not even thought about gambling yet at this tender age of 16, I knew I had to find something different to the norm.

    The ideal scenario would have been to work for my Dad, he had built up his own window cleaning business from scratch and watching him work for himself as his own boss was one of my early influences, as I kept on thinking deeply about what I was going to aspire to, and I wanted to be like him.

    The down-side to all this was that my brother Jeff, who was ten years older than me, was a much better worker than I was and our Dad didn't give him the chance to work with him, so I always knew it would be even slimmer for me.

    Jeff ended up moving to London to find employment, it seemed to spell out clearly that I wasn't going to be climbing ladders with a bucket and shammy anytime soon, but you never know till it's there in black and white, so only time would tell.

    It was of no surprise that my Dad had his own business, he was always motivated with a dream of wealth. He always had a get rich quick scheme on the go and was like an early version of Del-Boy, years before the real one existed. He dabbled in antiques to the degree that he had a huge collection of old pots, pans and plates everywhere in the house and more Victorian telescopes than Galileo.

    My Dad was also talented with his hands, he could make anything out of a lump of wood, and one of my fondest memories of him, was when I was around ten years old, when one day, he took me out with him, we went around the corner to look in an antique shop window, where he spotted a Welsh-dresser, he then stared at it for ages, and he appeared to appreciate the design and craftsmanship that it took to build it during the 19th century, but while perusing, there was something else that he noticed, and that was that it had a similar base to the chest of drawers he had at home, minus the wooden shelves.

    He seemed to want one himself, so decided that he was going to make this chest of drawers into a replica of the Welsh dresser and then he would own one himself at home, certainly a lot cheaper. He came back home from work the next day with a ton of wood from somewhere, as he prepared himself to start the process, he walked to the shop several times a day, always taking notes of the size, shape and dynamics of the dresser.

Out came his saw, his plane and a ton of sandpaper and he went to work, focused entirely on his project, working patiently, until finally, after several weeks, came the last stage, as he stained all the wood to make an exact match, and to his credit, he did an amazing job.

The finished product was identical right down to the screws and brackets, it looked like he had bought the dresser from the shop itself. It was a privilege to see such a talent at work while he was doing it. He was wasted because believe me, he never even used a tape measure during the whole time, it was obvious that he had missed his real vocation somewhere.

A couple of weeks passed and one evening we heard a knock at our front door, two well-dressed guys walked in with my Dad, whom he then took upstairs, my Mum and I were listening at the bottom of the landing, even though I was young, I was old enough to be curious, I wanted to know what it was all about. It soon transpired that the men were antique dealers, he was only trying to flog it as legit! he wanted them to believe it was an authentic Victorian Welsh-dresser!

They didn't buy it though, I don't know how they could tell the difference, I couldn't.
So, it wasn't the appreciation of the old and uniqueness that made him want one at home, it was the price tag of £500 on the Welsh-dresser in the shop that caught his eye.

He tried a couple more times to sell it, but again to no avail before he eventually dismantled the shelves and turned it back into a chest of drawers again.

The next sign of his ability was a couple of years later when he built an extension on our house, with brand new bricks, doors and guttering, we thought he must have spent a fortune on materials, but around the corner, new houses were being built and our porch looked the same colour brickwork as these half-finished homes, but again, when he had completed the job, it looked like a professional builder had been at work.

Everyone down the street offered him money to build one of these outside their home but he politely declined, I never knew why until I asked him one day and he said,
"every time one of them got a leaky roof, they would be knocking on my door expecting me to fix it," which I found quite educational and an early lesson, as that when you do something for someone that involves parting with their money, they never let you forget it, and I was to learn more about this from a certain person we will come across later, but back to this current time.

My Dad enjoyed working for himself more than his old job as an inspector at Yorkshire-Water, where he would examine if ground floor workers had correctly laid their water and drainage pipes and checking all was hunky-dory. You would think this type of job would have paid well, back then it didn't, and he found he earned more working for himself, but without the same level of responsibility, although he was expected to keep his customer's windows clean of course.

Jeff left School at the Easter of 1972, during the glory days when Hull was a thriving import and export city, and at best he managed to get casual work between periods of unemployment, despite this our Dad still wouldn't take him on, always spouting the same words,
"it just wouldn't work."

Sometimes he stated that the business was only big enough for himself and he didn't earn enough to employ anyone.

Jeff left home for seasonal work every year around March, but always came back for a few months then left again, and repeated this cycle for a few years and each time our Dad was asked why he didn't employ his own son, which would allow him to remain in Hull, but the same reply as before,
"it just wouldn't work."

One year while away, Jeff met someone and was soon married, we knew then he wasn't coming back to Hull to live anytime soon.

A few weeks after I'd left school, the conversation came up again about what I was going to do, my aunt was down and looked at my Dad and came straight out with it,
"are you going to take him working with you Bernard" of which he replied the same words that I had heard many times,
"it just wouldn't work."

It wasn't a surprise to me, and we all assumed he just liked working on his own, until a few months later, he came home with a guy none of us had met before, we soon found out it was someone from his schooldays.

He looked as if he was in his mid-fifties and despite being very friendly, he looked out of shape, with a few extra pounds and a middle aged spread, and although I wasn't the most athletic individual, even I could probably have lapped him in a cross-country race, and it took no figuring out that he smoked forty roll-your-own cigarettes each day.

My Dad then introduced him to us,
"this is Ron," and I never thought anything of it at that point, he just appeared to have invited an old mate round to the house, until a few minutes later, my Dad came out with the crème de la crème,
"as from Monday Ron is going to be working with me," my jaw hit the floor! I was stunned,
"what? no way, your pulling my leg" was my immediate thought but I dare not say it loudly, sadly, he wasn't. Jeff wasn't good enough to work with our Dad, and it was made clear that I wasn't either, but this guy was?

Despite this, I didn't see it as Ron's fault and I couldn't blame him, even if I had, it was impossible not to like him, he had a warm and chatty personality.

Everyone knows someone like Ron, and even more so, someone that looks like him. If you made a movie about a famous person, you might struggle to find someone to double as Winston Churchill, but you could find twenty blokes that are Ron's doppelganger, bald, with a small amount of grey-hair growth just above his ears, silver glasses and a cloth cap, and a cig paper hanging from his lips, and he was one pigeon away from being Hull's version of Andy Capp.

Ron was an only child during the second world war, spending his whole life in Hull, which was one of the heaviest hit cities in the UK. There were many times that he lived in fear as he ran for air raid shelters as the sirens sounded. You never knew when the Nazi's were going to drop their firebombs, and after the attacks, Ron would witness soldiers placing sandbags on the loose flames. He also experienced many other wartime activities, including rations, and often sat listening for updates on the radio with anticipation and many other things you only see and hear about in a museum now. Above all though, he grew up with strong family ties.

After the war had finished and in later years when his National service was over, his Mum, whom he was close too, sadly passed away and some say he was never the same again, this could have been a factor to his mindset being what it was when I met him because he lived like there was no tomorrow, every day to the full as he found it difficult to cope with normal responsibilities of everyday life and as time passed he drank, smoked and gambled as a kind of comfort.

Yes, Ron was a gambler, and he was one of the first to show me the variety of the way people bet differently in the world of gambling, as he was nothing like my Dad, who always put a betting slip on hours before racing began and checked the results at the end of the day.

Just before he bumped into my Dad, betting and drinking ended up transcending his life downwards and before he knew where he was, he found himself living at the Salvation Army hostel on Anlaby road corner, known as William Booth house.

He also discovered that he had mates already living there that he knew from his days in pubs and betting shops, that were gambling addicts and alcoholics, most of these had hit rock bottom too, so when he was given his new room and lodgings in William Booth house, he may have been skint but he was never lonely as he was in good company with like-minded people, but gambling got him into trouble, as you've probably already figured out, he was compulsive with a tendency to chase his losses.

This happened when temptation was put in front of him when an unbelievably irresponsible decision by the hostel's warden was laid at Ron's feet. Every two weeks, he and several of his buddies all visited the employment exchange to sign on the dotted line and receive a giro in the post a couple of days later, which was delivered to the pigeonhole in the reception.

For whatever reason, the warden arranged for the residents to take turns going to the post office to pick everyone's giro's up, before distributing the money out when the allotted person came back, but when you think they all had problems which culminated because of a lack of cash, which is why they were living here in the first place, it was sheer lunacy to do what he did and he was asking for trouble, and you couldn't make this up, and what happened next, was bound to happen.

The week arrived when it was Ron's turn to collect everyone's benefits, several of them then signed the back as Ron was volunteered to pop to the Post office and collect them all for everyone – as well as his own.

A quick question here, would you send someone to collect your money that had a drinking and gambling problem?

Ron did indeed cash them all in just after lunchtime, and on his way back he went to William Hills instead of William Booth.

At first, the intention was to have a bet with his own money. If he had a decent day, it would not have gone the way it did, but he couldn't hit a donkey's ass with a banjo that afternoon and once his own money had gone, he tried to win it back with the pocketful of cash he had, which, of course, was everyone else's money. He lost the lot and had to go back with tears rolling down his face and was inconsolable.

The Salvation Army supervisor was the person that met him before the residents could lynch him up, but rather than throw him out of the building or punish him in some way, he went to the hierarchy and pleaded Ron's case that he had an addiction and needed help, not punishment.

They put Ron only one offer on the table, and this was on the condition that he agreed to get help, and providing he went along with this, they would organise a collection and used some of the funds in the office, and all of the lost giro monies were then reimbursed to the residents of which Ron would have to pay back in instalments, and the help would be in the form of attending regular Gamblers-Anonymous meetings.

He agreed before being told that there was to be a further condition, the hostel supervisor had to accompany Ron to the meetings to make sure that he went. Ron agreed to this and he was thrown a lifeline and did as was suggested, although he didn't have a choice.

What would have been the alternative to the second chance they gave him? The Police may have been involved followed by a trip to court.

Gambling wasn't understood as an addiction in those days, perhaps it still isn't, he may have gone to jail, which leaves the million-dollar question, would that have done him potentially better?

The reason I say this is because after Ron had done all that was necessary, he didn't want to stop gambling, he was never back at the point where he broke down mentally as he got away with it, that may have been the moment that he wanted to address the problem, once he was given a way out, he didn't face any consequences beyond being forced to go to a meeting with a roomful of people that he didn't know.

He did the mandatory stuff, sounded convincing and sincere in the room but the opportunity the supervisor at William Booth house gave him, literally reset Ron back to the person he was before he went off with the Giro's that day, he then resumed gambling again, and this was the very point where he met my Dad.

Although he was back in bad habits, the opportunity to clean windows also meant a new lease of life and the mistake had already been forgotten by him, he accepted the chance to work with glee and conviction and was a model employee, turning up on time and fully appreciating the extra cash which my Dad paid him daily, which was perfect for someone who enjoys a drink and a flutter on the horses.

My Mum even packed him and my Dad up every day, the same thing, cheese and tomato sandwiches wrapped in silver foil, and a kit-Kat. My Dad would even lecture Ron for eating his chocolate bar before his sandwiches, to which he would reply,
"it all mixes no matter what order you eat it," this was Ron to a tee, down to Earth and likeable and we all thought the world of him.

Ron always arrived before 8.00 am, which was the time my Dad would set off, this allowed him his mandatory cup of tea with three sugars before the day's work began, and here I would chat with him, to some memorable conversations. To his credit, Ron was open about the mistakes he had made and talked about the perils of gambling in a brutally honest way, this should have sparked something in me to never venture into a betting shop, but I didn't want to walk into the front doors of a workplace either and go through what I did at school, but working with my Dad was now well and truly out of the question.

So why did my Dad employ Ron and not Jeff or me? The simple answer was that Ron was happy to get paid and run, with no further thought, whereas Jeff and I might have worked out how much he earned in a week, which may have been different from the amount he told my Mum, who had two jobs at the time.

The only time I saw my Dad and Ron in action together was on an occasion when I was on the bus heading down Sutton road, and spotted them through the window as I was going past, they were both up their ladders on the opposite sides of the street, my Dad was always skilled and accurate with an amazing eye for detail, but he was never fast, but I could see that he was several windows ahead of Ron.

The partnership may have worked well for both parties for reasons mentioned, but with a quicker pair of hands, how big could we have built the business up if it was a family firm? Jeff and I could have made our Dad a millionaire before he retired, if he could make money with Ron's tortoise speed, he would have prospered with our younger and faster legs.

Despite Ron being a reliable employee to begin, as time went on, he began to let my Dad down, and Thursday in particular, became a day when Ron would have appointments or ring to say he was ill, my Mum and I knew it was going to happen before my Dad did.

He was grateful when he first started the job, just as he showed gratitude when he was given another chance after he lost everyone's money at the hostel, but nothing lasted long because Ron had an uncontrolled gambling addiction and like other people with the same problem, he had tunnel vision to his own agenda.

Ron worked for my Dad for a few more years, but he was later kicked out of the Salvation Army hostel for reasons unknown, was this due to his gambling again?

He was soon rehoused and found other employment as a night watchman for cash in hand, and he didn't need my Dad as much anymore and began to let him down even more.

Still, he was a top-notch bloke and eventually my Dad sold his round and retired due to arthritis, Ron stayed in touch for a while but tended to spend more time on Holderness Road, where his new flat was located, with a two minute walk to the local Ladbrokes and the Elephant and Castle pub next door, everything he needed to make him happy.

From late 1983 till halfway through the following year, I signed up for a youth training scheme, or YTS as they were known, now many years defunct, they were designed to train young chaps up with new skills that could be transferred into the workplace.

I initially chose bricklaying, but after a similar to School environment that saw me working with a bunch of people my own age, I jumped ship as this was an area of my life I wanted to leave behind, instead I signed onto a welding and fabrication course and didn't look back, and with more older people around, I was focused and completed the training and tests and received a City and Guilds certificate of competence for Mig, Arc and gas welding.

We also had a project where we worked at Hull marina, and everyone that goes there with me hears how I welded some of the safety bars onto a few of the railings.

I left the scheme with a new skill, sadly I never got any interviews, my City and Guilds meant nothing, employers of welders wanted apprenticeship served, but this was my first sample of the real-world workplace.

City and Guilds qualifications have a nickname – Sitting Gills, which is cute, as well as ironic because it is sat at the bottom of a drawer somewhere, although, even many years later, I'm still proud of it.

The Thatcherite government meant I was never going to be able to laze around all day while I figured out what I wanted to do after welding didn't work out.

The initial placement in the bricklaying department, albeit only for a single month, relit my fear of being stuck in the wrong kind of workplace, I also remembered that my Mum was bullied herself when she was a cleaner at Park road Primary School, for two years her boss stopped talking to her and tried to make her life there unbearable, but my Mum was tough and could give as much back, till eventually it went to the head office and her employer moved her to another school, but I wasn't as strong as her, unfortunately, I was still scarred mentally, and I knew that whatever age a person is, the type of situation you think you have left behind can follow you.

All this convinced me that I needed to find another more ready skill, outside of the engineering or building industry, something that I would be happy to do long term and where I would be appreciated, I knew what I wanted, I just didn't know how to find it.

While I was pondering this, my thinking changed fast when I ventured into a betting shop for the first time, coinciding with me reading an article about a guy who made a living as a punter, it began to appeal and the more I thought about it, the more it looked like an opportunity until I could see it clearly.

I wanted to be a professional gambler, a person who wins at the game, with working for an employer as the only reluctant alternative if I couldn't make it, so I was motivated.

What followed for the next couple of years was a contest between work versus gambling, and I knew which one appealed the most, and after seeing my Dad become his own boss, I wanted to be the same, and only success as a punter would give me that.

In real life I had seen my Dad and brother lose, Ron almost lost more than just money, my Uncle David liked a bet too, and he was always skint and constantly borrowing off his Mother, so this is how gambling was presented to me, as a losers hobby, where there was only one winner, the bookmaker.

My Dad was a rare breed, a gambler with a car, but he needed it for work, but generally, there was a joke about the gambler having no transport while the betting shop owner had a Rolls-Royce, until now, that is what was in front of me, the evidence, but here I was, believing that I was going to be different and buck the trend and re-invent the wheel.

What I didn't take into account was that the guy in the article was as cool as a cucumber, whereas I felt like I had been robbed for every bet I placed that lost, as if the money had been stolen off me and it complicated things because winning was more about temperament than ability alone.

From here it was a choice of getting my act together and bet shrewdly, or be a 9 to 5 slave, and if that had to be the case, then I had to be choosy, as I didn't want to be in a place that had micro-management, intimidation, or me working the hardest whilst getting a reputation of being a slacker, being set up to fail, working in skewered atmospheres or having people talking about me negatively when I was out of the workplace, and this was all I could visualise from working for a living.

After a few months of betting and getting nowhere, I knew I didn't have time on my hands and wasn't ready yet, and would have to find something for the short term but again, what could I do?

It was only after I booked my first ever driving lesson that it dawned on me, what if I could pass my test quickly? Could this be the answer?

Driving for a living took up a small proportion of my thoughts, as it looked like a job where your left to your own devices, your boss and colleagues were unlikely to be sat in your vehicle pulling you to bits or insulting you, it looked like a position with freedom, just what I was looking for.

In addition, I watched adverts on the TV for Yorkie bars every night, where a handsome guy in a denim jacket was driving his truck with a chunky chocolate bar in his right hand and a beautiful blonde sat on his left, this appealed as I was very impressionable.

You'll have noticed that I said a small proportion of my thoughts were geared towards driving as a form of employment, this was because the majority of my grey matter was always hooked on gambling for a living, and again being able to drive would help me in that area too, especially when I would need to visit all the northern racecourse's if I was to become successful in chosen field.

As I was barely eighteen, I still felt like a child as I sat behind the wheel for my first driving lesson at Quick pass in Saville Street.

This was a company that had a guy on a desk who would book your lessons with the firm's trainee instructors and they operated solely at this base, put simply you turn up at the headquarters for driving tuition, they never came to you.

It felt scary as I was in control of a car for the first time, as I ventured down a busy Anlaby road and around town in my first hour, I didn't expect to be driving for some reason but when you think about it, how else would I learn? But I soon got better as my confidence grew.

The instructors kept leaving and I had three different people teaching me within the first two months, with them being trainees, they probably qualified and went on to better things, either that or I was the world's worst driver.

Instructor number three stayed longer than the others, he was called Tommy, he was more eccentrically dressed too, sporting light blue jeans and a shell suit top, complete with mirrored sunglasses and a red baseball cap that had his long ponytail sticking out of the back, I don't ever remember this look being cool but it was certainly the 1980s for you.

He asked me to apply for my test after the very first hour driving with him, which I didn't hesitate to do. It came back a week later for a date two months away.

The lessons were £6.50 but he used to encourage his clients to gamble the odd 50 pence piece with the toss of this very coin,
"heads or tails" he would shout – if you won the lesson was £6 but if you lost it would cost you £7 and you had to give him another fifty pence. I didn't think of this as gambling despite mentioning it here, but technically it was.

After ten lessons with tommy, eight of them cost me £7 and only once did I get the hour for £6.

I was beginning to think it was a two-headed coin before he told me of an occasion where it went wrong for him, he lost and the winning client then said,
"double or quits," which ended up with Tommy losing for the second time in a row, before the chap once again said, "double or quits," after losing a 3rd time Tommy realised if he were to lose again, he would not only have given the guy the lesson for free, he would owe him money as well, so one toss of the coin was just a bit of fun, beyond that, it can spiral out of control.

The test arrived, I felt I drove well and if I had passed on my first attempt, I would have felt a sense of achievement, but I didn't, I had four fail-marks.

I thought I had done enough so the disappointment was hard to take in. I blamed the lack of continuation with different instructors and proceeded to put my test in again but decided to change driving Schools, this was cemented when Tommy called me at home and said he was leaving himself and did I want to go with him privately. I had nothing against him but didn't feel he was right for me, so I decided to search again but I didn't have to look hard for very long.

One of the customers on my Dad's window cleaning round recommended a guy called Tony Stephenson, who was ex-army and did it for future ambitions as he wanted to be an examiner, he was the top driver and the best mechanic in the motor pool during his time in service, so, one simple telephone call and it was set in motion and I had found my new instructor.

Tony came to pick me up at the house for my first lesson, which was different from having to walk to the driving school in town, and he did a mock test with me, of which I thought I had driven well, but afterwards he let me know his thoughts on my driving,
"your roundabout procedure is appalling, your approach to junctions is laughable, I think you're a long way off being good enough to pass your test," he then tried to inspire me,

"but, I am going to make you ready, a bit of work and we'll get you there."

I was confident he would do the trick, but over the next few weeks there were too many of his putdowns and not enough encouragement and this had a detrimental effect, and although it was obvious he was very focussed and thorough, I felt his brand of teaching didn't work well for me as an individual and the strictness put me off as I would often hear him shouting,
"no, no, no, no" every time I made an error, with each 'no' getting louder than the previous, or he might say,
"I could teach a chimpanzee to drive better," which again didn't help.

His remarks made me drive worse if anything, but would I get in the car one day and everything gel together? Would his methods work?

I wasn't producing the goods on the roads, but maybe I would on the test? I knew time would tell, as his pass rate was impressive, with 90% of his clients passing on the first time of asking, and the 10% of fails went close, but with a single week to go before my test things came to a head as the lesson was drawing to a close, he had been putting me down for almost the full hour and as we were on the home run, it all went pear-shaped, suddenly, he had to use his dual controls to brake the car as I was about to crash into another vehicle as I tried to turn right at the Queens Road junction onto Beverley road, just as another car was coming forward, as he yelled at the top of his voice,
"are you mad, you were about to cause a head-on collision," followed by,
"that was dangerous driving at it's worse, do you even look where you're going? you're shocking as a driver."

I had never felt more relieved to arrive home, I was battered emotionally, physically drained and mentally, I had nothing left, except the feeling of being useless and embarrassed to the degree that I never told anyone about this, until now.

It was hard to put this behind me, even when the day of the test came. He picked me up promptly, gave me a pep talk, telling me to put everything I have into the test and fight for the licence, then he took me to the driving exam centre, this time at Salisbury street down Princes Avenue, where it was sometimes held in those days.

Onto the test itself, and I drove terribly, at one point I stopped at a junction going uphill and began to roll backwards, I also clipped the kerb on one occasion and flew out of a junction so fast that the examiner made a noise to suggest that he had jumped out of his skin.

No surprise, I didn't pass and was given a sheet with six fail-marks, which was two worse than the previous time, Tony was far from happy,
"nobody has ever failed on this number of faults before with me," he said before I sarcastically replied,
"well, they have now."

He drove back and I could see him shaking his head a few times, he never said another word until we got to the house, then he spoke,
"you were good enough to pass that test," I then said,
"I know, I had a bad day," of which he then shook his head again, I paid him and then climbed out of the vehicle.

Maybe I was capable, as he suggested, but it was too little too late as far as I was concerned, and with me nearly causing a crash only a week earlier, I didn't feel I was ready to pass just yet and accepted this verdict.

It wasn't nice telling my parents of another fail, which was the only part of the story I told them.

I could easily have never gotten into a car again after this but from somewhere came the determination to move onwards and forwards, and I put in for test number three the next morning.

I just needed to find a new instructor, and whoever it is, they couldn't be any worse than that guy, Tony Stevenson, surely?

It was a relief to be finished with Tony, lessons with him felt more like a boot camp in the Marines than learning to drive. He had come recommended by one of my Dads customers, and it just so happened that at work the next day, my Dad was telling another client who received his window cleaning services, about my driving experiences, who just happened to be a new driving instructor himself, albeit a trainee, he was called Don, and he ended up saying to my Dad,
"send him to me, I'll get him through that test."

He came home and told us of this, and after a short discussion, we decided to give him a chance.

Don lived in a four-bedroomed house down Ella street on Newland avenue, with his third wife and five kids and that was all I knew about him at this point, but this gave me an image already, but without me having to do another thing, my Mum and Dad sorted my first lesson, which was another pickup service.

The day arrived and we waited and wondered how he would compare to my previous two disasters, Tommy would turn up a few minutes late and end the lesson slightly early, Tony Stephenson, being ex-army, was the opposite, very prompt, and regimental to the letter, but this guy Don turned up fifteen-minutes late for my initial hour, we didn't think he was coming at all until he eventually arrived,
"sorry I'm late," were his first words, and I can't remember what the rest of the excuse was, but first impressions and all that, but there was more to come.

He stepped out of the car and continued to introduce himself, he was a short sappy guy, scruffily dressed and looked like the last guy on Earth that you would think taught people to drive, he had a shifty look, more like someone who hadn't actually passed their test themselves, but let's not judge a book by its cover, as this novel looked like it had been well used and worse for wear.

Upon climbing into the car, the seats were full of dog hairs, the upholstery stained yellow with nicotine and cigarette butts on the floor, in fact, the whole car may as well have been an ash-tray as every time he put out a cigarette, he lit another.

It would have been nice if he had opened a window, but he didn't, and I was too timid to ask. It was hard to breathe in the confined area filled with blue smoke, it was as bad as the betting shop on a Saturday afternoon.

Despite the late start, he brought me back on the exact time when the lesson was due to finish, and then took his money, no reduction despite robbing me of a quarter of an hour.

This type of timekeeping continued for weeks as my test approached, and he was certainly more interested in smoking and looking at a busty woman out of the window than he was in teaching me to drive. If I had an hour's lesson at 11.00 am, he would likely come at 11.05 am and drop me off at 11.55 am, I never got the full sixty-minutes that I was paying for.

On one occasion, whilst driving near my test area down Chamberlain road, he spotted a small branch of William Hills that even I didn't know existed, hidden away at the side of a pub,
"I want you to park up outside that shop Chris," as he strolled in and left me in the car and came out ten minutes later and said,
"Chris, can you give me the money for your lesson now?" as he then went back into the bookies and eventually came out with a face like a wet weekend,
"I shouldn't have gone in there, but I had a tip for a sure thing," I wasn't interested as I could have told him there was no such thing and I had only started gambling a year before myself at this time.

If that had been an isolated incident it would have been bad enough, but on another occasion, he stopped to buy a carpet from a guy sat in a van at the side of a road, and even had me get out of the car and help him bend and manoeuvre it in the back of the vehicle, I then got back in the driving seat to find I couldn't see through the rear-view mirror because of the huge rug, and had to drive back not been able to see what was happening behind me, but wasn't this against the law?

I knew this even then that if we had been pulled over by the Police because my view was obstructed it would more than likely have been me that got the fine. Again, he had come late even on that day and dropped me off early just as before, even when there was all that carpet business in between.

If you added in all the visits to shops, mate's houses and long chats to attractive cashiers in petrol stations with the fact that he always charged me the full price you can imagine the outcome almost before it happened.

I knew that if I were to pass the test, it would have been despite Don, not because of him, as it happened I was unsuccessful with four fail-marks.

When I arrived home to tell the bad news again, I mentioned Don's methods to my Dad, which up to now I hadn't been vocal about,
"I've learned the difference between John Player special cigarettes and Benson and Hedges king size and how to stuff a large carpet into a small car, but not how to drive adequately enough to pass a driving test," my Dad replied defensively,
"I clean his windows down Ella Street that's all, he told me he was a good instructor, he said he would get you passed."

I knew It was my fault for not speaking out earlier and putting up with his shenanigans, but I was pondering what to do next.

That night Don rang the house phone,
"I've got some places available for lessons up to your next test, but I suggest you have two lessons a week so I can teach you properly," I was stunned by the cheek of the man,
"what?, no thank you," was the politest way I could tell him I wasn't interested; I wouldn't have gotten in a car with him again if he was the last instructor on Earth. I told my Dad who responded,
"I hope you weren't rude to him; I clean his windows; I don't want to lose any of my customers," it was now my turn to be on the defensive,

"I wasn't, I just told him I am not taking any more lessons, that's all."

My Dad continued to clean Don's windows after all this had happened, so at least that side of things never went wrong.

Test four was during my time living down south, in Stevenage, a normal guy teaching me for a change but a point of interest was that he came from Wakefield in West Yorkshire but had lived in Hull for a year before he re-located down south, he remembered Beverley road and had drunk in the Swan pub, which was the closest boozer to where I was currently living, small world but Wakefield, Hull, London or Mars, the result was the same, another fail but with three marks this time, so, getting better at least.

Test number five was booked for Stevenage again, but with everything that happened in an eventful year (as per the first Insanity of Gambling book), I eventually settled back in Hull before the due date and switched it to there, and with new ambitions and a bid to re-invent myself, I was of the mindset that I was determined to make it as a full-time professional gambler within five years, passing my test was on my list of essentials.

Despite all the practice behind the wheel, I still had that near-crash on my mind, but my way of thinking was that I had improved enough to be a wary and careful road user and here I went again, as the date of my test centre switch came through, and it was only three weeks away, so the next step was to look in the Hull Daily mail for someone to give me yet more driving lessons.

My next instructor looked like Tim Brooke-Taylor from the Goodies, but the laugh was on me as despite feeling comfortable with his laid-back attitude, test five ended with two fail-marks, but I was getting even nearer now, the best I had driven on the day that mattered, I felt unlucky at coming so close, almost over the line, It was hard to drive that well and not get what I had been putting time and effort to accomplish.

After this, and for the first time, I stayed with the same instructor for my next test, which if your losing count, was number six. I thought I was more ready to pass than ever, but Groundhog Day as I failed again, but with four marks this time.

I was beginning to think that it was not meant to be, I just could not pass that test and every time had been different, the scores from the examiners went up and down, after I came close with two fail-marks, the next was back to four again, I was confused as when I got near, I was suddenly far away again, and each time were for things I'd not failed on the previous test, I had spent so much time money and effort and I still didn't have a licence.

Jeff had started driving lessons at the same time as me but he passed on the second attempt, his partner Pat started driving for the first time after I had failed my third test, she passed too before I had taken my fifth, a few people I knew had been successful on the first or second attempt and I was getting more and more frustrated and wondered if it was worth it.

I was thinking that if I had put all the money I spent on lessons into a pot, I would have a small fortune, although to be fair, we know where that would have gone, but I didn't think that, my thoughts were that I had nothing to show for all my hard work.

I felt sorry for myself because I was losing on the horses, after what was supposed to have been my transitional period of achieving my dreams of winning through patience and discipline, which was found lacking, and of course, I couldn't get my driving license and was on the verge of giving up, I would often call myself a 'born loser'.

The work versus professional gambling was coming up short on both counts, as I couldn't get the desired licence to drive, which was what I wanted to do if the betting failed.

I spent some time deliberating, and I concluded that I was getting nowhere and finally decided to call it a day and not waste any more time or money, which added up to the inevitable outcome that, despite it not being what I wanted, I was at the end of my tether.

That was until I went home the following day and found that despite my reluctance, my parents refused to give up, even if I did,
"Chris, we have sent away for another test, give it a final go, please, just one last attempt," I could see their determination, "you have nothing to lose and we are paying for your lessons."

It was a shock and I was caught off-guard, I was genuinely grateful to them even though I didn't want to go through it all again, but I felt I had no choice, I went along and thanked them, I was touched that they believed in me, again, even if I no longer cared about the licence, I now wanted to try for them.

A new driving School had opened on Beverly road, so, my Mum booked me a course up to my test, which came through quickly, it was in a month, so it wasn't going to be a long build-up.

The first lesson came and in anticipation, I said to my Mum, "I hope I don't get another instructor like Don," but it was a welcome start when the new chap parked outside the house five minutes early, he was also called Chris like myself, only I wasn't the double of Jan Michael Vincent like he was, and first impressions were good.

The lessons went smooth, no carpets, baseball caps with hair hanging down, waiting outside friends' houses or ex-army personnel's shouting at me, just straight and informal hour-long lessons, in Chris would often say to me,
"if you do anything, and I mean absolutely anything at all, no matter how trivial, look in the mirror," and if I had a quid for every time he repeated this statement I would have been rich, but the test arrived and it was those words that were stuck in my head.

I did what Chris said and when the examiner said after twenty minutes of driving,

"I'm happy, let's take a short cut back, I've seen enough," it felt surreal, I was thinking,
"surely I haven't passed, I think I have," as I had tingly sensations as if I were in a dream where I had achieved the impossible of attaining something that had previously been unreachable.

This realisation transpired to where I was, still out on the road and I suddenly became more nervous, knowing if I drove back and made a mistake, it would be snatched away from me.

My nerves where on tenterhooks as I knew I had it in the bag, as long as I didn't do something stupid like clipping a curb or drive through a red light, and with Chris's voice still in my head, telling me to keep looking in the mirror, I steadily drove it back to the centre, but the ten minutes it took to get there felt like ages.

I parked up, turned the engine off and answered a couple of highway code questions when he said to me,
"that is the end of the test and I am pleased to tell you that you have passed," finally the words I had wanted to hear for over three long years made my heart fill with joy, although I knew I had done it, I still needed to hear him say it.

I was ecstatic, and I was now finally getting that elusive driving licence after six failed attempts, now it was time to tell the two people who had got me to this point, but first I planned to be mischievous and as I arrived home, I tried to pull a sad, miserable face, but as my Mum and Dad looked at me out of the window, I couldn't hold it back and a smile appeared from ear to ear, and I could see my Dad fisting the air.

It was all thanks to them and they were always non-drinkers otherwise it would have been a bottle of cheap champagne, so a cup of tea had to do, but I couldn't show my gratitude enough for them never doubting my ability.

It was a pleasure writing out a thank you card the next morning with Chris's name on it and delivering it to the driving school, I didn't know if I should have done more, he had helped me in ways others hadn't.

It was hard to imagine how things would have worked out if I had passed on that first time of asking instead of the seventh, although we shouldn't think like that it is hard not to surmise, it would have saved me a lot of grief, but when I weighed up all the evidence, I knew I wasn't ready back then.

I recollected about the time between my first lesson and passing the test, over three years in the making and it felt like a rollercoaster, it wasn't a surprise to find that obtaining my driving license had as much madness as my gambling did.

So, this left me with a dilemma, I still wanted to be a professional gambler, but now as a backup, I could take a driving job until I got there.

This new ability meant, either way, I would need that license, either to work in this area, or to drive to the racetracks, this was going to come in handy one way or another, but for now, I could at least attempt to do a day job that I would actually enjoy, or would I?

So, work versus gambling was now taking a more interesting twist and whichever way I went, I could now legally sit behind the wheel of a car.

In the four years since I had placed my first bet, every time something positive happened along the way, I was left hoping that it would lead to better things, all I knew was, this felt like a gamechanger and I was ready for something new.

CHAPTER TWO

It was an enjoyable experience staring at my new driving licence, it was printed on green paper within a plastic wallet, with all my eligibility, I could even drive a 7.5-ton vehicle. I couldn't help but smile at the thought of driving lessons being a thing of the past, now it was all about what to do next.

I felt achieving something like this would help me on other levels, I somehow believed this accomplishment would assist in maturing me and having a knock-on effect towards reaching my ambitions with the horses, because while I may have been a million miles away, in my head it was about a small change, a tweak, a bit of growing up and I was there, and this was always in my psyche.

It was only a driving licence, but I already had visions of me travelling in my car to race meetings, such as York, Lingfield, Ripon, Doncaster and so on. I did say 'my car' there, which was a long stretch from reality, where I could hardly afford to keep my rusty bike on the road, yet I was seeing myself parking outside northern racetracks with a wad full of cash for a day's productive punting on the horses.

I carried with me a constant faith that my time would come, luckily for me on this occasion, I didn't get built up too long before things came crashing down to reality street, as the first time betting after this so-called change in me, didn't last a day, and what a shocker it was, one I will always remember.

It started with me walking to the corner shop to buy the Racing Post, and after returning home and spreading this out all over the floor, armed with my pen and paper, I was of the belief that I was commencing a new phase of my life, and I began studying the contents to shortlist some good value punts for the day ahead.

This was the focused me, in a good place and in love with life itself, believing I would finally be going places and all the suffering at the hands of the bookies up to this point was just me learning my trade.

The afternoons betting didn't start too badly, an hour in the bookies with a winner and three losers, I counted up and found myself fifty-pence down, while an average punter would look at this as the price to pay for the enjoyment, let's face it, the difference between breaking even, or losing a small amount of chump change, probably won't make a significant difference to your life unless it's your bus fare home and you live at the other side of town, in that case, no matter how small, it would become money you couldn't afford to lose, this wasn't even the case, I was a ten-minute walk from my house, and I don't know if it was my temperament, or being a bad loser, I couldn't accept losing even this tiny amount of money.

This is when the switch kicked in and every bet I placed from this point lost, I even tried to back two greyhounds in the same race in an attempt to shake things up and get something first past the post, but when these were the last dogs to pass the line, I knew I was up against it, walking away felt impossible.

I was compelled to stay in this zone, feeling angry while at the same time existing in a zombified state, lashing out with no regard for consequences, increasing my stakes till eventually, my money dwindled, then I was soon backing longer priced selections as my luck felt in short supply, placing what I had left on rank outsiders as they were the only ones that could get me back what I had lost.

When I had no money left, I ran out of the shop as quickly as my legs would carry me, determined to get more cash and get back again, as there was still two hours of racing left.

I arrived home to borrow money from my Mum, I then rushed back to the betting shop and that went the same way, so I did the same again, sprinting back to the house, where I then asked to lend some more, and it was the same story yet again.

I knew I couldn't ask for money for a third time, but my brain was working in overdrive, I just had to carry on, I couldn't stop.

An idea came to me, and this was put into action when I arrived at the house, I entered my bedroom, opened the drawer on my bedside locker and grabbed a pile of my comics.

They were DC and Marvel, all superhero stuff, and I cherished them, I was proud of my collection and knew they would be worth a fair amount one day, although they meant more to me than money, some were over twenty years old, and with no regard for what I was doing, I put them in a bag and took them to a second-hand comic book shop hoping to sell them and handed them to a lady who worked there.

   She took her time perusing through my collection while I was getting more anxious by the second, I felt desperate to get something to bet with, before she finally said,
"these are not in mint condition so I can't give you the full price that we would normally pay."

   There was nothing wrong with them, she was looking at vintage Superman, Batman and Wonder woman comics from the late 60s to early 70s and I didn't count how many I had but there must have been at least twenty of them in her hand, when she said,
"a fiver for the lot!"

   I was floored, I was expecting her to say £50 and my heart wanted to take them back home but the desperate gambler in me said,
"yes, ok, thanks."

   I was still £100 down and what was I going to do with £5? I placed £3 on a 4-1 shot in an eight-horse handicap, and a £2 forecast on my horse to win and a 10-1 shot to finish second.

   Guess what happened? I got the forecast right, the first two home, but unfortunately, the wrong way around, the horse I wanted to finish in second place beat my selection, I knew my luck was out, because if somehow I had staked a £2.50p reverse forecast I would have recouped all my losses for that day, I was on the right line but near misses are the same as getting nowhere, they pay nothing, and this made me feel even worse.

   I went home in a foul mood, everything lost, I had borrowed twice so I was also now limited till I got paid again, and to make matters worse, my precious comic collection had gone too, all because I couldn't accept losing 50p.

   I went to the comic shop a few days later and looked in the racks, she had only put them for sale between £3 and £5 each, and I got a fraction of that and if they were in such bad condition how could she justify this?

I couldn't do anything about this now, it would have cost me close to a hundred quid to buy them back, but all I could think of was that fiver she gave me, I didn't want to part with these in the first place for any price, but gambling cost me heavy that day, I lost something that was a sentimental connection to my childhood.

Pain is not always a physical thing, because I was feeling it big time emotionally after this, it was as if my addiction had taken a bite out of me because that chunk remained missing and it hurt for a long time.

This left me pondering as I was back to considering real work aspects again and it felt the time to put my driving license to good use as the scales of professional gambling versus working for a living tipped towards the latter again.

As far as being out of work went, the government were turning the screws and didn't take any prisoners. The Prime Minister, Margaret Thatcher, wasn't afraid to call a spade a spade, especially as the Conservatives were now in their third term of office, unemployment was no longer an easy option, one to one interviews with benefit advisors were held regularly to see what you were doing to find work, the cushy 1970s where a distant memory, in the days where you could simply turn up at the dole office every two weeks, sign on a dotted line and receive a Giro posted first class, two days later, no questions asked, just a friendly,
"see you in a fortnight."

This was advertised as if it was a way to help the individual rather than just pay-out, but it felt more like they were applying pressure, often the threat of having your money stopped and rumours of a change in the law where you had to do community service before you could be paid out, this never happened but I lived in fear of it.

To cut a long story short, me walking into the employment exchange to sign on and then say to them,
"I don't want to work; I want to try to become a professional gambler first," would not have gone down well.

Gambling certainly hadn't worked out the way I had hoped, I often wished I'd never betted at all, but the dream was what I craved, and I still believed it would happen, one day.

They didn't have to worry about my authenticity at the employment exchange anymore, I was now there looking for work, although reluctantly I knew I had no choice, it was almost as if they had a gun pointed at my head.

I knew I needed changes and the way I looked at it, I would be better to embrace it, as if I was putting my life in a bag and shaking it up, so it was new territory and who knows, maybe something positive could come from it? I had worked in the Shredded wheat factory, completed a welding course, but now I wanted to do something that I would enjoy doing for a while, and this is where I wanted to put my driving license to good use.

I had chosen the route I wanted to go down myself and I applied for a few jobs that appealed to me, and I soon received a phone call from a haulage company, and the conversation started with a couple of questions before I was invited for an interview for the position of a van driver, I was asked if I could come straight away, of which I agreed, I then pulled on my best shirt, tie and suit, polished my black shoes that were a size too small, all in the quickest time possible, and I set off walking as I knew the area well.

The place I needed to be was located near the beginning of James Reckitt Avenue, close to the Punchbowl pub, and directly opposite on the other side of the road was a small row of shops which I was familiar with.

Starting on the left, there was a fish and chip takeaway, which like every other chippie in Hull, claimed to make the best patties in England, next door was a betting shop, ok now you know why I knew this area so well, and as we work our way along, there was a mini supermarket, and finally, completing things was a Barbers shop on the corner called 'Johns', this looked a good old-fashioned place for a shave or trim and was complete with the red and white stripe pole and a sign outside saying 'gentlemen's haircut - inn', which let us all know that it catered for men only, and not the place for a lady who wants a perm with purple highlights, but in an interesting irony, the barber who cut the men's hair was a woman, and almost certainly not called John.

She had short spikey blonde hair and always wore tight red or black cycling shorts, and a clingy orange t-shirt, and on occasions when I used the betting shop and found myself stood outside waiting for my horses to run, I noticed that she always attracted the attention of the same gang of teenage Schoolkids, who I had witnessed walking past several times to peer at her, their hormones must have been racing overtime.

If we ventured several yards further around the corner, there was an insurance shop stood on its own, but the same lads showed no interest in that.

It's amazing what you notice when you bet like I did, after placing my slip, and never watching my races, I'd walk around the block until the horses had crossed the line, I observed all sorts, but I'd never noticed the haulage firm where I was currently heading.

As I approached, I saw a small building containing offices on the left and a large gate on the right that led to a yard, which was locked, but I assumed the vehicles were kept there. I saw the sign above the door which said, 'Norfolk Haulage' and then I knew I was in the right place.

I nervously walked into the building, in a degree of pain as my shoes were squeezing my toes together, and the back of my footwear was now cutting into my Achilles heel, and as I approached the reception, I was greeted by a stand-offish middle-aged woman who told me to take a seat, which I did for at least half an hour, until eventually the guy I was here to see, came out and invited me into his office while slurring his words slightly, he looked like he had been drinking.

He was scruffily dressed in well-worn jeans and a Dennis the Menace style top with a few days' growths on his face and greasy flyaway hair. He looked like a cross between an alcoholic and Freddie Kruger, but not the owner of a haulage business.

First impressions where that if Don the driving instructor had a long-lost brother, here he was. He didn't even tell me his name but began asking questions, getting straight to the point,

"I don't need you, over there are loads of letters from guys begging for a job," as he pointed to a pile of unopened mail on the window ledge,
"so why you? I could pick any of them right now."

With this and other questions in the same tone, I answered them with an air of confidence that comes from a guy with nothing to lose, indeed, I wasn't desperate for this job because of my impression of the place, and his abrupt attitude, so it was a mystery as to why I lied when he asked me about my work history in relation to the vacancy and I said that I had driven all over the country for a firm which I knew no longer existed, I also told him that I was experienced in handling the larger commercial vehicles.

I'd first started fibbing four years earlier to cover my gambling losses, it had now evolved to the stage where I was just a pathological liar, but It worked and I was given the job, instantly thinking.
"what have I done?" and
"am I crazy?" but it got worse when he then said to me,
"you get yourself here tomorrow at 6.00 am sharp," which was a long way from
starting on Monday as I would have expected or waiting until he had received references before he employed me.

I was not impressed with him, or me, I wanted to turn around and tell him I didn't want the job but I just couldn't do it for some reason, and it was then that I shook his hand and made my way to the door, but he wasn't finished and I never forgot his parting words as I left, I did not know if he was serious or joking when he finally told me his name,
"I am called John, but you can call me boss," and hearing his name made me wonder if he was the guy who owned the barber's shop across the road, and was that his girlfriend in the shop? I couldn't imagine it; she might trim guys beards, but she surely wouldn't put her fingers through this guy's hair?

As I hobbled out of the office with my feet getting worse by the minute, I was soon walking like a penguin to take the weight off parts that hurt more than others, I felt like I was in a bad dream, and the blisters I was developing were the least of my problems.

I couldn't comprehend why I said what I did in the office, and I now had to back this up and I felt sick to my stomach at the thought, I had acted crazily and made ridiculous claims, the furthest I had driven was to Withernsea on the east coast on a quiet Sunday when my Dad let me drive his car, even then I nearly crashed into a Ford Fiesta that was innocently parked on the side of the road, which was not good when you consider that there was hardly any traffic that day.

I also underestimated the skill needed to drive as I thought that as almost everyone had a car – it must be easy; the only form of transport I ever owned was a second-hand bike and a cheap lock to secure it to a lamppost, which meant I hadn't even developed the practical everyday skills as a road user and here I was, a brand new haulage driver about to start a job at the deep end.

This was yet another time to reflect on why I gambled, to be successful and avoid feeling like I did right now, like I wanted to throw up and then run away and hide.

I went home and couldn't eat my tea; I couldn't stop thinking that I might not be here tomorrow night. Boss-John then rang me and told me the codes to get in the office and where the keys and pick up points where hidden, although there would be a list of addresses, and a card in the glove box with which I could buy diesel from any garage.

He spoke for ages but I didn't like his tone and his voice grated on me, I felt out of control as it was everything as he suggested, with no scope, which made him come across as if he owned me, he never gave me a choice about when where or how we did things, everything sounded like an order, not helpful tips.

I'd known him for a few hours and had physically only spent twenty minutes in a room with him, but already I felt like I hated him, and that I had made a huge mistake by telling untruths. Was it gambling that made me this person or was it me, if I hadn't spent over four years losing myself would I have been in a different position? Somehow it all connected to what was going wrong around me, and with who I was now.

I couldn't sleep that night; I knew I wasn't experienced enough for this, so I thought an early start was the best way for me, as I arrived at the outside door of the office for 3.00 a.m. and gained access with the code I had been given, I managed to get in the other necessary places too, again with more codes to find what I needed, it was like clockwork and everything was left exactly as boss-John had said. I then went to the yard with the vehicle's key and instructions in my hand and walked up to the van, which I hadn't seen until now, it was here that I got a shock, it was huge, massive, I could not believe I could drive the thing in front of me with a normal driving license.

Thoughts came in my head of the near-crashes I almost had in a small car, now I was controlling this monstrosity, I was scared, and my heart was racing ten to the dozen.

Figuring out how to open the van door seemed yet another task, but despite this, I was soon sat behind the steering wheel looking at the first address of the three locations I had to visit, and I took a few minutes to read the directions that I would be going from the notes I had made the night before, no sat-navs in 1989 so it was of luck that I had a UK road map from home that I brought with me.

The journey would take me to York, Newcastle and Berwick-upon-Tweed.

It was now, more than ever that I was regretting lying to get the job, as I turned the key to start the motor, and took a giant gulp, and said to myself,
"here goes."

As I moved out of the yard, it felt surreal, very different to the driving lessons, which is all I had known up to this point, this was the first time I had driven unsupervised, and what a way to start!

As I turned left, I felt like I was taking a juggernaut onto the main road, I just hoped that I could adapt quickly.

I drove down James Reckitt avenue and headed towards Beverley high road, here I was York-bound, I was nervous and didn't know how I wasn't hitting the cars parked on the side of the road, but as it was the early hours of the morning, I had time to familiarise myself with the vehicle as there was very little traffic about.

The van was pre-loaded and by the time I was on the motorway I was cruising and began to gain confidence; it was that first steady half-hour that made the difference and finding the first premises of the day came easy and it was still only 5.00 a.m.

I didn't have to do anything as it was a large yard and a guy came with a fork-lift-truck and did all the work. I was thinking how easy his job looked with the amount of room he had to work in, and he didn't seem stressed in any way like I was, it looked like he had all the time in the world.

I then set off again, this time for Newcastle, which was a pickup before another drop-off.

Weirdly enough, I was surprised how quickly I got to my next destination, I had thought that it was a lot further than it was, but as I wasn't taking any breaks, I was there for 6.20 am.

Again, I found the place easily once I arrived in Newcastle, and it was almost identical to the previous stop, except the guy there was loading my van this time, not taking stuff out, and once more I was watching with interest as he manoeuvred the fork-lift-truck, whilst wishing that was the job I had, it looked grounded, skilled and the guy was not going all over the country under pressure like I was.

It wasn't difficult finding the motorway again, and as I was cruising along, I found myself thinking more relaxingly about what I was doing, I didn't know I had the talent to drive something like this when I had set off, and here I was having done two of the three stops already.

I saw a petrol station signposted, and made my first stop outside of the designated pick up and drop off points, I filled the van up with diesel after remembering Boss john had mentioned that the vehicle takes this, otherwise I may have put petrol in, that would have been interesting but thankfully I got this right. I then paid with the card Boss-John had given me, and then took a few minutes out to compose myself, because despite being pleased with the progress, I was still anxious and soon set off again.

Things seemed to go downhill after this mini time out, and I had an awful job finding Berwick-on-Tweed. I went past it, around it and everywhere but in it, until I eventually got there and found the place I was meant to go.

This business's premises were very different from the previous two I'd stopped at that morning and smaller in comparison.

A guy was there waiting for me, showing impatience in the light of wanting to unload, I wouldn't mind but I had arrived much earlier than if I had set off at the time I was told, rather than the middle of the night, but here, I showed my lack of experience by parking the van outside in the street, which seemed miles away from the loading bay.

"Mate, you need to reverse the van in there," he said, pointing to a narrow alley that wasn't much wider than the vehicle itself, he then let me know the reason,

"I can't unload from there in the street."

He had a tone in his voice rather than politely asking me, so I went out to do as he requested. Firstly, I had to swing the van into the middle of the road before I could reverse it, and I nearly hit another car in the process, forcing another road user to swerve to avoid hitting me, I then received a middle finger sign from the driver as he went past. It took me a few attempts to get the angle right and when I did, I took it back slowly, very slow in fact, as there was an inch of space at each end until I got into the yard.

I considered what I had just done to be amazing driving, I never knew I had the skill to reverse a van that size backwards through such a tiny gap, and as far as I was concerned I was doing the job to a high standard, but my heart was still racing from that near-miss with the car.

After the guy unloaded we were finished and he told me that was it, I could then see him rushing away to the office where he made a phone call. I wondered if he was ringing Boss-John. I didn't care I just wanted to get in that van and drive away.

Once I got through the alley again without scraping off any of the paintworks, I went towards the coast and parked up, and took a stroll down the beach and tried to enjoy the sea-air and sample the place while I was there. I still had no appetite what-so-ever so fish and chips were out of the question.

I liked the look of Berwick-on-Tweed, although I was thinking that I would like to have seen it under better circumstances, I did think it was Scotland, where I had always wanted to go, I didn't know at the time that I was still in the north of England. I tried to take in what I saw but I was dreading the thought of the drive back and wanted it over and done with, so I only stayed on the beachfront for ten minutes, no photos though, we didn't have mobiles, let alone camera and video phones so I knew I would have to rely on my memory.

As I returned to the van, I was now more familiar with it, and strangely, it didn't look or feel as big as it did the first thing that morning, but being halfway through the day journey wise, it was now all about getting back again and with no stops to make I estimated I'd be home by 3.00 pm.

To make sure I could get back efficiently I needed to make sure the van had sufficient fuel, so firstly, I popped to another petrol station and filled it up once more with diesel, and after paying for this with the card, I was on my way and soon out of the town, and back on the main roads intending to drive without stopping.

Initially, things appeared as straightforward as they possibly could, but all roads looked the same and I saw nothing memorable, but I kept on driving thinking I was going the same way back that I came.

I cruised along the motorway for what seemed an endless journey, slowing down only when I came to roundabouts or junctions, looking for any signs that said Newcastle, York or Hull, eventually, I spotted a signpost in the distance and approached it with anticipation, and as I got closer I saw '63 miles to Blackpool' in big white letters, I was shocked! I had somehow gone in the wrong direction.

I stopped at another petrol station and asked a couple of drivers who I thought might be familiar with the roads, to advise me which way I should be going, of which I was told that I needed to turn around and go the opposite way back.

Feeling sick was something I had been getting used to in the last twenty-four crazy hours, but it was worse now as my anxiety levels hit new heights, as I was closer to the west coast rather than north Yorkshire.

I drove for two more hours, and turned onto another road, still not knowing if I was heading home when I finally noticed a sign for York, I had skipped Newcastle altogether, this meant I was now going in the right direction, so I carried on driving.

I didn't see the York sign again during the next spell with my foot down but carried on regardless, and soon stopped at another petrol station and noticed the time, it was 4.00 pm, but I had long since given up on getting back at the time I planned.

I started the engine and set the wheels in motion again, although fearing that I may have turned off somewhere that I shouldn't and was going the wrong way, but the panic was over when I saw another sign for York, fifty-miles this time, which meant it was maybe an hour away, the feeling of relief came rushing through me. I drove like a man on a mission and eventually got there.

York was packed with traffic, I had looked at the time at every opportunity but failed to contemplate it was approaching rush-hour, and I was gridlocked for a while until I eventually came onto another dual carriageway, and it wasn't long after this that I hit the town of Selby. To my dismay, there was more traffic, but this was caused by a toll bridge which was twenty-pence to cross, even in 1989 this wasn't much then either.

I eventually came to this and drove over it, and a guy who looked like Ricky Tomlinson from Brookside was collecting the funds with a bucket, but I had a brainwave, the traffic was getting lighter so I decided that I was going to drive away without paying, so I put my foot down, but a few yards later I got stuck behind another car, and saw the bucket man running after me, waving his fists and looking angry, calling me every swear word under the sun and I had no choice but to open my window for him, I knew he wasn't going to be friendly,
"oy you, you have to pay like everyone else, you're lucky I don't turn you back around and tell you to clear off," all this fuss, I thought, over a twenty-pence piece, so I dropped it in his bucket and replied,
"sorry fella, I didn't know about the toll, honestly,"

"yeah course you didn't, you tried it on and thought you'd get away with it," was his comeback and he was then swearing obscenities about me again while ranting at his co-worker.

I was soon moving more progressively with the traffic easing down further, and relieved to get away from this Mr Angry who seemed to enjoy confrontation, I hoped when he was telling his mates later that evening about me and how he stopped Selby city council from being robbed from a Hull van driver, that he added some zeros on the amount to make it sound more impressive, he didn't exactly foil an armed robber with a sawn-off shotgun, but then again, why didn't I just give him the 20p in the first place?

I then drove for around half an hour looking for the Hull sign when I spotted something I didn't expect to see, a 'welcome to York' board at the side of the road.

Somehow I had got lost and ended up turning 180-degrees back to where I was an hour earlier.

After driving around at the end of my tether I found another exit of which I went through, again, I was not sure if I was coming or going till I eventually saw another sign saying 'Beverley 20-miles ahead' and I then knew, after all this time, that I was nearly home.

It was now 7.00 pm, and with the traffic a lot lighter on the road, I could relax for the first time since I left Boss-Johns yard seventeen long-hours ago, and barring something stupid, I knew the worse was over.

I finally arrived in Hull and drove the van back to the yard where boss-John was still there, despite being 8.00 pm. He welcomed me back by immediately telling me that he could have done the same journey in less than six hours, and how I would be able to do that too, I could only get quicker according to him, nothing about extra pay though, I had been driving since the middle of the night till the following evening, but I knew I would not be paid for that long, as any surplice outside the agreement they allotted me would be classed as my fault, not that I had signed any form of contract in the first place.

I began to walk home totally deflated but relieved when boss-John caught me up and offered me a lift home, he then came out with a sports car that must have cost a fortune, he didn't look like the type of guy that would drive something like this, but I visualised myself in one of these in the future from gambling winnings, because there was no way I was working this way for a living if the day I'd had was anything to go by, as the whole thing felt like an inspired moment telling me to get my act together.

For the time being though, I felt trapped in a job that would take its toll on my mental and physical health, and it was to get worse before he left after dropping me off home, Boss-John told me that I would be driving to Durham the next day but the yard I needed to be in for the first pick up didn't open till 8.00 am so there was no need to get in before that time.

I didn't want to go there at all and that evening I made the decision that I knew I had to, and it was a no brainer, I was going to work the next day which was Friday and then hand a weeks' notice before I went home, thinking that I may as well get a week and a half's pay first, but little did I know I wasn't going to last that long.

It was 7.55 am the next morning when I arrived and Boss-John was waiting for a call about my delivery, so he showed me the yard, he pointed to the sweeping brush, then the guttering full of leaves and told me how he wanted it to look when I had finished, he then told me his wife and son work there so not to slag him off or it will get back to him.

After spending at least half an hour clearing the wet leaves with the yard brush, I went into the office and found out that the lady that I first met at the interview, who I described as stand-offish, was his wife, and not the blonde across the road from 'Johns' barbershop, mind you, I worked this out already.

I asked about my pay, as I had been told nothing, and had a nice chat with his lovely other half, she had an attitude that stank. I was trying to find out a few details when she told me, "you're on a trial, if your considered worthy after a week you will be offered a position," I wasn't told this, so I was stunned as I carried on listening,
"we will talk about Salaries next week," she then finished off talking down at me by putting me firmly in my place so there was no doubt in my mind,

"where your boss tells you to go, you go, and you will be as efficient as possible, professional as possible and as quick as possible," of which she then closed the door as I was about to speak, to let me know the conversation was over.

I thought I was getting paid for the full day that I had already done, it transpired that I was getting nothing for it, not for the first week anyway, I was assuming they would treat me if they were not paying me, but as I was broke, I didn't want to waste my time while these people benefited from having me work for nothing.

Back in the yard, just as I picked up the brush again, Boss-John came out and told me to get in the van, where I was to take it to a place on Hessle road so it could be loaded, then I had to drive it to an address he gave me in Luton, the night before he had said Durham, I was confused, to put it mildly.

I knew where this was as I lived a few miles away from it when I spent a year in Welwyn Garden City at Jeff and Pat's house. I soon arrived at the pickup location, a guy with a fork-lift then skilfully manoeuvred the package that I was to deliver, once again I was looking at him and wishing I had learnt to drive one of those instead, he didn't seem stressed or rushed.

The package was twice the size of the van, it went in, but it stuck out the back by a clear two feet. The doors had to be tied to stop them flapping and I looked at this with my mouth wide open.

"Do you think I am safe to take this," I said to the guy on the fork-lift, he was young, I was 21 years old myself, so he was probably the same age as me.

"If it was me, I wouldn't drive it, if you take it you're responsible, not your employer,"

This is what I was hoping to hear and it made shivers go down my spine at what Boss-John wanted me to do, I had passed the end of my tether stage the previous day when I nearly ended up at Blackpool, I couldn't believe what I was doing.

I saw things in black and white, I was working for a bad boss, I was stressed, unhappy and still hadn't eaten for two days, and yet another long trip, and I could not face another day like the one I'd just had, my morale was in the toilet as

Boss-John and his wife had constantly spoken to me like I was a piece of crap, and I thought about him making me sweep that yard, I knew it wasn't right.

I politely asked the guy to unload it and I rang boss-John and his wife answered, now that I was assertive she was suddenly as nice as pie to me, and she didn't know what to do and told me to come back to the yard. I then drove back where boss-John was waiting for me,
"wait in there" he yelled pointing to the office, he was on the phone to the young lad shouting at him, his wife asked me if I wanted a drink, I didn't want anything from either of them even though the back of my throat was dry despite necking a bottle of water a few minutes earlier, it was too late for her to act civil as far as I was concerned.

Boss-john walked in and I started our conversation,
"it was dangerous, I couldn't take it as I was responsible"
"if" was the next word I got out before he interrupted with a barrage,
"if, ifs and buts, if I had been born a woman I might have been working as a prostitute down Waterhouse lane and not running a haulage business," he then spoke of the package,
"if it sticks out you can put flags on the back, different ones for different lengths, it could have been double what was sticking out and still been transported legally within the law, and you were covered to drive it," his tone then lowered as he explained how he normally gives all his drivers second chances but asked me what I would do if I was him,
"I would sack someone who did that," I said this in a way that was telling him that this is what I wanted him to do, not just to say what he wanted to hear, I didn't want to work there, simple as.

He then left the room and another guy came in who was probably his son and explained that I didn't need to come in anymore, and that it was a trial that I had been on, which I already knew 'after' I had done that long haul the day before, and that they would keep my name on file.

I would have respected him more if he had straight sacked me as if I was a first-round loser on 'the Apprentice' TV show, but I was very relieved and left the yard, I still hadn't eaten for

thirty-six hours, I would have been a sure winner at a weight-watcher's weigh-in, but for the present, it was a stroll home, I needed the space and air you get from the solitude of a walk, as I cut down the old Wincolmlee industrial estate, then onto Fountain road, feeling like a weight had been lifted off my shoulder, until, after half-an-hour, I arrived home, where I could smell food and I heard my Mum greet me with the words,
"we are just having a bacon sandwich; do you want one?", I knew I was through the other side of the nightmare when I said,
"yes please, I'm starving."

It's odd how you can look at a choice in career and view it as something you can do for the rest of your life, a job that fits around you and one that allows you to pace yourself and coast along, but when you get there its nothing as you expect.

I was grateful to be back to where I was two-days earlier, but I was not thinking 'turning point', this time, which had been the most overused word's in my vocabulary in recent years, but it was clear to me that I needed a break after I was treated appallingly by Boss-John who to me was now just John, not my gaffer anymore, and I never wanted to be cohered like that again, as relieved as I was, I felt angry at what I had been put through, and all for nothing as I never received a penny for my time there.

Right now, It's no surprise that gambling for a living appealed at an all-time high but my finances were at their lowest, especially after the latest calamity at Norfolk haulage, add this to the last betting binge just before this, when I lost my precious comic-book collection, and with the temperament I had I could not do it, but I felt this was another lesson, that would stack up with the others and take a step towards eventually defining what I would become, I strongly believed that one day, I would emerge that new man.

Things took an interesting twist quickly, as something else changed my life, I met Sally within a month of that driving disaster, and only a few weeks after this I found out I was going to be hearing the patter of tiny feet in the not too distant future, I was going to be a father.

Soon I moved out of my parents' house and into my first council property up east Hull. I tried to be responsible and it wasn't long before I found work in a fish finger packing factory down Hessle road, this lasted six weeks before I was fired for being too slow, but with shocking working conditions including management timing workers with stopwatches and minimum breaks, it wasn't for me, but at least I got paid for my exploits, which is more than I did at Norfolk haulage.

The only employees at that factory that seemed relaxed and did not look to be under pressure were the two fork-lift drivers, they appeared to stand around talking most of the day, and always the first in the staff room at break times, and the last out, again this remained in my thoughts.

My firstborn, Lisa-Marie came along, and life made sense, but I now visualised my whole future different, I thought less about holidays and cruises around Caribbean islands, it was now more home comforts, a large detached house with no neighbours, so we could blast music out, televisions in every room with the latest games and consoles, a cellar in the basement with the best wines, giving myself, my daughter, and any other kids that came along, the best living conditions.

I wanted a happy home, with everyone sat around the dinner table at set times as a family, but this was the basics and I yearned for even more.

I wanted to take my family out for treats in the best restaurants, watching them being served exquisite cuisine cooked by Michelin star chefs and served by posh waiters, and they were going to have it all, and never want for a thing, and I had a picture in my head of gambling financing it all, but I wasn't near any of that yet.

This dream stayed with me, although I was currently living on a rough council estate in East Hull with little or no money in my backside pocket, I hadn't even started to get off the ground, but with new-found focus I again believed I could achieve, but before I could say the word 'nappy', another baby was on the way.

At this stage, I was beginning to know what the old woman who lived in a shoe felt like.

Despite being more contented with my life than I had ever been before, gambling was still with me on an emotional and psychological level, but I couldn't deny that even with my fantasy, reality was in front of me and I knew that I would have to work for the short term, I couldn't get away with it for long, but for now, I had to re-think everything about my life and situation.

The gambler within me was like a secondary existence, it made the excuses in my head and left me believing them, that I was going to be rich but the only way I could do this was to keep in touch with horse racing, so I didn't lose my ability.

Reality check now, what ability? I was broke and threw away every chance I had by putting my gambling first, but I had the vision that I would be prosperous one day, and to do this I needed to keep myself up to date with betting, yes, I was a level below naïve, but I somehow fed myself this and it took excuses to new boundaries, even by my standards, this was a mind of a gambling addict at work.

The problem I had was I liked to study the races in the morning, by making myself comfy and spreading the racing formbook and newspapers containing runners and riders all over the floor, and going through it with a fine-tooth comb, striving to solve the puzzle of what was going to win the races, finding an edge, discovering something that no one else had found and exploiting it, but with the distractions in the house that weren't at my Mum and Dads place, it was difficult, so I needed to think of a different tact.

The big money and rewards were going to come later as far as I was concerned but in the meantime, I remembered something I had seen in the Sporting life, as I planned to do something I had never done before, I was going to try system betting, something fast, easy and profitable.

My Dad was always into systems, he liked to pick his horses by glancing at the papers, he would do everything from bottom weights to following trainers in form, even backing horses that had won the corresponding race a year earlier, he made them up as he went along but the one thing he wouldn't do is spend hours looking at the formbook, I was the complete opposite but decided to give his way of thinking a chance, with a difference, I wanted to find something that worked and showed a profit if there was such a thing.

There was an ad running from a guy that claimed to be selling a system catalogue on the cheap, for just a fiver, I showed the article to my Dad and he took an immediate shine to it, and he then went to his top drawer, reached in and pulled out a five-pound note that had been torn and sellotaped back together, and said,

"I'll buy it, you can pay the postage costs," he didn't need to ask me twice, and I was then on my way to the post office to buy a postal-order and a stamp, rushing to catch the 11.30 am collection, so it would be there on Monday.

My Dad and I had bought a couple of books from the paper before, and often received circulars offering us tipping services or more expensive systems, most likely because the sellers may have sold our name on to others in the game, to add to their mailing lists.

We had a quick response, as Tuesday morning, the day after it had been received, I was back at my parent's house when a large letter fell on the mat, I instantly knew what it was.

I opened it to find a small book that had been homemade with a computer. I can't remember what it was called except it had 'systems' in the title and it provided what it said on the tin.

I skimmed through it with great fascination and upon reading found out that, according to him, there were thousands of horse and dog racing systems out there and they sold on average, between £5 and £100 each, but no more such prices for us, his lucky readers, because he had bought them all, and with his trusty photocopier he was offering them to us for a quid each, but the book with the list of the systems cost an initial £5, but he claimed it was large and detailed, but after this, it was only ever going to be £1 for anything we saw in it.

The catalogue also had customer feedback onto which of them worked the best, I could not have been more impressed, I was expecting it to be a con, but the guy seemed legit.

I discussed the findings with my Dad and it's easy to guess what we decided, we bought five systems that we liked the look of, and rather than get a postal order, we took a chance and put a five-pound note in the envelope, affixed a stamp and dropped it in the mailbox.

The systems came back quickly, they were, as described, one or two sheets of paper photocopied for us. There was also a list of updates as more systems had been added, again all £1 each, and we kept on buying them infrequently, and we had fun reading them, and they ranged from possible potential winners to the laughable.

One such example of a bad system was when we received an A4 sheet which contained just three sentences, it was called ' the huge priced winner method', and it told us to back every horse in September that had finished 4th, then 9th, and then 4th again in its last three races, and this claimed to have scooped a 50-1 winner.

I am sure this was after the event and it wouldn't be a surprise to find a horse at that price with the recent form like that, but we had a chuckle or two trying to find the right system.

Another laughable system was for Greyhounds and you needed to be at the track and look at a certain way the dogs walked. I didn't take this seriously, surely they all put one paw in front of the other when they approach the traps?

After some deliberation, we shortlisted just two, they were called the 'classy winner' and the 'double top' systems.

I'll make this as informative but as brief as I can for anyone who has no interest or knowledge of horse racing.

First the Double top system, it was for the flat season only, which ran from March to September in the days before all-weather tracks, and current season only. The horse had to be carrying top weight and a minimum of two outings and needed to have either won both its races or come second in one of its other runs if it's been out three times or more.

To make this simpler the form had to read like this: 1st,1st (in the last two runs) or 1st, 2nd, 1st or 1st,1st, 2nd (last 3 runs).

This one was easy and could be done briefly from any newspaper.

The classy winner system was also for the flat season only, and this was straightforward too; you back a horse that takes the lead at the two-furlong marker and holds this to the winning line.

The theory was that hitting the front at that stage meant the horse had to fight off challengers as the other runners would have been going for it as well, leading more than two-furlongs out could have meant it had stolen a lead and not had to battle its way home, if it took it up later than this, again it might not have had to deal with other challengers coming up to overtake.

You would back the horse in its next three races after it had performed this feat, this was easy enough but you would need a paper like the Sporting life or the Racing post as they delved into details of a horses form that you don't get from a daily newspaper like the Mirror or the Sun.

Now that I had sorted this out, I aimed to save money up for these systems as it was early in the year and weeks away from the flat season, so I had time on my hands and between then and the present I wanted to tinker with small bets and try to show profit in time before I had the opportunity to bet with bigger stakes, which I hoped would help put me where I needed to be.

I knew what I was doing, I had a plan and I was motivated, I had reasons for being patient and had a lot to prove to many people, above all I wanted to have the life for myself and the family that the guys in the professional gamblers biopics had. So, the rest of this book is about how I won my fortune? If only! I may have had everything set in place, what I didn't have was a sound temperament and didn't know the meaning of the word 'wait'.

When the flat season was underway, I had nothing saved up, but I knew it would be a few weeks before the horses had enough runs that allowed the systems to kick in anyway.

The double top claimed to give an average of ten to fifteen points profit a year, so for a £1 level stake, this would be £10 - £15 winnings. For a 'grand per bet' stake that would be between £10k and £15k profit. I wasn't in the latter category with what I could put down but lovely thought for easy money and no study, if it worked that is.

The Classy winner system claimed slightly more but the logistics were the same.

I was excited on the morning that I looked in the paper and saw the first horse that qualified under the double top system, I was fairly flush for a change and I put £20 on it to win before racing began, but, it lost. It looked weighed down with ten stone of jockey and leaded-weight, as it went back-paddling early on.

When it rains it pours, and only the next day on borrowed money, after an afternoon of chasing when the double top went down, a classy winner system selection was running, and it was late in the day. I started with a tenner in my pocket, but by the time the main horse was running, I had to ask the bookie if he would allow me to put my last 40p on it, it then won at 7 -2 and the £1.62 I received as I didn't have enough to pay the 4p tax on the bet, went on the next greyhound race, which got beaten by a short head at 5-1, the same old story.

A strong double top ran a few days later, which fell on my payday, tipped by all the papers, I had £200 to last two weeks at this time as I was between jobs, too lazy in other words, and I put half of this, which was £100, on this horse.

It started as the 6-4 favourite and I was thinking of what I would do with the £150 profit when it won, but it didn't, nor did it finish in the frame, it could have been 4th, it could have finished last, but my money was gone whatever position it ended up crossing the line.

I saw none of the race, so I was hoping there was some way of getting my money back, did it run? with its form how could it not place? I was checking the screen and hoping against hope it had been pulled out of the race and was a non-runner so I could get my money back, as I couldn't afford to lose this much.

I was now in a bad place, as always nobody knew I had lost this money, there was cash missing from the house from the day before, that I had lost without telling anyone, and I owed even more out and the only way I could get around it was to lie and borrow over my head.

I told Sally that I didn't get paid as she wasn't there when I drew the money. I double and treble lied to everyone and juggled one fib to cover another and the money must have done a fifty-mile journey, but at the end of it, even though it was my fault, I wasn't prepared to be the one that suffered.

I stalled her further for a couple of days, then I gave her £20, and then made out that I had seen a bargain at the travel agents and needed a deposit, that we were going to Spain in six months, but we had to suffer for this month, this was so that I could leave her on a pittance while I had gambling money.

I went along with this lie, and I was going to either book us a real holiday or make a story up that it had been cancelled, every day Sally was asking me about passports and I would say we didn't need them till the month before so they lasted longer, they last for ten years, so why would I have made us wait?

Optimistically, I believed that I had a chance of winning the money and could then pay for the holiday there and then, but I never got close to this, so there were only one of two solutions for me, either come clean or tell more lies and as per always, I chose the latter so I wouldn't look bad.

Sally believed everything I said and sure enough, I eventually had to say that I received a phone-call, again conveniently while she was out, that the airline had gone bust, but we were getting our money back, but it would take a few weeks.

She was watching the news on the TV avidly for the next two nights, expecting a report on an airline that had gone into liquidation, I then implied it was a small flight company, and that it was only briefly mentioned when it first happened, it would have been on if it had been someone like Thomas Cook, yet more lies but she was getting wiser to me now.

I paid her what I could, but she kept asking me for weeks where the money was, and when we were getting it back, and she never let up, so I told another lie that I had found yet another bargain, but taken it to my Mums for a Christmas present for when the second baby arrived, there were no depths to how low I would stoop, she never saw me getting any calls or any of the bargains I was constantly finding, but she knew clearly that the man of the house was a liar.

While all this was taking place, I lost track of any 'classy winner' system runners and wasn't sure if I had missed any Double top horses, but out of the blue, one was running, and it started at 4-1, I put £20 on it. If it won I was going to give Sally half the money to gain some credibility back, I was aware I was running low on trust, but again, it lost and didn't even look like winning like the others.

A few days later another was running in the evening meeting, I planned to back it with the same stake but I spent the full afternoon chasing and as the betting shops were closed I put a slip-on with what I had left and this one finally won, and at a good price, 6-1, good news? I didn't say what I had on the horse, I put my last sixty pence on it and had a whole £4.20 to come the next morning.

I couldn't help thinking that had I put £100 on it like I had a previous loser that I thought had more chance because it was a shorter price, I would have had £600 profit, and the holiday in Spain could have been real, it was 1993, even £20 as the previous double top would have netted me a £120 profit, nice money in them days.

As far as the systems went for the summer, the double top did ok after the shaky start to the year, I saw a couple of them win at 2-1 and 7-2 as the flat season drew to a close, I observed a few points profit but it could have been more or less as I am sure some ran without me knowing.

The classy winner system seemed to give a winner out of every three on average, again from what I caught. Had I followed them both for level stakes I would have been quid's in profit, but even when I got a winning system in front of me, I couldn't make it pay.

I didn't want to bet anymore, and I wanted to provide and build from the ground up again.

I knew it hadn't worked the last time I had tried paid employment, but I looked in the local paper every night at the job ads, and something else caught my eye, an advert for fork-lift driver training. I had remembered the places I had worked, and the guys who drove these always looked unrushed.

I recollected the times I had seen them in action, the factories, or when I was on the road for Boss-John, always wishing I was doing that job. Now I had an opportunity staring at me in the face.

The Advert was a small box near the vacancies page, and for £300 they would put you through an intense 3-day course and if you passed, you received a certificate and was qualified to work as a fork-lift driver. Just one problem, I had a £1 coin in my pocket and needed another £299 to get on the course.

Ok so did I get the money? Well the Bank of Mum and Dad was the obvious answer so I went around to the house and put the kettle on, I wanted them comfy with a cup of tea when I asked them, the worse they could do was say 'no'.

I convinced them that I was committed to my responsibilities, but they said a big fat 'yes' and the next step was to book the lessons.

I wanted to focus on where I was now and the short term, not looking too far ahead, and I needed work that I could do, so the first step was the training and I rang and booked the course for two-weeks-time, offering to pay the next morning in cash.

My parents knew I always paid back, my Mum then walked into her bedroom and I could hear the lid of the black cat coming off where she saved up in case my Dad needed a new car, and she came out with a wad of notes and handed it to me. I then offered to pay back at a set monthly amount, meaning it would be off early in the new year, and I could have a new career into the bargain.

Every time I had money like this I felt nervous but I went early the next day to the centre, which was down Cottingham road before the bookies opened and paid for the course and was set to go.

So after observing fork-lift truck drivers in action and liking what I saw, I had preparations to become one myself, it looked like a well-paid job with a fairly high degree of skill to it, I was confident I would end up doing the same as the guys I had earmarked, so it was all easy and straightforward from here, right?

CHAPTER THREE

Here I was again, on the verge of learning to drive, but something new. It was hard not to think about the hassle I had trying to get my car licence, but at the same time, thinking that this is what I should have done in the first place, fork-lift truck driving looked the best job ever, and from what I had witnessed, it seemed to involve sitting around all day drinking coffee while waiting for vans to come to the yard, then lock and load.

When the first day of the course arrived, I hadn't even left the house and I was already a bag of nerves, I was pacing up and down and feeling anxious because I knew there was a lot at stake, I had one chance because of the higher costs involved, I knew I couldn't keep taking tests on the fork-lift until I passed, as I could with normal car driving, and look what happened with that?

The training always began on Tuesday's with both a written exam and a test on the Friday of the same week. I left the house earlier than I needed to, so I could take a steady stroll to the centre, hoping to calm myself down and psych myself up at the same time.

I tried not to overthink the past, especially with my track record of driving tests, but it was hard not to have it in the back of my mind, as I didn't fancy another disaster trying to get the certificate, there was not long to find out though, I knew that I would have the outcome in front of me in seventy-two hours, and would regroup then, for now, I just had to do it.

As I turned onto Cottingham road, I could see the centre and I knew this was it, I took a deep breath as I approached the building and walking inside to the main reception, I was then given directions to where I needed to be.

As I walked towards the area where I was told to go to, I saw buses parked with L-plates on, this told me that they taught public service vehicle driving too, I was certainly not thinking of this for my future, so there aren't any stories in the next chapter about me taking out a bus-load of passengers around the city, which is a shame as I am sure that would have been interesting and something would have gone pear-shaped.

I saw the office the receptionist had described to me, and as I got nearer I noticed the door was open, as I peered in, I spotted a guy, who looked in his late fifties and a younger chap around the same age as me,
"you must be Chris? come in here and take a seat," said the older man, and I knew instantly I was in the right place.

He introduced himself as John, yet another person with that name! and the other student was called Mike, who worked at the warehouse of a department store in the city centre that is no longer with us, called Willis Ludlow's, Primark was destined to own that spot a few years later.

John liked to be called JB and thank goodness for that or I would have had to have changed his name for the sake of this story, too many John's so far and every one of them had given me grief of some kind, but not as much as another 'John' was going to in the future, but that was to come later, but in the here and now I was ready to start, we now know JB was the instructor and Mike was here to get his certificate just like myself.

I sat down, and as we were strangers, a chat and a mini bonding session was the next thing on the agenda. I soon took a dislike to JB as he made us coffee's, he didn't ask us if we preferred tea or a cold drink, he literally made our mind's up for us, and with the hot beverage, also came milk and sugar sachets.

What did leave a bad taste in my mouth wasn't the choice of the freeze-dried coffee he used, it was the opening of his hatred for all things non-British and ethnic minorities.

If I had needed to change his name for the story it would have been easy, I would have called him Adolf, and this was after only ten minutes.

Previously, JB had been a coach driver before he began teaching and told us the story of how he refused to take a minibus that contained a small group of Muslim people who had booked this in advance

I disliked his bigoted attitude, my brother's wife Pat was of Caribbean origin and the only reason I didn't like her was that she was a nightmare to live with during my stay in London, not because of the colour of her skin.

I hated people that had an attitude like JB, and I knew that if he even had a whiff of knowing I had mixed-race nephews he would fail me on the final day, he virtually said as much in the opening hour.

To make things worse, Mike was agreeing with every word JB said and it wasn't long before I found out that he was just as bad, but I wasn't joining in, I refused to even nod my head, even if it meant failing at the end of the course, and I stayed silent while these two racists swapped their views. Mike was already driving a fork-lift at work but had to get this certificate to do it legit.

So, great! here I was asking myself if anything normal was ever going to happen to me, even this had to have a twist, as two Klu-Klux Clan wannabees that can already drive a fork-lift, sat with me, having their ongoing conversation about their outdated views of white supremacy.

Mike went as far as to say he had a partner at home that owned a business, I had no doubt it was a woman as he was probably homophobic too, and then he confirmed this.

She earned twice as much as him, but this didn't stop him criticising her lack of cooking skills, so, his Victorian-age view of a woman and a kitchen seemed to continue to create a consistent portfolio of him.

He then mentioned that he played football and went training most evenings and she used to complain he was out a lot, of which he was bragging of his standard reply to her,
"my football comes first and always will, and when the season ends the five-a-side indoor matches begin so stop complaining."

He talked about her like she was a lodger, and as they didn't have any kids, I couldn't surmise what hold he had over her, he wasn't exactly Richard Gere. There was surrealness about him, his views didn't fit someone his age, which he confirmed was 24, a year older than I was.

The training was undertaken in a confined area consisting of ten isles, each of these had three levels, top, middle and bottom, and it was going to be all practice from here onwards, as JB gave us a demonstration on how to lift pallets with the forks from one place and put them down in another.

We were to take turns, and Mike went first, and not surprisingly with his experience, he did what he was told the first time of asking, then he climbed out as I approached the fork-lift truck for the first time in my life, and I sat down expecting to make a fool of myself, but to my amazement, I didn't! I soon picked it up, I took longer than Mike, but it wasn't anywhere near as hard as I expected, as I forwarded, reversed and lifted pallets while swinging the truck around to place them elsewhere, I sighed with relief, already believing I would be able to pass the test on Friday, even after this one short attempt, but there was no complacency or over-confidence, remembering what it took to get my car license, this left me feeling that I had the right balance in my approach.

As we continued, I felt that I had it in the bag within an hour, the truck was limited to the number of things that it could do, so it didn't mean rocket science, and as I improved, Mike didn't look that much better than me after a further hour.

I came on further leaps and bounds as we finished the day off, I knew I was well on my way.

On the way home, I would normally have called day-one a success as far as learning what I needed, but it was hard to get the morning conversation and all that bigoted stuff that I'd heard out of my head and this stopped me from feeling on a high.

I was cursing my lack of principles for not walking to the main office and demanding another instructor, but I never had the power of easy choice through my lack of money, even this course was done with funds I borrowed, which meant my parents had a vested interest and wanted me to pass, I couldn't do it in secret, but if I could, and this had been the case, I would have considered writing it off, but I had a child and another on the way so I had to think of them, but with spare cash, there were other centres I could have gone too, but that wasn't an option, I couldn't buy my way out of anything and I cursed gambling for the place I was in.

My addiction had not only eroded me financially, the knock-on effect was that it also reduced me as a person, but I took a small comfort that there was this part of me that would always hate attitudes like JB and Mike, I worried about how much more my addiction would take from me though.

Right now, I would have loved to have written the money off, left the course and made a stand, instead, I was going to go on and complete it, while at the same time feeling I was letting my two nephews down by continuing to associate with this pair of fascists.

The only way I could look at it was that it was only two and a half more days, I told myself to get that bloody certificate and forget about these people if I could bring myself to call them that, to simplify it, I was going to take what I needed and ignore the parts I didn't.

Day two came and I approached the centre with a different tactic, I was aware of what could be ahead and decided to be prepared and come flying out of the blocks, and as we started things with coffee's, my plan was to speak more than the previous morning and dictate the conversation, first sport was on my agenda, especially as Mike was a soccer fan, and then I told them of my time in London, anything to stop them airing views that I did not want to hear.

This worked to a degree, but we got the story of JB's love of everything medieval England, he certainly had views dating from then, he revealed that he was a member of a club called the 'golden lions of England', where everyone would meet up, dressed as kings, queens or knights, or anything from the chosen period they were theming at the time.

JB had recently re-enacted a historical battle on a field between England and Scotland. It was all probably innocent enough and more likely full of people that enjoy this type of history rather than have attitudes like his, but not for me, I couldn't imagine anything worse than being dressed in a kilt and seeing JB charging towards me in a suit of armour.

Soon it was more practice on the fork-lift truck, of which I carried on from where I had left off the day before, moving pallets from one place to another, but JB advised me later in the day that the test had a time limit and I needed to speed up a little more, so the focus was on this and a couple of errors then came into my driving, but this may have been my concentration wavering a little rather than because I was rushing about, but I only needed to get it right on the test, to me, it was about practising hard till then. I was determined to give everything I had to get that certificate.

The third day went better, JB was in the office for coffees but had to leave the room for half an hour and when he came back it was straight into more practice. It was tiring as the day went on, I threw everything I had into it knowing the test was the next day, I knew this was the whole point of intensive training, as I went home satisfied with both my progress and my efforts.

It seemed a long week but the final day arrived and I knew it would be the last time we would meet in the office for coffee, but there was a board displayed that wasn't there the previous mornings, which showed our paths to get to where we currently were.

This display stated that Mikes employer had paid for him to undertake the training and test to obtain his fork-lift certificate, whereas mine had 'private funding' written, in other words, I paid the full price, and Mikes tuition was totally free.

He came across as a guy that always got the best, a successful wife earning mega-bucks, a lifestyle where everything evolved around him, and now this.

I didn't know why, but I thought he had paid it himself, whereas I went into debt for mine, and if I failed, I would be paying it off for the next year with nothing to show for it.

Shortly after this it got even more interesting with another revelation, he mentioned that he only drove the fork-lift at work now and again, it was only a small part of his job, there was no pressure on him to pass, and no outlay meant he would lose nothing either way, but to me it was everything.

Again, after the coffee, it was straight to the bays for more lifting and moving before the tests. After an hour's practice it was time for the exams to begin, JB then asked who wanted to go first on the fork-lift, we both did, so it was a question of who got it over with before the other.

The format was that one of us would do the written questions while the other did the driving and then swap over. If I had gotten it all for free, I may have been inclined to let the other person go first, Mike wasn't like this though, he wanted everything his way, it ended up being decided by the toss of a coin,
"tails" I shouted before Mike could say anything because if I won it would feel better knowing I didn't give him a chance, and as JB's hand came up, it was indeed a tail, I won,
"I am going first then JB," I said, Mike then looked at me, I could see anger and annoyance etched on his face, if JB hadn't have been there, I could tell he wanted to do everything from punching me on the nose, to running over my foot with the fork-lift truck, but this just added to the delight I was feeling, as I was happier inside than any time since Tuesday morning, the guy who liked his bread buttered on both sides didn't get his way, it felt like a result.

I was motivated, ready and willing as I sat on the truck for the last time, I was also anxious, nervous and sleep-deprived after laying away thinking about it most of the night, I just wanted it over with and didn't fancy the worse outcome, which was telling my Mum and Dad that I had failed yet again at something else.

The test was straightforward, consisting of a series of manoeuvres, marked by giving the operative a starting score of 100%, and for every mistake, points were deducted, and you had to have a final tally of 70% or above remaining for a pass, which was a clever way of doing it in my humble opinion.

I looked up at the numbered bays and pallets that I had been moving around for the last few days and had little problems, I had to get it right now though as none of that mattered, and I began moving the fork-lift to JB's voice and instructions,
"Shelf three middle to shelf six tops," and so on, as I swung in and out with the truck.
Any time I took a wrong angle, I could adjust in what was called a 'shunt', and the first of these were free, but any additional adjustments meant points were taken off.

JB didn't pass everyone and had failed many people, so it was not hung and dry.

The first few moves where done quick and efficiently, this went exactly as I had planned, which was getting off to a flying start, and it was a good job I did, as mistakes started creeping in, then after slowing down and completing a few flawless moves, I misjudged a couple of approaches and took three shunts at one of them.

Even at this point, I still had scope to make a couple more minor errors without putting myself under undue pressure, and I needed it, because I began struggling, even forgetting to do silly things like look both ways when I moved in and out, all the things I'd practised, and I had to then take my time even more.

JB reminded me that the test had to be completed within an hour, and of course, there was the written exam, of which Mike was already undertaking in the office.

I speeded up as the clock reached the final quarter, and finally completed my last manoeuvre and placed the forks flat to the floor, turned the truck off and stepped away from it.

He then told me I had a score of 71, and when I looked at the time I had taken exactly 1 hour, not a second to spare. I passed by the skin of my teeth; I wasn't worried about the written exam. Mike was sat drinking coffee when we returned to the office, he then told me how easy it was and that he had finished it in less than twenty minutes.

JB then called for a break for lunch, which must have been torture for Mike, I no longer wanted to see him suffer and despite what he appeared to be, I felt sorry for him, but I thought of that first day and my nephews, I was human though, I knew for sure that JB was a total bigot, Mike may have gone along to keep on the right side of JB, it was possible but then it came down to the fact that he shouldn't have said the things he did, but he was a young guy and I thought that one day, he might change his outlook, I hoped so.

As we left for lunch, I knew Mike would not have appreciated the hour for dinner right now, but as we left the building, we were in a different place, I had done the worst bit, the driving test and a multiple-choice questionnaire to go, I was in a better place than him, but all roads lead to Rome and it wouldn't be long before the course was over, two-hours from now. We left the building separately, but both headed down Cottingham road.

Mike headed to the Gardner's Arms pub that was just across from the centre, whereas I went a little further, up to the junction and left onto Beverley road, to a row of shops and I was ravenous, especially now the pressure was off.

First stop was the chippy for a well-deserved treat, well that was my intention, but there was a large queue, so I decided to wait till it was smaller, and went in the betting shop next door for a short while, the same four words again 'that was my intention'.

No surprises what happened next. I had planned to get a Pattie and chips but here I was having a flutter on the early races as National hunt often started around midday, soon the £10 note I had was down to a couple of quid, I should have cut my losses and bought my dinner but instead, I carried on betting and I couldn't get any form of a winner, a couple of second-place finishes, yes, a first past the post, no!

I left the shop skint and hungry, and when I looked at the time, I realised that I was due back at the centre in a quarter of an hour to do the written exam, and it was a ten-minute walk.

On the way back, I felt disappointed as I had seen the sign outside the chip shop all week boasting that they won an award for the best patties in the city. This was weird because the chip shop near where I lived bragged the same thing. We have always been proud of our patties in Hull, you couldn't get them anywhere else in the country, but everyone claimed that theirs were the best.

With no hanging around, I was immediately given the exam paper as soon as I arrived at the centre, JB told me to pop and see him when I had finished. Once I had answered the thirty multiple-choice questions, I did as he asked, I knew I needed 70% to pass on this as well, which was the same as the driving test, but I was confident as it was straightforward, I wasn't cutting it fine this time, and I had a much higher score.

While I was in the driving test area, Mike was attempting his manoeuvres, while JB had one eye on him, and the other on my exam sheet, he quickly told me I had a couple wrong, but all the rest were correct, and he held his hand out to me and said,

"congratulations, you've passed, you will receive the certificate in the post in seven to ten days."

I was chuffed to bits. He then said Mikes test would be over in a while, and if I wanted to wait in the room and make myself a drink, I could.

I hadn't eaten since the previous evening and because of this, I was feeling weak, this influenced my decision as I thanked JB, then told him I wanted to go home and tell my Mum and Dad, not that I had lost all my money betting on National hunt handicap races. I then turned and wished Mike luck while signalling a thumbs up, then I left the building for the final time.

Telling my parents that I'd passed felt as much for them, as it was for me, I loved the rare times I could give them good news, this wasn't on a par with that day when I came home successful after my car driving test, nothing could beat that, but this was a solid second.

Later that evening (and every day since), remained this lingering curiosity, Did Mike pass? Did he come back from the pub intoxicated and mess it up? I never knew, but I wished I had stayed, I wanted to go back in time and stand in that queue in the chip shop and stay out of the bookies, or hang around instead of being a wimp, I wouldn't have starved in an hour.

Did my mood change significantly after losing money, and influence me leaving? If it did, then this is a weak example when you compare it to other things that had happened because of my addiction, with much bigger losses and consequences, but countless times like this have occurred, moments that have been forgotten between the worst incidents, I only remembered losing that tenner because it fitted around me not knowing Mike's result, but there were hundreds of times when losses like this happened, that I can't even remember. These are like little straws that work together unknowingly manifesting themselves on eventually breaking the camel's back, in the form of the gambler.

A few weeks later, I rang the centre to find out the outcome of Mikes test, but nobody knew, so I asked for a contact number to reach JB, but I was informed that he had left to do another job, and they wouldn't tell me where, so this quickly hit a dead end.

I never saw Mike again, even when I walked past the back of Willis Ludlow's loading bay, he was never there. It would have made sense with them both seemingly vanishing, to find out that they had run off together to get eloped somewhere, it remains one of my regrets that I didn't wait that day.

There is one thing I did know, in the tug of war in my head, between 'working for a living' versus 'professional gambling', work was now in the driving seat – no pun intended, and with my brand new spanking fork-lift certificate, which added an additional qualification to my armour, it was time to get a job that fitted the description of my new skillset.

Firstly, I worked on how I was going to sell myself, because, at the end of the day, I only had three days actual experience, but I had worked in a haulage yard, albeit that was for less than two days, but I didn't have to let a potential employer know that, I just had to make sure that my story wasn't too far-fetched as I would have to live up to what I claimed.

It was not like telling a few lies would be a shock to my system, but I had to remember the position I got myself in with boss-John, although from what I had already seen on my travels, fork-lift driving looked like an easy job, with decent, unrushed working conditions, banter in the yard, and half the day playing cards, while waiting for wagons to come into the yard, surely I couldn't have got this wrong?

I typed out a CV in the library, exaggerating the factory work I had done, stating I had been a fork-lift driver in some of them, especially the places that had since closed.

Once I had completed this and was happy with it, I applied for some of the jobs advertised in the Hull Daily Mail.

A few of the ads were for different types of fork-lifts that I'd never heard of, like side loaders or counterbalance, whatever they were I didn't know, I stuck with what I had learnt and stayed within the remit of what I had physically done.

I didn't get any positive responses in the next month, but my luck changed one morning when I was walking down Holderness road, I ventured past a packaging company that had a sign outside advertising a position for a 'shrink-wrap operative'. I didn't fancy this job, but I needed work, so I went in and asked about this and they took my details and landline number, I told them I had a fork-lift qualification and experience, although the poster didn't ask for this.

No sooner had I arrived home, the phone rang, it was the company, and could I come in for an interview that very day, they needed a new fork-lift driver. It was a Monday afternoon and I had only passed the test five weeks earlier, but I didn't care about the logistics.

I quickly put on a shirt and tie and I was thinking of all the positives. I may have hated working for Boss-John, but I was going to mention this in a glowing account of what happened there, in other words, lie. As the company no longer existed to check up, I planned to say I was there till it closed, and there was no proof of me leaving under a cloud-like I did.

I felt that I had a skill, so I was sure the pay would be good. My imagination was carried away as I pictured myself being offered something in the region of £300 and upwards per week to do the job.

I arrived at the reception where the same polite woman that took my details greeted me, she was also the lady that called me back. I was only sat a couple of minutes when the managing director and owner of the company came in and introduced himself as Tony.

He talked with a very posh accent and dressed up in what must have been the sharpest suit I'd ever seen in person, complete with a pocket watch and cufflinks. I guessed immediately that he didn't come from around these parts, East Hull.

He asked a couple of questions and then passed me a pen and paper, and told me to write a couple of sentences, you could tell this was probably from his educated background, he had most likely attended one of the posh universities like Oxford or Cambridge, in fact, I wouldn't have been surprised if he had been a member of the annual boat race, probably the only thing I had never bet on up to this point.

"What School did you go too," he said looking at my handwriting
"Sir Henry Cooper" I replied, he probably thought it was named after the boxer and not the former Mayor of Hull.

He paused and went into a long silence, staring at my writing, but eventually said,
"know what, I am going to give you a chance, you start tomorrow and its 8.00 am till 4.00 pm, and the pay will be £90 a week."

I was shocked when he said this, ok, I knew the figure I thought up was overinflated, but I used to pack shredded wheat five-years earlier for more money than this and I did not have to drive a bloody fork-lift to do that, not even a hundred quid. My excitement was gone and when I told people that evening I lied and said £120 was the weekly pay, even then I would get the same response each time,
"what? is that all you get for fork-lift driving, is that all?"

They were right, but I had to look at the bigger picture, it was about getting my foot in the door.

I turned up for work the next morning and Tony showed me around, he talked and jested with the workforce, who earned him his living, so he knew where his bread was buttered. He also introduced me to his wife, who was the finance director, and told me his son Richard, who was coming in later, was the floor manager where I would be working.

I was then taken to meet the foreman, he was called Kevin, who was also one of the other fork-lift drivers, there was also another, a young chap called Ed, who I met next, who did the same job as Kevin and me, everyone else on the floor packed and shrink wrapped products.

Finally, before he left to go back to his office, Tony showed me where I was to clock in and out, at the start and end of every shift.

Being a new person was enough to make me nervous as I walked across the shop floor and saw everyone looking at me, but the bit I dreaded the most followed, as I was shown to my fork-lift truck.

I let off a huge sigh of relief when I saw that it was a match to the one JB taught me to drive in, all the controls were in the same place. I was then left with Ed, who showed me what my job entailed and then told me to get into the truck, of which I then asked if I could have a few minutes to get my bearings and the feel for driving a fork-lift again, I didn't think this was unreasonable but I could tell this opinion wasn't shared judging by the look on his face.

It wasn't too difficult though, and I soon picked up some pallets that had been wrapped and proceeded to load them onto the lorry, when the foreman Kevin shouted at me at the top of his voice,
"Oy, don't just leave that there"
"what do you mean? I have done what you asked" I replied, he then continued in a similar dismissive tone,
"use your fork's and push the pallet to the back of the truck, we have more to load up," I had simply left them on the front of the empty wagon, and this was down to my inexperience, he could have told me nicely, I had only been there half an hour after all.

I soon corrected this but felt angry because everyone was watching us, and this is not how you want to be seen, especially on your first day, I wanted to build up a reputation, and I had one already, as someone that was useless.

Two hours later, when I thought things were calming down and I was getting into my flow and the morning mistake was forgotten, I was loading another wagon, and just as I was putting on the last pallet, that had to be placed on top of the others, which was done by lifting it up high with the forks as I approached, I failed to notice the shutter roof in the loading bay as I was attempting to stack it and caught this as I drove forward, and half of the products ripped off and went all over the floor, suddenly Kevin's voice was in its full vocal range again as he yelled at me, "that is a waste and if it's damaged it can't be repacked, you're costing this company time and money."

I was in plain view with nowhere to hide as everyone stopped what they were doing to look across at the noise and commotion, it was probably exciting for them, but I had never felt embarrassment on this scale before, I felt sick, I hated the job already.

While we were waiting for the next lorry to come in, I talked to a couple of the lads that were packaging, one of them was called Doug, and he proceeded to tell me it was the best job he'd ever had, he claimed to have been the manager of a large tool hire company, but it wasn't a patch on what he was doing now.

Doug looked about 18 and I didn't believe a word he said, but he and the co-worker sat next to him showed me one thing, they resented me, they probably thought I was on fantastic money, and earning a lot more than them. This was clarified when Doug started asking questions,
"how do you get a licence to drive a fork-lift," I replied,
"just pay £300 for a three-day course, pass a test and it's as simple as that," his face dropped which told me this sort of money was out of his range,
"maybe you should have paid for it when you were a high-flying manager of a tool hire plant," I said in a lowered voice as I walked away, knowing he was unlikely to hear me, but enough to know I was being sarcastic, at this moment though, I felt like the only 'tool' in the place being hired, was me.

Tony popped down to the shop floor and looked around, before gazing angrily in my direction, I was hoping that his focus was on someone stood next to me, but it wasn't, as he pointed to the sweeping brush, and then proceeded to tell me that is what I needed to be doing, and not standing around, this was confusing as Mark, Ed and a couple of the packing operatives were doing the same as me, stood there doing nothing, but it was just me that had to sweep the floor.

There wasn't any doubt in my mind that someone had told Tony what had happened earlier with the shutter roof.

As I picked up the brush, one of the guys on the shop floor shouted,

"the vans back."

Now it was time to load the wagon again, nothing better than the fear of making another mistake combined with being shouted at three times in one morning to spike up your concentration to the maximum, as I did a few lifts and drops with no problems, or so I thought.

"you're going to have to load quicker as that van has to go back and forth several times and we are all on timescales," said Kevin, again letting me know he was the foreman.

Late in the afternoon, a chap I hadn't seen up to now walked into the area and made a beeline for me, he wore light blue jeans mixed with an expensive-looking tuxedo, and black shiny shoes that you could see your reflection in, enough clue's for me to guess who he was, and I was right, this was Tony's son, Richard.

He removed his jacket, revealing a shirt and tie, but then rolled up his sleeves, to mimic the fact that he lived in two worlds, the upstairs offices and the shop floor where he was currently standing, he had blonde hair and to give an image of what he looked like, he was the double of the villain from the James Bond film Skyfall, played by Raoul Silva. That movie may have been made many years later, but this guy had a licence to humiliate right now, and true to form, most of the bad guys who confront 007 have a weakness, and his was that he couldn't pronounce the letter 'R',

"I'm Wichard, my old man tells me your having a few pwoblems", he then got into my fork-lift and started giving me lessons, I could tell instantly that he had started in this very place with the other employees before being promoted to the number two for the company, but, to be honest, he was amazing on it and drove it quickly and effortlessly, he was without a doubt, the best driver in that place or indeed, anywhere I'd ever seen, I wondered if they taught fork-lift truck driving at Oxford or Cambridge?, but currently, I felt like a guy who had sunk the boat in their annual race.

After half an hour talking to Kevin and Ed like they were his long-lost friends, while I was sweeping the floor, Richard disappeared upstairs again, and normal activities resumed.

I went home without further incident, bemused by the day as a whole, thinking that in the workplace, I had thought that it was an unwritten rule that everyone is nice to the new person on their first day, to welcome them, and problems usually start later, when they get to know you, none of that seemingly applied here.

Here I was, in yet another position that I didn't want to be in, I had to vastly improve or leave, no other option. I slept better than expected and decided I was going to give everything I had on day two.

After arriving, it was the sweeping brush in my hand for me, as the loading bay hadn't opened yet, and I found myself in another conversation with Doug, as he looked in awe at a manoeuvre that Kevin was undertaking on the fork-lift, squeezing down the tightest space to take out a pallet,
"that is what you call a fork-lift driver," he said, I could tell this was aimed at me as he continued whatever issues he had.

Initially, I walked away after the hint, and let Doug have his moment, but after the previous days humiliations were still fresh, something inside me wasn't going to be outdone by anyone today, I got in my truck and did the same move that Kevin had just finished a few moments earlier, squeezing into the same space, as I fetched out an identical pallet, I then turned to Doug and said,
"not bad eh, are you impressed?, I can drive these too you know".

Doug may have looked away without answering me, but it felt like my first win in the place, as I parked up and stepped away to resume sweeping the floor, with a smug look on my face.

It was obvious that the young lad had a problem with me, but why was he so jealous?

When I spoke to him again later that morning, I tried a different approach, as I explained that I was on low wages, not whatever he thought I was getting paid, thinking that if he knew he was receiving the same or more than I was, for much easier work, that he might come around, but he didn't, and as the day progressed, it was still etched in his face that he didn't like me.

Richard was around all afternoon, most of it spent talking to the elderly drivers in the loading bay, who had broad Yorkshire accents, which suggested they were from Wakefield or Barnsley, and they were your typical old fashioned northerners, the type that rolled their own cigarettes and drank mild at the local working men's club, playing link up bingo on a Friday night, but what didn't fit into the conversation, was Richard's incredibly posh voice, as he was trying to talk in a down-to-Earth fashion, but it wasn't working, you could see he was brought up very differently and privileged, he would probably carry his Financial Times newspaper tucked inside a copy of the Sun to appear to be one of the shop floor lads, but he was crème Fraiche and caviar, not baked beans on toast.

Between all the socialising with the long-serving employee's, Richard was keeping tabs on me as I went about my work, but, as I was determined to win my place and turn things around after a disastrous first day, I kept on working hard in front of him, offering any assistance to the production workers, I even filled a bucket with hot soapy water and mopped out the loading bay, but he kept pointing out other jobs I should have been doing.

I didn't feel as if I was slacking in any way or missing things on purpose and I couldn't know the format of the place yet, I only loaded what I was told to do and the same with unloading but several times I would hear Richard say to me,
"move those Cwates Cwris" (That's crates and Chris),

The hours passed, and despite trying my best and doing better on this second day, I still felt as if I was the talk of the place, and I was criticised by Kevin for the lack of pace that I was doing things, despite feeling like I had speeded up significantly.

I looked at the clock and it was approaching 3.00 pm, everyone was preparing for their tea-break, but I had a different plan, I was going upstairs to see Tony.

As I nervously approached the top of the flight of stairs, I could see Tony's door was ajar, but he was on the phone speaking assertively to someone.

He spotted me and waved for me to come in, in a way, a sign that his office was always open to employee's, maybe that was the idea, and it gave me the confidence to ask what I needed to know,
"thanks for seeing me, can I ask you, how am I doing?",

I felt like I had asked a stupid question, and I knew what he was going to say, especially as I could see he was a no-nonsense person, judging from the phone call he had just finished,
"ok, let's talk about this and I'll be honest, I don't think you're going to make the grade," oddly enough, this is what I wanted to hear, I didn't want to work at this place anymore, he carried on, still firm but in a calm professional manner,
"You're a nice lad, and I don't expect you to be pulling wheelies on the fork-lift, but I think I could get on it right now and do as good as you, and I've never driven one."

As much as my pride wanted to think differently, I knew he was right. In time there was no doubt I would have reached a better standard, but I knew this wasn't for me, especially when he put firmly on the table what he wanted on his factory floor,
"we are first-class here, and we work at an effective speed."

This pricked something in me, as to how could he expect a top-class performance while paying paltry salaries? but I didn't say what I was thinking, instead, I replied,

"sorry I let you down, I am happy to leave at the end of the day if you want me to," he then replied,
"You can finish off the week if you want, you started Tuesday, but I am happy to give you a full week's pay."

   This was music to my ears, and despite the generous offer, I knew what I wanted,
"do you mind if I finish today?, but I don't want to leave you short-staffed,"
"no, that's fine" he replied.

   He finished by letting me know that my pay for the work would be sent in the post within the next two weeks.

   I resumed back downstairs again and found it was quiet, Kevin was gone for a while, my guess was that he was upstairs getting a briefing from Tony about me, this seemed evident, as when he did return, neither him, Ed, or Doug spoke a word to me for the rest of the afternoon, they were probably all glad to see the back of me in different ways, Kevin's reason seemed because I wasn't up to the job and he wasn't prepared to wait for me to get to the standard, and Doug's was that he was simply jealous of the status of my position, even though my pay didn't reflect this.

   Once 3.50 pm came, I looked for my clocking out card, so I knew where it was, I wanted to grab it quickly and be the first out at 4.00 pm, but it wasn't there, I then said to the guy next to me,
"blimey, they don't hang around," going on to explain that it was my last day, he then suggested that they were most likely sorting mine out first with me leaving, as they would be taking me off the books.

   Whatever the reason, I didn't see any point in staying around, so I waited till nobody could see me, and sneaked away five minutes from time, nobody had left their posts and Kevin was missing again, so off I went as I turned left onto Holderness road as I headed towards Witham for the walk home.

I didn't regret the last two days at this point because I felt it taught me something valuable, as I now knew driving and warehouse jobs didn't suit me, whether the work was on the road, in the loading bay or on the shop floor, I did not want this again.

I remembered seeing the fork-lift truck drivers at the various factories I'd worked, and on the road for Boss-John and convinced myself it was an easy cushy job, before that, I believed driving around the country making deliveries was also tailor-made for me, boy oh boy - I couldn't have been further from the truth.

This was another pull in the tug of war between working for a living and the prospect of being a professional gambler, and it turned in such a degree as I strolled over Cleveland street bridge, that it may as well have been flashing in bright lights in front of me as it was the only way forward I wanted. Work versus gambling was now a no contest in my mind.

A week later I received a cheque for £350, not only had they paid me for my work, his wife who was the accounts and payroll manager located and retrieved some back-tax that I was owed. I was stunned. I owed my Mum £260 at this stage as I had made my first instalment and once the cheque had cleared I paid her back in full, of which the remaining £90 went in my back pocket.

The way I now looked at it, the fork-lift certificate was paid off, as if I had gotten it for free, and in the mix of things, I kept this on my CV to make my whole portfolio more impressive, I just didn't mention that both my jobs, on the road, and in the loading bay, each lasted two days, not that I intended to have to use this, it was for show.

A further few weeks down the line, a new baby came into my life, my son was born in the February of 1992, with all the Johns in the story so far, what did I call him? You guessed it, 'John', you couldn't make this up.

Even with a new distraction, what remained with me for a long time, was the overwhelming conclusion to the reason the type of workplace's I had been in, weren't right for me, it was my demeanour, I stood out in the crowd and was noticed whereas others passed by as if invisible, add to this that I was tall, lanky and a little weird looking with my flyaway hair, which culminated in a lack of fluency that prevented me being able to camouflage in, perhaps there was something lacking in my attitude too, my personality was passive, Kevin the foreman looked like he would knock your block off if you said the wrong thing to him, whereas I came across as if I would see the other person's point of view above my own, which often led to me apologising profusely, even if I was in the right, I just didn't work as an individual in what I had done so far.

Gambling hadn't helped me either, I always stated that my choice to do this stunted my development and growth when I became an adult, often losing myself and my mind, temper tantrums would be commonplace and most days would be spent in a depressive state because of what I was inflicting on myself, nothing had stopped or eased the addiction so far, and that continued to be the case, as the second child, a dream home, and failures in the workplace, all the things I thought would change me, didn't scratch the surface, it was stronger than me, even though I went along with the belief that I would sort out my temperament problem, I couldn't change what I was.

I took the knocks at work personally, and it should have told me what was in front of me as clear as crystal, I had simply made the wrong decision for my career path, I failed to go down the avenue that was right for me, and it took a while before I realised this before I could re-set things again.

So where was my place? I knew it wasn't driving a fork-lift for poor wages while some guy in a suit was making fat profits, or managers standing over me with a stop-watch, and certainly not driving around the country getting lost in a light haulage vehicle, which ironically I never got paid for, while the owner was driving around in a sports car.

I wanted something more worthwhile, to help people, and I accepted my career was more academic, and despite leaving school at 14, I re-sat my exams as a mature student, and eventually found my place in working life, which was health based admin work, something that I could go home at the end of the day, earning a living while at the same time feeling that I have also contributed something back, in a way, a different form of job satisfaction that making money from gambling would have provided, but for me, it was something real that was in front of me and not a fantasy.

Now it's time for the star of the show, sadly that's not me, I was the centre-piece and protagonist in the first 'Insanity of gambling', but, even I have to move over as we now raise the bar even further without the aid of a fork-lift truck, as I am proud to introduce Mr Choc-Ice-John, often mentioned in the previous book, with a promise to tell his full story, and it's worth the wait, fasten your seatbelts for the next few chapters, as we go on an even faster rollercoaster of insanity.

CHAPTER FOUR

Individuals that I'd met in betting shops always seemed that little different to those that I'd come across from various other walks of life, with interesting personalities, as punters who gambled were the most diverse people I'd ever met as the establishment had no real pattern to the type that would hang out there.

You could spend all day in a public library and meet people there, but would you remember them at the end of the week? you would know what to expect, nothing off the scales.

If you went to a gym, you'd witness a lot of sweating from lycra-clad fitness enthusiasts in the aerobic section, others pelting it out on the treadmill or emulating the Tour-de-France on the stationary bikes, and in muscle corner, there would be a hoard of beefy guys grunting loudly as they lugged heavy barbells around, but everyone was there for a similar purpose, and a single-minded pursuit of achieving their agenda, but again, you would struggle to remember them in a week, but spend some time in a bookmakers shop and it's a different story.

The Beverley road branch of William Hills was my usual haunt, I went in other shops as well, but this was my local, and it was close to the area where I grew up, which made it my Dad's regular betting shop too. I felt like I belonged there, which is far from being a good thing when you consider my story.

In those days, it was situated on the left-hand side of the road if you came from the town centre. It was very small with little room to move around, barely enough space to fit the few screens they had. It contained a counter at the back, just big enough for two clerks to sit, and with the congestion came so much cigarette smoke that you almost needed a fog lamp to find your way back out again.

Despite being tiny, the personalities that occupied the space where big, we had the 'coffee shop man' as my Dad and I used to call him, his real name was Alan and he was so loud that you knew he was in the shop before you opened the door, dressed almost head to toe in white, from his chefs apron to his full head of grey hair, he would look like the world's scariest milkman if you entered the shop as he was stomping towards the door after his horses had lost, yes, he was a bad loser, and before you think it, I have little room to criticise.

Alan and his wife co-owned a café, situated on the same block as the betting shop, they had their roles in the business, she would do the cooking, take orders and keep the café clean, often employing family members to help out, and he would ride his bike all over Hull buying the cheapest sausages from various butchers, and manky meat and eggs that had been reduced at the market, plus tins and teabags from the avalanche of cheap stores that was currently flooding the city.

The coffee-shop man spent an equal amount of the day in the bookies, as he did peddling the city and working in the cafe, but his light work clothes never had a single food or grease stain on them, so it was easy to guess that he stayed out of the kitchen.

It's difficult to say how much gambling affected his business, but he didn't seem to win very often, most days I would witness him going berserk, blaming the jockey, the horse or anyone he could call a four-worded profanity.

Often, after the day was over, Alan was sometimes seen knocking on doors on his way home attempting to sell leftover meat or fish to anyone who had the right price.

Another regular in this shop was Harry, who was nearly 80, and Hull's oldest lollypop man, working at the local school crossing. He also played top division pool for a pub team, again he was the city's most senior league player. We called him 'the placepot man' because this was the bet he did every day without fail, where the aim is to achieve six-placed horses at a single meeting, and if you managed this, you scooped the dividend, which was announced at the end of the day.

It was a bet that wasn't likely to come in often, I would regularly ask him how things went the previous day, expecting to hear the same thing each time,
"I got five there, but one horse let me down."

Harry was a lovely guy, he never changed his expression, win or lose, sunny or rainy outside, he was always the same friendly chap, the total opposite of Alan, who was the nicest man walking when he won, however, he would snap and push you out of the way when his horses didn't come in, these two showed a complete contrast in personalities in that shop.

One of the most amusing characters was Len, but my Dad and I dubbed him 'Ragman'. He would always carry a small lady's purse with him, and after a morning collecting scrap on his bike, he would lay out every penny, generally, on multiple bets, he usually followed tips, or backed the favourites from the newspaper.

He would show us his purse in the morning and there would be nothing inside it, then later in the day he would open it to show that it contained several hundred pounds, he'd claim all his horses had come in, but before you knew where you were, it was empty again.

He had good runs, followed by bad, but his money would be up and down like a yo-yo. He was always convinced that when he was winning the bookmaker was on the phone ringing the course to stop his horses in their tracks, he used to try to get his bets on during the dying seconds thinking he had outsmarted them before they could pick the phone up. It was clear that he had mental health issues, but he was cleverer than all of us as he was picking up his wad of notes from the counter, while we were losing. It was incredible to see the fluctuations; it was almost as if he had a magic purse that filled itself up.

From this one bookmaker, we now have three more members of the insanity of gambling club, but the shop's biggest personality didn't stand out in the crowd as the others did, but there was something strangely fascinating about this one guy, who I had seen a few times. He had something about him that drew me, a presence, and while we have just introduced some new characters, we are about to meet one that is more interesting than them all put together.

This chap looked like he should have been in the library that I referred to earlier, he was a tall, quiet guy who used to look intensely at the screen, with brown hair and stylish metal-framed glasses, his facial hair was the only thing that changed, alternating from clean-shaven to a full beard,

I had stood next to him a few times, but we had never spoken to each other, but I could feel an aura of mystery without him uttering a word. If he won or lost, there was no emotion in his demeanour. This was none other than the central character to the story, meet Mr Choc-Ice-John.

His intensity and concentration suggested to me that he was a guy that used his head, someone that wasn't here to play games, the way he gave nothing away suggested that he might be the guy I aimed to be, devoted to an ideal of winning, had I finally met a professional gambler in the flesh?

He would often be there for hours, but I didn't see him rushing to the counter to place bets, I guessed that his strategy was patience, waiting for the right runners to come along, he gave me a good first impression and as the analysis continued, I asked myself, could I learn something from this man?

While my journey had never properly begun, not yet anyway, was this man fated to cross my path and be a fellow Ronin travelling down the road between good and evil, would his influence be the missing link in my puzzle, was he the one to help me?

I was too nervous to speak to him and break the ice but it was him that approached me shortly after the first race was over one random Wednesday afternoon, I had just backed the winner and was walking away with a crisp ten-pound note in my hand and I could see him looking in my direction and

heading towards me, he was finally going to speak, and as he zoned in on me, he uttered his first words,
"is there any chance you could lend me £3 till tomorrow?"

I was shocked as this was the opposite of what I expected him to say and it came as a surprise that I wasn't prepared for, but after a few seconds, I replied,
"sure, here you go," as I dug in my pocket and placed three-pound coins in the palm of his hand, and this created a friendship and many other things.

It was a surreal feeling after I had built him up in my head, to then find out that he was not on the mantle where I put him, at least now I knew, looks can be deceptive, but this guy's whole persona was just as misleading.

Only a few minutes earlier, I thought he was a professional gambler, I still didn't know him very well, but that was about to change.

John gave me the money back the next time he saw me, which was a couple of days later, we chatted at length as we left the bookies together, both of us discovering that we had a lot in common, as we walked to the bus station, he was unusually relaxed as if he had nowhere to go and didn't have any concept of time, or responsibility to be anywhere.

Before we parted, I asked for his name,
"I am John, your Chris I believe?"

I didn't know how he knew who I was, but yet another person with that name, as the sea of John's that kept crossing my path, continued, so we now have him too, later to be dubbed choc-ice-John and when it came to the insanity of gambling club, this guy was to be a warmly welcomed member in the hall of fame, an iconic character if ever there was one and like all legends, he has a beginning and although we are currently in 1995 with the story, if this was a tv show, we would be doing a flashback right now, as we go back in time nearly 40 years to how it all began.

John was born in Hull in 1957, the second of what would be three siblings, the middle child sandwiched between an elder brother and younger sister, nothing any different to many other kids growing up, with sibling rivalry and a no-nonsense Dad and a Mum who he could confide in when he couldn't tell his other parent, a familiar setting to many people.

As a child, John grew up around the streets of Orchard-Park estate, before his family moved and settled on Anlaby road, where they resided on the Boulevard estate, close to the stadium of the same name, which hosted speedway events, and much more famously, it was where Hull FC played their home games in the rugby league.

Like all good things, the stadium was destined to close in 2009, but not before John became influenced with the sport, and he was to remain a lifelong fan of the team, who, during their time there, had three nicknames, 'the black and whites', 'the airley-birds' and 'the all-blacks', the latter didn't last very long and I am sure the New Zealand rugby union team befit this name better nowadays.

As he became older, John was above average intelligence, with no difficulty in mixing with other kids and making new friends. Naturally, his parents had high hopes for him, believing he was the one out of their three offspring's that was the most likely to succeed in later life.

Like myself, John would have annual holidays down the east coast, and a caravan in Hornsea was the usual destination although they occasionally went as far up the coast as the seaside town of Whitby, which was famous for the arrival of Bram Stoker's Dracula when he came to the UK mainland, according to the famous book of the same name.

But a claim to fame was closer to home, as 'Hornsea-pottery' was a hugely successful venture for the area, and this now-defunct business was once the heart and soul of this pleasant but unnoticed seaside town, starting in a small shed by two brothers, it eventually expanded to a large shop and warehouse, employing 700 staff at its peak as the products sold well.

Despite being closed in the modern-day, a museum now stands in the same spot, sporting some of the pots and tableware made by the business when in full operation, however, Hornsea Pottery and Count Dracula may not be the only icons you say in the same breath when you mention the east coast of England, it could be argued that another symbolic figure was created there, as this was the place where John had his first taste of gambling, as it was the amusement arcades and not the vases that took Johns attention.

Part of a trip to any of the seaside towns was usually a visit to the huge fun palaces, filled with fruit machines and games where you play with your own money, drop coins onto moving ledges to cause others to fall, sliding two pence pieces down a shoot where you win if you don't land on a line, and prize bingo played everywhere you turn, loads of ways to pass the time providing you had cash in your pocket, and Johns parents would allow their kids to play, seeing it as harmless fun.

Many compulsive gamblers that I have spoken too often state that they started at a young age at these old-fashioned amusement arcades on the penny games, I am not sure if I would say this is where his gambling started, I too played these machines when I was younger, but I still insist that my first trip to the betting shop at 17 was where I started going downhill, whereas John believes his spiralling started at the seaside when he was a kid.

It was obvious even then that he had a compulsive nature, and he hadn't even started shaving yet. As he grew into his teenage years and towards the end of full-time education, he was torn between staying on at school to sit his GCE's, or start work and begin earning, and he chose the latter after being offered casual employment as a labourer at Humber street, which was a thriving import/export area in Hull's docks.

The job lasted two months, and he found it difficult to find further work, making him realise that he had just been pure lucky to get that position, as nothing else materialised.

He soon regretted leaving school and felt he had made a mistake doing so, something his Dad agreed with, as he regularly told John of his disappointment.

Despite having time on his hands, it took a further two years before he made another life-changing decision, and it happened during the summer of 1976, which many of us remember as the hottest June, July and August on record, as he reached the magical age of 18, and he was now old enough to get married, buy alcohol and, you've guessed it, gamble.

It began on a Saturday afternoon in the Phoenix club on Hessle road, his family went there for years, and John had only ever been allowed a soft drink with ice, that was until his birthday a few weeks earlier, now he was feeling all grown up as he could now order a pint of Worthington's bitter, and as the alcohol set in, he discovered that he didn't have to venture far from one age restricted pastime to another as the place had a betting shop joined onto it, situated upstairs, and it wasn't long before he climbed the single flight to have a closer look.

John entered the betting shop and connected instantly, and the first thing he noticed was that he was the youngest by a clear twenty years, but the room oozed atmosphere and character all the same, with sights and noises familiar to this type of business, and the first thing that got his attention was a loud 'thump', as a bet was placed and a number was stamped onto the punters slip as a receipt, and then it was torn in two, with the bookie keeping half for settling.

Newspapers were pinned on the wall with drawing pins, showing the form of the runners and riders, with sharp pencils nearby in containers, encouraging everyone to pick one up and write out a bet, some punters waited anxiously for results to be displayed, and John could tell by the look on some of the faces who couldn't afford to lose.

The main selling point to him was the look of the challenge, and the dynamics of working out what would win, and the reward if you could pick the right horse. It was tailor-made for him and although he was intoxicated when he came, that wouldn't have made any difference, he was here to stay and had found his calling, this was love at first sight, even before he placed a bet.

After watching what everyone was doing for a sustained period, he picked up a pencil and wrote the name of a horse on a slip, followed by displaying his chosen stake and taking it to the counter, the lady took this plus his money, he heard that familiar noise again, a 'thump', the same as before but this time it was for him, as he officially placed his first bet.

He was hooked immediately, it seemed such fun and although his first selection lost, he placed another bet in the next race, only this time it came in first passed the post, as he backed his maiden winner.

People comment on how addictive racing is, they often blame exciting commentary, where you shout your selection on as it runs, that it creates a buzz as if you were sat in the saddle, you live every stride your horse takes, but food for thought, there was none of this, just a guy ringing the tracks to get the results for him to then write them up on a blackboard, not even with different colours, everything was written in white, and often it was noisy as the chalk scraped along, snapping if the piece was too long and looking for the box to get out another when it wore down too short.

What was exciting for John was watching the clerk approach the board, then as he began writing, waiting eagerly to see what letters came out first, he'd know before it was fully displayed the outcome of his bet.

John had two winners that afternoon, and nothing beat the feeling he got from receiving free money that he didn't have when he first walked into the shop, and as he left that day, he couldn't stop thinking about his afternoon, so much so, that he was soon there again, and it hardly took any time at all before he was on the slippery slope.

You can usually tell the time you change as a person because of gambling when you start telling lies to cover your tracks or bend the truth more than you did before.

The next stage that follows this is when people get wise, and stop trusting you, and right now, John was about to go through his initiation into the madness of the betting world.

Johns first consequence because of his gambling, happened only a mere four weeks after he placed that first bet at the Phoenix club, he had already been bitten by the addiction in this short space of time.

John's father would expect his son to run errands for him, even though he had left school and was now a young adult didn't make any difference, and this was one of those occasions as he asked John to pay his electric bill for him, which was just under £40.

What his Dad asked of John was simple, to take the statement and the money to the cities local provider, located in the centre of town, the Yorkshire Electricity Board, or Y.E.B as it was better known, and hand it all to the person behind the counter at the rear of the shop, then bring the receipt home, it was that easy.

On the way there, John popped into the betting shop, innocently, as he had a fiver in his pocket and never intended to use his Dad's bill money, but once he lost the cash that was his, he experienced a loss of control as he bet a small amount from his Dads funds, with no thought of what could happen, and when this went down, he dug out some more, then this carried on as he chased to get the losses back and try to win something for himself, and consequently lost everything that he had on him, and he was amazed how quickly it all happened once he had crossed that line.

With quick thinking, he knew he had time on his side as his Dad was old School, paid his bills the day they came in, which meant it would be a couple of weeks before a red demand letter was sent in the post, so John thought he could then slip in and pay the bill when he got paid himself and nobody was any wiser.

Upon arriving home, he was greeted with his Dad who started the conversation,
"Did you pay the bill like I asked" in which John now, even at this early stage looked at him straight in the face, showing off his new talent, lying to people with convincingness,
"yes, I did, its paid Dad,"
"show me the receipt then," was his father's super-fast response, John then pretended to go through his pockets raking through every bit of paper,
"It's here somewhere," he said in an Oscar-worthy acting performance,
"next time keep the receipt; you know I like to hang onto these things in case there is any comeback." was his Dad's way of wanting to believe him, but he had his doubts, but John had gotten away with it for now.

The domino effect of losing this money meant that when he got paid and laid the cash out to put right what he did, it would leave a hole in what he had to live on and in effect go without something else, on a larger scale it may have meant the Caribbean cruise would be in danger of being cancelled but in Johns case, it was just money he had lost and it meant him going without it himself.

This did leave him strutting around, feeling agitated and worried about how he would manage, but he knew what he had to do and eventually, the day came where he was paid, and he took the bill out of the top drawer in his bedroom, where he had hidden it, and set off to pay it once more.

John knew that when he had sorted this out, the sixty-five quid he cashed in at the post office, would be reduced, but it still meant John would have a tenner left to last him two-weeks until he was paid again after he gave his Dad the usual £15 for his board and lodgings.

It was early so he went home first and settled with his Dad for his keep, and this is where he should have gone straight back out, headed to YEB and paid the bill, using his head and being productive before the betting shops opened, but no, he hung around till the afternoon and then set off to pay out what he should have done over a week earlier, only he went into the bookies first, again.

Just like previously he didn't intend to lose the money, but he did not plan this last time either, he only went in with the idea of betting with what was his, but he wanted to make a little bit more for himself, it all went wrong and he lost everything in a repeat of that other occasion, now, he couldn't pay the bill once more.

He set off home thinking of what he could do to dig himself out of this hole, and an idea sprang to his mind, as he rang YEB from a phone box in town, putting in his last twenty pence, which hurt him because he could have had a bet with it, such was the mentality of the gambler, as he spoke to an operative on the other end of the phone while pretending to be his Dad, but he failed on one of the security questions, which was the password that was set up on the account, but quick as a flash, he stated that he had forgotten, and explained that he didn't want to know anything confidential, he simply wanted to have time to pay the bill and asked them not to send a late payment demand letter.

They explained that it was out of their hands and that they were printed automatically from another department, but by this time the person on the other end of the phone was wise to John and refused to help him any further.

He was in even deeper trouble now, and after a sleepless night worrying about what he could do, it was at breakfast the next morning that a glimmer of light appeared, as his Dad asked him to pick up a present for his daughter Jackie's birthday, who was Johns younger sister by 18 months, and his Dad made clear what he wanted,

"get her a nice watch for me, I don't know how much to spend, but I want something a bit special," John gave the facial expressions as if he was on the same page as his Dad, as he replied,
"£80 would get her a great watch, I've seen a few at that price," but his father was having none of it,
"I don't want to get her a bloody Rolex son, here is £30, get the best you can."

John then left the house, and in the desperate situation that he had gotten himself into, walked into YEB and paid a fiver off the bill, in the vain attempt that this payment would stop a red-letter from being sent out, even if it did leave an outstanding balance.

He then went to the cheapest watch manufacturers and found he could get something pretty decent for £25, but he only wanted to spend around £15 and use the remaining tenner to try to win the rest of the Electric bill, he then went for a walk to another watch shop, but he never made it and ended up in the next bookmakers on his way.

Initially, he only bet with what he saw as the surplice from the juggling he had done, he lost this, and then the money for his Dad's gift went the same way, as he walked home penniless again.

John had twice been put in a position of trust and failed badly on both counts, but before he placed that first bet at the Phoenix club just over a month ago at this time, he was a person that could be relied on.

For years, he had run these types of errands with no issues, but now he was someone that would let you down.

Despite being overwhelmed with the mess that he was in, John's desire and urge to gamble clouded logical thought processing, and he struggled to see what he was becoming or had already become.

Like any gambler or addict in trouble, his imagination was going off the scales, he had become a genius at making up lies on the spot that if it was a sport he would have been the world heavyweight champion.

As he returned home that day, his Dad, Mark and Jackie were all in the room waiting for him, and he had never had a greeting like this, as his father grabbed him and threw him up against the wall and said, through gritted teeth,
"I knew you would come back empty-handed," he then tightened his grip around John's throat and raised his voice even higher,
"you didn't go to the shop for me and I know you went in the bookies," quickly, John responded,
"Dad I did get the present, but I don't want to mention it in front of Jackie, I ordered it and it's coming from another shop as they had none in stock, it's lovely too, just what you asked for," John knew he was being rumbled and needed to be more convincing,
"give me till Friday and it will be here,"
"It had better be," were his Dads last words on the subject. Friday was Johns payday, he had this planned before he walked through the door, but the conversation wasn't over as Mark had his say on the subject too,
"I don't believe a word that comes out of his mouth anymore,"
"thanks, it's nice to know who my friends are," replied John sarcastically, as if believing his own lies.

Friday came and John was feeling anxious and left the house early, his first stop was to the watch shop, of which he managed to get one for a tenner, he then asked for it to be gift wrapped,
"we only do this for free if you spend over £25" replied the lady behind the counter, but it did come in a case.

John then went to pay the bill, and he finally managed to do this, although he would be left with nothing after he paid his board money, he had no choice though, but worse of all for him, he had no money left to gamble with, however, he felt relieved that the nightmare was finally over, but was it?

When he arrived home and handed over the watch, his newly found comfort zone was soon tested as his Dad asked to see the receipt for it, and another argument duly erupted, as John tried to talk his way out of this one,
"I'm sorry, I just don't keep them," his Dad then examined the present,
"so this is the fancy watch that they had to order because it's that good, this looks second hand or something that costs next to nothing," John laughed and before he could speak the next surprise came as his Dad spoke quietly at first to lure John into a false sense of security,
"do you know what came through the post today? I'll give you three guesses,"
"how would I know, I'm not psychic" replied John before his Dads voice went as loud as it could go
"a red-letter for my unpaid electric bill," as he threw it angrily at John,
"but I paid it Dad and I have the proof; I will get it for you", he then went into the hallway to his coat pocket and then proceeded to doctor the receipt in what little time he had, before handing it over,
"what am I looking at John, part of it has been smudged out and why is the date confirmation ripped off?"
"Dad, I have had it in my pocket for 2 weeks,"
"ok john, why is it £5 less than the full amount,?" remembering John had paid a fiver first in a vain attempt to stop that very letter coming, but he was now going to reverse all that around in an attempt to convince him that he had done no wrong,
 "I should have told you, Dad, I had to pay that fiver today, that's why you got the red letter, I had a job interview and couldn't afford any shoes, that is why I was sheepish, you have got to believe me," but his Dad was far from convinced,
"ok show me the shoes and I might believe you," John was quick to respond hoping the speed of his answer would make him sound legit,

"I wore them for the interview and gave them away as they were too tight,"

"you always have an answer to your lies don't you John, I don't know you anymore," his Dad was as red as a beetroot at this stage with rage, but Mark walked through the door to stir things up even further, putting his weight behind the lousy quality of Jackie's present and repeated what had already been said, but more inexorably,

"this watch is crap, and you say it's in demand at a posh jeweller, your scum John and if I had my way this family would disown you."

John thought everyone was being dramatic, the watch was there, and the bill was paid, but there was no easing off as his Father and Brother hadn't finished and as a tag team they both took turns to go at him, but his Dad's voice was louder than Marks,

"I'm not through with you yet, but I am going to warn you now," while pointing his finger an inch away from his son's face,

"if you ever pull any stunts like this again, don't bother coming home as you won't live here anymore, and I will batter you into the middle of next week."

This was the lowest point of Johns young life so far and he had been gambling for less than six weeks, it all happened so fast.

Mark may have been making things worse as if he was twisting the knife further in, but an hour later, came back to see John again, and, as he had calmed down, he showed his more compassionate side, as he had some words of comfort and advice for his brother,

"this is what gambling does to you, for your own sake please stop now, you will soon be able to repair all this, and people will trust you again, so you shouldn't gamble any more, make today a turning point in your life,"

"I will do that, I don't want this anymore," said John, and at this moment, it's hard to guess what percentage of him meant it.

The weather may have felt more like the Costa Del Sol than the north of England during that summer, but the heat was on John after his family made it clear that they didn't like what was happening with him, and over the next few months, he was in a position that would feel familiar to a lot of gamblers, as he didn't stop betting, but he told everyone that he had, just for a quiet life and to get them off his back, and because it's what they wanted to hear, things were otherwise uneventful for a while, but this wouldn't last.

Every time John had a winning day at the bookies, he couldn't help but think that it should have happened this way when he had the bill money in his pocket, and who knows, his sister may have got a better watch, but this was his thought processing to a tee, what he wished had happened rather than thinking that he shouldn't have gambled in the first place with other people's hard-earned cash, one thing was for sure, he wasn't compromising with his new-found hobby, but could he tweak things in the future?

John had already learnt a hard lesson about gambling, that he didn't seem to win when he needed it the most, or when he had dug himself into a hole, but could he turn things around? he would soon know as another opportunity presented itself, unexpectedly.

Three months after the disastrous errand, it was late morning and things had settled down, it was almost as if none of it had happened, John was getting ready to leave the house as it was late in the morning, when his Dad shouted his name, upon arriving into the kitchen to see what he wanted, he was taken aback,
"John, I want you to pay my gas bill for me, it's £35, so do what I ask and bring me the receipt afterwards, I want the family to trust you again and this is a chance for you to get back on track son."

John was grateful for this chance and he was determined not to mess up this time, as he took the money and headed for the door, his Dad wasn't finished,

"you made a mistake last time and I want to get you on good terms with your brother and sister again, don't let me down John, this is your chance to get back on the right side of us all," he then proceeded to hand over a shopping list and some more money,
"pick these up for me and if there is anything left you can get a taxi home if you want".

John headed to town to pay the bill, which in those days was paid at a place called 'British Gas showrooms', who were the only provider available in the '70s, it was a large store full of cookers, heaters and boilers, with ready-available finance and free fittings, it was located in the centre of the city, and like Y.E.B, there was a counter to the rear where payments were taken.

John had no money of his own, but he had a plan and it was a simple one, do everything he was supposed to do, shop on the cheap and what was left he could gamble with, he could walk home with money left for the taxi, he just needed to execute it all this way, but would he?

As he got off the bus, the first race was about to get underway and John re-thought things and looked at the facts the way he saw them, he had been gambling months, not years, and believed you had to be at it for a longer sustained period before you became addicted, and this led to a false sense of security as he viewed what happened last time as just a case of silliness, of which he felt he was now a wiser person because of it, as plan-A, became plan-B, and he changed his mind and decided to go into the betting shop first, but determined to only use the portion of the money that was his.

We have mentioned the weather that year already, despite being the back end, the going on the racecourse was still firm ground, the results had been positive for favourite backers and this was on Johns mind as he looked at the form of the first race of the day which was at 1.30 pm, of which he placed a small bet on a fancied runner.

This didn't go to plan as a rank outsider priced at 33-1 caught his horse on the winning line, it was a result he never forgot, had he won, things may have been different, as the next two hours were spent chasing his losses, and the money he had in his possession, dwindled until it was all gone.

John was in an all too familiar situation, this was Deja Vue and it was not because he wasn't wiser, it was that he underestimated the addiction, and its presence was strong, it was almost as if he couldn't walk past the betting shop before he did the errands.

After the event though, John was annoyed with himself and he did not have a clue what to do, if he went home he would more than likely be thrown out after his Dad had given him a few bruises from his awaiting fists.

Once again John had let his Father down, and just like previously all he could think about was how to get out of the situation he had caused for himself, but he was in bigger trouble now, as he had scope to stall things last time and give himself space, he didn't have that luxury on this occasion, it had to be today, he thought about going home and saying he was mugged, as this was how desperate he was, but he knew the family would see right through that, although he hadn't discounted the idea totally, he wanted to come up with a better solution first.

Fast to think as always, there was an answer to his problems if he had the guts to cross a boundary, his aunt Glynis.

She was his Dad's older sister and lived in Beverley, and for his plan to work, her husband needed to be out and as he worked away with North Sea Ferries a lot of the time, it was not just possible, but probable, it was just about getting there and taking his chances, and as he didn't have a bean to his name, he set off on the most original and oldest form of transport – his legs.

He walked for an hour and a half at a brisk pace before arriving at Glynis's house, he nervously knocked on the door, she answered but was surprised to see him, and after the shock of him turning up out of the blue having not seen him for six years, she invited him in and put the kettle on, thinking it was a friendly visit.

John looked and listened around, it was soon clear that her husband was nowhere in sight, this was his chance.

She believed John when he told her he was in the area and simply wanted to see her, she then chatted and made him his usual cup of tea with three sugars, John then actually dared to complain it wasn't sweet enough, as if you could believe that, considering where he was and how he got there.

"Aunt Glynis, I need some money for a surprise for my Dad for his birthday, it's £50 and I can give you it back next week," he said as he put his plan into place, and he wasn't lying about this, it was indeed his Dad's birthday in a month, but that was not the reason he wanted the money.

By telling her this, he thought Glynis was unlikely to call her brother as it was about a surprise to him from his son, he covered all bases with his story.

She went into her pot where she used to save up for a rainy day and soon handed John the money.

His Aunt had memory problems and was in the early days of developing dementia, John wasn't aware of the scale of this, but she was showing signs in front of him.

It was late afternoon and John decided to make tracks back, and needed the bus, but had no coinage, but as luck would have it when he was looking for somewhere to get change, he didn't find a betting shop, he found a garage and bought himself a packet of peanuts, a can of Pepsi and a bag of Jelly babies for his sweet tooth, you may have gathered that already.

Just before he left he remembered the shopping list and decided to buy the things that his Dad had written down, but above all, keep the receipt.

He then found the bus stop and didn't have to wait long before he was on his way back to Hull.

As he arrived in the city centre, he flew off the bus and ran to British Gas showrooms and they were closing, he banged on the door, out of breath and almost in tears as he shouted, "please, please let me in, I have a bill and I have to pay it tonight," his luck was in as the lady on duty was good-natured and despite being just past 5.00 pm, she let him come in to pay his bill.

After a huge sigh of relief, he walked the rest of the way home, he needed the fresh air after what he had been through and the space to think straight.

When he arrived back at the house, Mark was there but Jackie had just left, he knew he was going to get a reception similar to the time before, and sarcasm was in the air as he handed the bill and shopping to his Dad, first Mark quipped, "we were worried about you John, we were about to send a search party, out seven-hours to pay a bill," but John hit back, "I had other things to do, the world does not revolve around the both of you."

There was an air of confidence in his reply because, despite the obstacles, he had delivered and felt in his mind that he had no one to answer too, they didn't know about Glynis and he wasn't going to tell them, to him it was about what appeared on the surface, but the smugness was short-lived as a few moments later, Johns Dad had something to say,
"let's get this straight, you leave at 11.30 am this morning, but pay my bill at 5.05 pm, and all the cheap supermarket's that you could have gone to for my shopping, you went to a bloody petrol station, do you think I am made of money, those places cost the Earth," Mark was laughing and this prompted John to say,
"I did what you asked, don't hassle me," as he walked out the door and once again, he had experienced another occasion where he had got himself into all kinds of bother, because of his addiction to gambling and the consequences of betting with money he couldn't afford to lose, in this case, someone else's.

In reflection, this was another time he should have thought about stopping gambling, it was obvious that this was the sort of life he was going to have if he continued, however, part of him felt a buzz from the excitement that he had just had, although too close for comfort, something in his personality enjoyed it, all the same, the stake on this day was his home, his well-being and his future, and somehow he came up trumps, it was like betting with something more than just money on the line, it spiked his adrenaline and gave him a rush, a dangerous high as his addiction enjoyed a more exciting form of kick.

John called his Aunt Glynis just over two weeks later intending to come up with an excuse for not paying her back but didn't mention the money and she didn't either, it seemed she had forgotten, and when she struggled to remember him coming at all, was her dementia causing memory loss?

John didn't want to rip his Auntie off, and he intended to pay back, but he wasn't going to rush to do as it was clear she couldn't recall it and he wasn't going to remind her.

Glynis became ill a year later and sadly died, and cruelly, her husband was halfway to the Netherlands when he received the call, and it took him two days to get back. John wished he had won a decent amount of money as he wanted to pay her the money back what he borrowed, especially as she bailed him out at his lowest moment, but accepted it was too late now.

As we go forward four years, It was getting more difficult to find work as we hit the year 1980, but Mark decided that John had too much time on his hands, as he put in a good word and got his brother a job in a rival office, as a junior. Mark arranged the interview, lent John his suit and drove him there to make sure he was on time, and soon after he left the office, the job was his.

This position had duties not mentioned in the job description, as it wouldn't sound good describing the role as the guy who does all the crap work that nobody else wants to do, like sorting the post and answering the phones, filling out the tedious forms and carrying trolleys with files from one office to another, the mundane dull tasks that anyone who has had two promotions would never want to do again.

Let's now go to 1986 and he had held this position for six-full years, despite many warnings about time-keeping because of long lunch-breaks in the betting shop, but that was him to a tee, he always bet when he had money, sometimes a third of his wages in one hit on a strongly fancied horse on his payday and he'd end up chasing for the rest of the afternoon, often having nothing for a full week if he didn't back any winners.

Gambling with money you could afford to lose gives you a thrill, but when you stake everything you have, and it becomes a must-win, the adrenaline spike is comparable to that of a drug, and that is what John needed, the rush that came with it, getting out of situations he had caused became another thrill-ride. Some paydays he already owed all his wages out, but when he didn't it was the type of betting he enjoyed, and occasionally it was all his wages on a horse if he fancied it to win enough.

John had horses that he followed, and one was running on one of his paydays, it was called First Bout, it was favourite in the paper, he staked £100 and left as he had to go to work as he was on a final written warning because of betting affecting his performance and punctuality. The horse drifted in the market, but that didn't stop it winning, and its starting price was 6 - 1.

John's Jaw hit the floor when he peeped in and saw this result, he was soon at the counter to pick up his winnings, It was a sorry state of affairs in those days with the 10% deduction for betting tax and the £700 he would have collected had he paid this, became £630 that he was owed, but he was still happy with it as this was a large amount of money around that time, and his biggest ever win up to that point, You could buy a house in Hull for under twenty-grand then and a pint of Stella at your local pub for under a quid, so this shows how much it was worth, but it didn't go straightforwardly.

As he handed in the slip, they did not have enough cash in the shop to pay him, they rang around to see if any of the neighbouring betting shops had any spare, but none of them did, they told him to come back in the morning.

He had no money and couldn't get his hands on any either as this was everything he had, all on that horse.

The waiting, the win, the combination of the two forced john into a position where he could think and this, in turn, brought some form of clarity to his mind, John was used to a constant feeling of being broke, working for the bookies as we would call it, but at this moment, it was what if?
"what if I take this tomorrow and never bet again?" he said to himself.

He momentarily thought about walking away with this profit, you may have worked out, he had been gambling for ten years by now, yet this was the only time he considered stopping.

Ok, he wasn't in profit if every bet he'd ever had since that first time in Phoenix club was considered, and in the long run, he had lost a lot more than this, but what a way to go out.

Despite the most serious consideration to walking away from gambling for good, he withdrew the money from the counter the next day almost as soon as his lunch break started, and immediately put £200 on an even-money shot that looked a sure thing, he did this without thinking of what he had considered as if he was possessed when he stepped into the bookmaker's shop, it was only when the bet was placed that he remembered.

The horse came second, he did not need to have laid out this much on the bet as he had won a substantial amount already, it was the addiction and the thrill, as the money he picked up would have been enough to last a few months, giving him some comfort as he was used to having nothing.

He lost it all back by the end of that day and as he was always secretive, neither his Dad, Jackie nor Mark knew about this, what they didn't find out about they could not whinge about, was the way John looked at it.

The trend was set, John was a different type of compulsive gambler as he liked the feeling of having his back against the wall and the tingle of joy and the calming of his heartbeat when horses came in that he had heavily backed. The adrenaline spike was a fix to him.

Shortly afterwards, he had another big win, when he had a £150 bet on a horse called Duckinton, which won in a photo finish at Redcar at 3-1, he paid the tax of £15 on that occasion and drew £600, a profit of £435, not bad for two-minutes work, again this was nice money that would have allowed him to buy things he wouldn't normally be able too, but after a rise came the fall as in a change to fortune things took a mudslide as he got onto a losing streak, one of the worse ever, and straight after he had his two biggest ever wins.

This could be argued as the worst thing as far as a gamblers mood and emotions go, if you lost all of the time, you somehow stay in the same mindset, you even get used to it, but to win big, then lose it quickly, then another sizeable pick up before you give it back again, can put you on an emotional rollercoaster and the highs going straight to lows and back up again, can affect not only how you feel, but highlight how you behave in front of others.

John's employer had seen a further decline in his behaviour around this time, they were never happy with him, but of late his work was suffering as well as his timekeeping, and while he was away from the workplace, they were devising a way to get rid of him, and while he was at work, his family were meeting, considering disowning him as they too had enough, and in the middle, john was unaware that the net was closing in on him, but he was soon going to find out.

Rock bottom was a regular place that John was used too, and on Monday morning he was taken to the office on arrival and was told he was being laid off, which was a polite way of telling him he was sacked, everyone there was fed up of him and his lacklustre efforts and overall performance, but they did give him a fortnights notice, using the excuse that they couldn't financially sustain several positions within the company, and as he had holidays to use up, he could leave at lunchtime if he wanted and not come back, although it later transpired that he was the only one that lost his job.

The knock-on effect of having his employment terminated rang more alarm bells throughout John's family, who were already beyond tiredness of the problems that came with his gambling, and at the end of their tethers with his lies and underhandedness, so once they had soaked up the news of him being jobless again, they formed another meeting on the Tuesday in Johns absence, and it was left to Mark, to tell John of the family decision.

They had to wait as John had been out all day, being out of work meant a visit to the employment exchange to make a fresh claim for unemployment benefit, and when he returned home Mark was waiting for him, and John had barely taken his coat off when Mark dealt the latest blow,
"mate, I hate to be the bearer of bad news after you have lost your job, but we have had enough of the gambling, it's consumed you and you've changed since you first stepped in the bloody betting shop," at this point, John didn't know what was coming next and couldn't have guessed what Mark was about to say,
"we want you to move out and give Dad some peace, it's not fair on him or us, and although we will pay any bonds if needed, and get your furniture, you're not getting any more money off us for anything, we are done with you till you stop."

He knew that this wasn't an empty threat as it had been on other occasions, nobody was going to lend him any more money, he went from being skint but employed, to out of work and homeless in two short days.

John had only seen his home as a bed and the job as regular gambling funds, it was how he wanted to live his life and he felt everyone should have let him do what he wanted, as it was his choice and he was happy.

Now he was going to have more responsibility with less coming in, he was also being forced to run a place and all the gun-ho stuff needed to be curbed, but could he do it?

While it was being sorted out, John knew that he still had two-weeks wages to come, but he currently had no money to bet with, but he remembered seeing a shop offering payday loans, so he fished out his last payslips as proof of employment, that is at least what he wanted them to think, that he was still working.

He didn't possess a passport; you don't need one to holiday on the East coast of Yorkshire.

There are good and bad loans, but he wanted it right this minute and took every document he could find including his chequebook and cheque guarantee card, and scouted around town to the increasing lending companies, the first one he found accepted him, but they then gave him a choice, he could have £50 or he could have £400, and guess what he chose? damned right, the latter amount.

This was to be paid back at the extortionate rate of £74 for ten monthly repayments, that's £740 for a £400 loan but he could save money if he paid it back quick, he had the option of paying £480 within a week.

With those rates of interest, I think I am in the wrong profession when you can make money like that for just lending it. My parents would have owned a Villa in Seychelles if they had charged me this rate of interest every time I borrowed from them.

Before they gave him his loan, he had to agree to sign 10 predated cheques, somehow in on the proviso of everything going on, he never realised he would need to do this when he brought his chequebook, he had never used it before, it was incredible that John's bank had given him this in the first place, but they saw him as someone who got his wages paid regularly with them and gave him a few extra additions along the way, they never knew him.

The money was presented as a cheque that he could cash at the bank, this is how money was handled back then, and this was deposited in his account in minutes upon leaving the shop, but would take three days to clear, he would be paid from his former employ shortly after this, so at this point, he could have taken it back but all he saw was £400 extra to bet with, he never thought of long term or consequences.
72 hours passed and the money cleared and John lost £300 on the first day and the remainder on the second, it had all gone as quick as a flash, as gambling bit him on the backside once more.

What did he do the day after this, still in shellshock, he initially stood in the bookies not knowing what to do, borrowing fifty-pence from wherever he could get it to bet small for a kind of fix for his habit, and all he could do was wait till his payday came, and his first cheque was due out the following day after this, he had a fortnights money so making this deduction should have been more affordable, it would have been the next nine that he had to worry about, right? wrong!

Even though he knew he had the first instalment to pay, there was no way he was going to stay out of the betting shop on the day he had cash, he wasn't going to be sensible either, he may have had the best intentions.

He knew the maths consisting of himself + the bookies did not add-up well when he had money, but he couldn't stay out, it felt like he would be ill or his life would end if he didn't have a bet, it was as if it controlled him and sure as the nose on his face, he was there as soon as the cash went in.

Soon all this was gone too, every penny lost the same way at the bookies, and John was deep in trouble – yet again!

He had caused a situation where he was looking at defaulting on a high-interest loan, he was scared more than the other times, but he didn't have the funds to even make the first payment anymore, so what could he do?

There was only one solution, to ring his brother.

He was nervous as he spoke to Mark, but he eventually explained everything as it happened as there was no point lying at this stage, his voice sounded like he was on the verge of tears, but at one-point Mark shouted the word,
"tough" at the top of his voice, but as John pleaded more, Mark stated that he needed time to calm down and said, "call me back in two hours."

This was a long time for an anxious man, but John knew Mark would bail him out but what would be the cost?

He didn't wait that long and was soon on the phone again, less than an hour later,
"John, I know you blow your money as quick as you get it, but you should buy a cheap watch, like the one you got Jackie, I said give me a couple of hours,"
"Mark, I am too nervous, I can't wait, I am sorry, honestly,"
"you don't know the meaning of the word John, come down to the house in the morning,"
"but I need the money today," said John in a voice that once more was about to turn into tears,
"It's the morning John, or nothing" was the last thing Mark would say on the subject, but John couldn't wait and started walking to Hessle, six miles and it was scorching outside, even more so when you don't even have enough for a bottle of water, but he eventually got there and rang the doorbell and was greeted by his brother at the door,
"so, you not only can't tell the time, but you also don't know what day of the week it is, you have a nerve, you know that,"
"I hate myself, Mark,"
"don't give me that John, you don't mean a bloody word that comes out of that mouth of yours."
He made John a drink and then didn't beat about the bush,
"It's the last time and I mean it, after this you're on your own,"
"Mark, can I borrow your phone to tell the loan people I am giving them the money tomorrow", but his brother already had a plan in place,

"Yeah sure, but you are not getting the money now, I am going with you, that is the first condition,"
"what's the second?" replied John,
"you go to gamblers anonymous, no ifs or buts," John nodded his head. If Mark had asked him to take his clothes off and run through the middle of town naked he would have done it, this didn't mean he wanted to though, but right this minute, he would have agreed to anything.

    The next day came, as arranged, Mark turned up and took John to the loan company, he didn't trust John an inch and expected him to put the money into one of his friends accounts, then take this back and gamble without paying the loan off, so he took no chances and checked everything he was doing and got a receipt as he paid the money to the loan company.

    Once he made sure that there were no clauses that would have left John in debt, he said to the lady in the shop as she counted the £480 in front of him,
"that's the easiest £80 you've ever made, your parasites, don't ever lend this guy money again or I will not bail him out again and I will have no sympathy when you don't get it back, think yourself lucky."

    As they left the shop, John then asked Mark,
"is there any chance I could borrow £20 and owe you £500?, I am so broke," to which Mark slung it on the floor for John to pick up and got in his car and drove off shouting,
"keep it, its the last time, turn your life around you idiot."

    Mark had bailed John out again, and from here there was a choice to make, it was clear what sort of gambler he was, this meant he was likely to always have these problems if he continued and the addiction would carry on eroding everything away from him as he was now losing much more than just money.

    After this latest fiasco with the loan company, what was going to be the consequences? was it already too late?

CHAPTER FIVE

So far we have covered the early years and influences in Johns life up to him placing his first bet and the subsequent first ten years that followed, as the flashback continues, John has just arrived home after a fierce encounter with Mark where a high-interest loan had just been settled by his brother.

Things weren't good at the house, his Dad was giving him the silent treatment, everyone was disappointed in the aftermath of the loan and it transpires that the threat to kick him out had been just that, empty words that were an attempt to scare him into taking action to address his gambling problem, but not anymore.

John didn't hear anything else over the next few days and decided to carry on regardless, but during that time Mark had been proactive in making the changes he thought had now become necessary.

Mark turned up at their Dad's house at the end of the week to tell John he had found him a temporary flat on Beverly road with a six-month lease and had also found him some furniture.

He further explained that this wouldn't have happened but the loan situation was the last straw and it forced his hand, this showed that his impulsive decision to take this out for a single days betting coupled with his reluctance to try to stop gambling did have consequences and things would never be the same, it also created a toxic situation at home and their Father couldn't take any more of it.

Explaining too that the first month's rent and the bond where paid, and that the landlord was happy knowing the social security would pay further rents along the way, Mark then asked John to pack everything as he was moving out that weekend to be in his new accommodation by Monday.

The flat was a self-contained living room, bed and kitchen in a large house, close to Queens road, John was amazed how quickly he had done this, and even more surprised when Mark took him to show him around, it had a fridge full of food and all setup, John was then given the keys knowing his own family had given up on him, he felt he had lost everything, but Mark was hoping this was a beginning and not an end, a turning point, especially as John still had to go to Gamblers anonymous as he agreed, but there were more questions than answers, they all wanted an end to the insanity, but would that happen?

At the flat, John began a new chapter of his life, but why had he changed so much from the person they all remembered?

Sure, he had done the things that he has done, and nobody put a gun to his head, but the guy had an addiction which continued to plague him because he enjoyed gambling.

We can be certain here that he doesn't enjoy losing money, and we know that a part of him gets a buzz from the excitement of getting out of trouble, as mentioned before, but what would he be like if he never gambled?

John had lost the person he was supposed to be in the addiction, and unless he stopped that person was very unlikely, ever to come back. The real John was consumed with gambling, and this helped create the mental illness and state of being that was influencing the person we were seeing, we know he wasn't like this before he walked into a betting shop for the first time and since then it had completely taken him over.

The reason for this sympathetic view is to be on a par with Mark, because, despite being outspoken and a no-nonsense guy, he had a heart of gold, and always did the right thing when push came to shove, but he gave everyone a hard time first because he believed in tough-love, not the cotton wool approach, but what John was doing puzzled him, and although he had forced John to agree to go to G.A meetings, he felt that he needed to know what he was up against, he had put in a huge financial contribution to help his brother, paying off his loan, setting up the flat at a cost to him, he was determined to finally get John over the hurdle and back into the family fold again.

Remember Ron? the chap who cleaned windows with my Dad, a similar story to John's, where he was forced to go to G.A meetings when he got himself into bother, though it didn't help him, Ron never had anyone as astute as Mark in his corner.

Mark planned to go fully equipped before he took John for the first meeting, so he did his own research into gambling problems, and went along on his own to another form of addiction, as he got permission to attend an alcoholics anonymous meeting, which was done by the members agreeing to let him sit in the closed room.

Upon listening to the members, he found the stories distracted him from his purpose, which was to transfer what he could learn onto his brother, knowing the persons present had changed their lives and stopped drinking.

He waited until the end and had a conversation with a couple of the recovering addicts, trying to understand the mind of someone with a similar mental affliction, and could it be cured?

The talk helped Mark, the two members gave him an account of their own battles with demons, and how they sought help when it went too far, one of the guys had previous problems with both drink and narcotics and ended up in Jail, and was supported through the prison reform group, he then continued the help on the outside, attending A.A sessions and completing the twelve-steps to recovery program.

There was a time these two people had lost the trust of their family, but they clawed it back with a will to stop and a determination to keep it up, then they turned their attention to helping others who were struggling with addiction.

Mark left with a better Insight to what could be done and the support he could give John, he remembered the decent and reliable young man his brother used to be, the kind of person that would do anything for you.

From an outsider looking in, this would seem to show that there was some glimmer of hope for John after his family had appeared to wash their hands of him, why would Mark insist that his brother participates in Gamblers Anonymous meetings if he didn't still care about him? that was never in doubt.

Mark saw this as a chance for John to make amends if he wanted, if he was prepared to address the problem head-on and face up to the pain he had caused for himself and others, then a fresh start could be on the cards and a chance to win his family back, all laid out on a plate for him, but it's worth remembering, Mark was doing all the running and the leading, John was merely following at this stage.

With fresh hope, Mark had it all set up to take John in his car for each session, and with his own secret liaisons with recovering addicts, it was now a last desperate attempt to make his brother see sense.

The meetings were held on Friday nights at the YPI institute, located at George Street in the town centre.

This was a large grade-A listed building and when you walked in, the first thing that would capture your attention was the strong smell of foist, similar to getting a shirt out of your old wardrobe that you hadn't worn in years, magnify that by ten and you have the aroma of this place.

Sights wise, as you venture further into the building, on the left was a picture viewer that was prominent on the wall, where you could look through a tube and see a section of photo's, and each could be changed with the click of a button, all taken by the resident camera club, this was updated every month, varying from flowers, mountains or landscapes, with a little imagination thrown in.

Further to the right along the same wall was the arcade game Space-Invaders, if you took a closer look you would notice that the screen had the same name displayed at the top of the high score list every week.

To play the game cost twenty pence, and you had to battle to save the Earth from evil Martians by shooting their flying saucers while they were in the sky.

Turn around and there was a board high on the wall, with the name of past chess champions from the annual competition held in this very place, dating back over sixty years, it was fun to see who had won the most as several surnames appeared more prolifically than others, suggesting certain players had dominated the contest, and you could see the span between successes.

Near this, a glass window emerged, which you peered through to see the reception, here they took payments and issued membership cards, as well as offering information about the facilities.

The place then began to look bigger, as there was an upstairs area, and a basement as well as two corridors leading to various rooms.

If we take a tour starting below, there was a weightlifting club if you walked down the stairs, but by the time you got to the bottom step, you would notice that the awful smell was even stronger, and you could hear metal hitting metal as the guys who trained there were slapping plates onto the barbells, then you would notice another room, which housed two full-sized snooker tables.

Back to the ground floor, where we began, there was another room ahead with yet another two snooker tables, there was no pattern to where things were located, more higgledy-piggledy if anything.

Now back to the hall and passed the reception again, a longer walk and we come to a small locked room on the left and a much larger area on the right with a glass door, and if you entered this, it revealed two huge mats, this was where Karate and Judo lessons took place, which ironically, I took part in for a couple of years, possibly around this time to bring in a parallel that is partly running between John and me in the story.

Lastly, we venture upstairs, here we see a spacious hall which could be hired for functions and events, especially as the smell wasn't quite as bad up there. Nearby to this, we find three very small, dark and dingy rooms that I haven't got a clue what they would be used for.

Where were the G.A meetings held? remember the small locked room on the ground floor that I mentioned, this is where the weekly Gamblers Anonymous group met up, the keys were kept in the reception area and these were given to whoever was chairing that particular evening.

John tried to get out of going on the first night by saying he had a headache, but Mark was having none of it, we may have seen a softer side of him, but as we have mentioned, Mark believed in a firm approach and didn't give John any scope to see any different traits in his personality except the tough one, as he responded to John's request,
"you're going and that is all there is to it, after what we all did for you, don't even think about backing out."

He wasn't letting John forget the years of sleepless nights that he had caused everyone.

That evening, as John looked out of the window, he spotted Marks shiny red Ford Fiesta, parking up promptly, a full 45 minutes before the starting time of 7.30 pm.

This was the agreement, and he then drove John to his first G.A meeting.

Mark knew in advance the Gamblers Anonymous rules, and It wasn't a public meeting, but he sought permission to sit in, and similar to alcoholics anonymous, it was down to a vote by the members to show they unitedly had no objection, they then allowed this to happen, normally it was closed off to non-gamblers.

This was a double whammy to John, as not only was he forced there in the first place, he was now in the position where his brother could hear every word he was saying.

After introductions were over John was given the first chance to speak and he opened-up and talked in detail about his addiction and came across as sincere, but was he saying what Mark wanted to hear, or was he trying to get something out of the session?

A month went by, the stories in the room were different each time, some had come to the meetings before things had gotten too bad, whereas others had lost their homes, livelihoods, families, or in some cases, all three, but that wasn't the worst of it, as Mark was left horrified, listening to members openly admitting to stealing from their own families, leaving dependents unattended to gamble, and ripping their best friends off, all to have a bet.

Mark was shocked when he realised just how bad the addiction was and still found it hard to believe that John had become ingulfed with the problem, although he was trying to remedy it.

John was in good company at the meetings, and each time an individual spoke candidly about how the affliction had changed who they were as a person, Mark felt sympathetic, but at the same time, he had an eye on John, hoping this was resonating with his younger sibling, showing him the extent of how bad gambling is to persons with uncontrollable compulsive tendencies.

Mark had always believed alcohol and narcotics were the worse forms of addiction, he now believed gambling was on a par with those habits.

When he spoke, Mark would often joke that he could be out doing better things on a Friday, like taking the Mrs to the local pub, and eventually ending up himself in the alcoholics anonymous meetings that he had attended a couple of times to learn about addiction, but thanks to his brother he was unlikely to develop a drinking problem, he repeated this attempt at humour almost weekly.

Something unusual happened a couple of weeks later, with a
rare account of honesty, John admitted in front of everyone in the room that he had gambled during the week in a moment of weakness, to which case, a guy called Jason, who had the strongest Geordie accent he'd ever heard, was very direct,

telling John that he shouldn't be wasting everyone's time if he wasn't interested in his own recovery.

Jason continued to look at John with disgust and wasn't quick to let it go, was this another attempt at tough love? at no point in that whole evening did he give John an easy time.

Although many people attend G.A and never bet again, some do fall off the wagon, in which case there is an option to talk about it and work to find a solution in case they find themselves in the same situation again. Mark talked to other members at the end of the evening, most of them agreed that one addict shouldn't talk to another in that manner and Jason was wrong to do so, as the room was about help, not judgment, but there wasn't a chance that Mark would let John know this.

Jason's method was to shame individuals that slipped up, and he often stated that it came from a good place, but John had attended enough sessions to believe that this was not the G.A way and Jason was nothing more than a bully.

John was smarting about it as he sat in the car with Mark on the way home, and made it clear that he would lie if he was to slip up again,
"that's where honesty leads you, I thought that place was all about telling the truth," but as planned, Mark did not show sympathy,
"that guy was trying to help you John, and what he said was right, you owe us all, and you owe yourself, that man actually knew the score and the effort needed, try listening for a change."

Mark, of course, was dealing with his own mixed bag, while disappointed that John had stumbled on the road to recovery, he was also more understanding of the seriousness of the problem, but it was a promising sign that the admission had come from John, but he was going to save his praises for later if things got that far, as he knew his brother was far from being out of the woods.

Deep down, Mark was proud of John for telling the room of the time he had slipped and gambled, but he didn't know the truth, remember, we are going by what John said, and he had a past of telling lies, so let's get to what really happened away from the meetings, John had gambled on more than the one occasion he owned up too, he tried to water it down to appear to show honesty in the room, but he hadn't even tried to stop, he didn't want too, and he was wasting everyone's time, except no one knew it. Did Jason have a point?

In the world of the insanity of gambling, there is often a twist that we don't see coming, and this was no exception.

It was the following Wednesday afternoon while John was on his way to make his customary but sneaky visit to the bookies, to him it didn't feel right, and he was questioning why a full-grown man had to do this secretly, and wondering why he had to go further afield to make certain nobody that Mark knew would see him entering, but while he may have been the one doing all the avoiding, it seemed he wasn't on his own.

John ventured to the William Hill's branch down Whitefriargate, confident that it was off the beaten track and secondly, he had a few friends who were regulars there and none of them knew his brother, he proceeded to look around to see if there were any of his mates in the shop, there wasn't, but there was someone he knew at the counter, it was only Jason, the Geordie guy!

John kept his distance as he didn't want to be seen, as he watched Jason align himself with the papers that were pinned onto the wall, and studying the form before turning to listen eagerly to the live commentary,

John ducked out of the shop but continued to observe from outside, making sure all basis in his suspicions were covered, Jason could have just been in the shop, he may have been there innocently, so John waited until he saw him write out a slip and hand money to the cashier, the basics of horse race betting, and after another ten minutes, he had seen enough evidence to prove that this guy had indeed done the exact opposite of what he said in the room.

This made John keen to go to the next Gamblers anonymous meeting, he had vengeance in his blood, and Mark had never seen John so enthusiastic to get there, which fed him false hope.

The day arrived and John was a man with a mission, to expose Jason as a fraud in front of everyone unless the guy confessed first, but if he did, he would then appear to be a hypocrite after giving others a hard time.

John walked into the building with a spring in his step, the musty stale smell that greeted everyone that came in, suddenly smelt like the aroma of a beautiful flower garden, because John had the opportunity to kick a home run with this guy's lies.

It was all to no avail, Jason never turned up and John decided not to confess to his own misdemeanours, the moment was gone. John was curious as to how he would have defended himself when confronted, but he would never know now.

Two more weeks passed during which time nothing changed for John, he still let everyone think he had made that one single mistake and was happy to accept praise for keeping away from the addiction when he hadn't.

The following week, everyone appeared to be present who was coming that evening when five minutes after the meeting had begun, the door opened and Jason walked into the room, "sorry I'm late" he said, and then continued to introduce himself, and when he said the date of his last bet, it was still the original time from four years back.

He lied about the recent bets he'd placed, how many other times had he been in the bookies gambling? but the momentum wasn't there anymore for John, who instead stayed quiet for the whole first hour and then told Mark he wanted to go home, that he didn't feel well. They went to the

car and got ready to go back to Johns flat, but Mark showed his suspicions,
"what's the real reason? there was only an hour to go", John then replied,
"that guy who shouted at me, the Geordie, I saw him in the betting shop a couple of weeks ago", after a lengthy silence, Mark attempted to put this into perspective,
"don't look at what he does, it's about your gambling, not his, half the room are liars and the other half are genuine, even I could tell that,"
"Mark I am not going back; I won't bet again but I don't need to go there anymore."

   It was not as cut and dry as far as Mark was concerned and he was not going to beat about the bush and he wanted to make sure his brother fully understood the situation,
"John, if you gamble, even once, I mean it we are all over with you, this is your last chance but I won't force you to go anymore if these few weeks of going to those sessions haven't stopped you I don't think there is any cure".

   The word 'cure' is misleading, making it sound like you can take a pill or some special prescription, it was all about wanting to stop, and that was the difference. Jason, the Geordie guy was split, half of him wanted to quit and the other half didn't, so the maths meant he would attempt to half gamble, of course, there is no such thing and he would have found himself back at square one each time until the whole of him wanted to stop

   Everyone in the room that had been successful in keeping the addiction at bay, all had the desire to do something about the problem, John didn't have any intention of stopping, but if any part of him did, it was wafer thin and the gambler inside him easily crushed any resistance.

   Leaving the help that was available meant that John was now at cross-roads with himself, things were now different as he couldn't ask his family for help financially, and no matter what, he was on his own two feet.

The chances of him living back at his Dad's when the flat's lease was up, was off the table the way things stood, they didn't want him living there while he was a gambler, so the short sharp shock that Mark masterminded, changed absolutely nothing.

So, what happens when a gambler is left to run a flat on his own, how did things pan out in the coming weeks?

When John couldn't pay his utility bills, he had to call the energy suppliers and ask for more time to settle up, this culminated in him accumulating debt, and the electric and gas companies fitted him with a pre-pay metre which was set at a higher rate to eventually pay his arrears off until he caught up, this was five months after moving in. Shortly after this, he received a demand for a tv licence, and as he couldn't meet the fee for the BBC service, he sold his television set, of which Mark had bought for him, this was done by placing an ad in the post office window, leaving his address visible, until one evening, a young couple rang the bell and bought it for less than half of what it was worth.

The money he was losing was more than the cost of obtaining a tv licence and keeping up to date with his energy suppliers.

As more time progressed, Johns instinct for survival had to grow stronger, as desperate measures were needed to counteract the damage he was willingly doing to himself, and he soon befriended new people in the city's betting shops in the hope of tapping them up when his money had run out, in other words, he was setting out his stall to get by without letting his family know he was still betting.

Every time he won a decent amount, his betting shop buddies would receive little treats from john in the form of money, this was to make sure he could ask them for something to help him when he was out of funds himself.

There were other options too for getting his hands on some ready cash when John's unemployed status reached a year, he qualified for budgeting loans from the Department of health and social security, who paid his benefits.

These loans were interest-free and paid back in affordable instalments lasting up to a year, but less pressure as the repayments were already deducted from the benefit amount – usually fortnightly.

These became a common thing and John applied successfully for these every few months, often blowing the lot betting, sometimes within a day, other times he would win and be able to railroad himself for a few days.

The knock-on effect of accepting the loans was that John would then have less money coming in, but it wasn't just about finances, and he couldn't see that every time he bet, the repercussions touched other parts of his life, filtering down to reducing him mentally, financially and even physically as he often wasn't eating or living properly. He was a mess, worse than ever, but one thing that hadn't changed, he still didn't want to stop gambling.

Manipulating how he appeared to his family was part of Johns portfolio as often when he did have money and had smartened himself up, he would visit his family before racing began, showing he had cash in his pocket, making them think he had turned his life around.

If he visited when he didn't have money he would simply say it was payday the next day, it wasn't unusual to struggle the day before a person's wages was paid in, or this is how he would make it appear.

He even bought clothes or shoes that were in sales and would take off the reduced label and leave the original price tag on the item to make it falsely appear that he could afford better things now.

Status was hard to achieve for John when you consider that his family had good jobs, own homes, cars, pensions and money invested sensibly. The way Mark had the ready funds to help John just before he left their Fathers house showed the difference between the two brothers' availabilities.

On one random visit, on a day when John didn't have any money to his name, he arrived at his Dad's house on a day that didn't appear any different to the other times he had turned up, which was usually twice a month on average, but it was now almost two years since he had lived there, and although Mark and Jackie had their doubts, his Father believed John had not had a bet in all that time, truth is, although he never asked for money, he because he daren't!

John was broke, more than usual on this visit, worse of all, he had no food in his house and none of his friends could help him, the only nutrition he had that day was from pinching a bottle of full-fat milk from someone's doorstep at the crack of dawn, John was desperate, tired and hungry.

He had walked six miles to the house knowing he could eat there, he had done this many times before, as there was always snacks and biscuits everywhere, and he could even sneak some in his pocket for later.

Each time he had completed his journey back, easy maths here would show that he had walked a twelve-mile round trip, that is half the distance of the London-Marathon, that's a long walk for a meal and a chocolate digestive, but it turned out to be more fruitful this time, when his father returned to the room, and opened his mouth to speak, not as natural as he normally would, he paused first as if he was deliberating before saying what he was about to,
"you're going to get some money John, I had an insurance policy out while I had the mortgage, which is now off, I've done this for your brother and sister too, don't waste it or I will wash my hands of you completely."

He was told it could be over £500, and John could keep it invested or cash it in, John's manipulating skills were through the roof by now, and he told his father what he wanted to hear, "I will put it away and won't touch it, Dad," and he even managed to keep a straight face, because the next day he set off on foot to a friends on Anlaby road, which was a mere three miles, half of what he had walked the day before in a single journey, this was an attempt to rustle up some food and to use the landline to ring the insurance company.

He spoke to a trained advisor who worked on the phones, and the guy explained to John that the policy covered a lot more if he kept it and didn't go for the money option, that it would bury him if anything happened, and the life cover that was at his disposal, the person on the other end of the phone may as well have walked out of the call centre and talked to a tree, because there was no way Choc-Ice-John would say no to a tenner, never mind this substantial amount.

The chap proceeded to tell John how to claim the money, they would send him a form and told him what security checks he would need in the form of ID, the usual stuff.

Next, they calculated the dividend John would be receiving, and he was stunned when he found out he would be getting an estimated cheque for £550.

He already had a bank account; but it was in the days when the department of Social-Security sent a giro rather than pay into a bank account, and he hadn't put a penny in since he lost his job two years before, he didn't know if it was still active.

He was told he would need such an account to cash this in unless he could sign the back of the cheque and trust someone, but he didn't.

John worried about how he was going to get his hands on the money if his account had been closed, but it was all to no avail as when he went to the bank, it was all still up and running, despite no regular money going into it.

The form came and was sent back immediately, then it was just a matter of waiting.

In anticipation for the cheque, he was looking for the postman every day around the same time, constantly walking to the top of the street to see if he was coming, then onto the phone to the insurance company to see where the money was, sometimes he had enough for the phone box, another occasion it would be a walk of several miles to make the call.

It took two full weeks before the cheque eventually came, and John had his coat on before it even hit the floor, it was then ripped open and tucked into his pocket.

He ran to the bank, expecting them to pay the full amount there and then, but was shocked to discover that he would have to wait three working days for it to clear, it was Thursday, of which he was then told that weekends don't count,
"next Tuesday at midnight," said the cashier, John was livid, she may as well have said six-months as he had no money for food or gambling.

Another reason that he wanted the money so badly on this day, was that a sure thing was going, a horse that he had been watching, that he 100% believed couldn't lose, and he now couldn't bet on it.

As it happened the 'good thing' lost, so the hefty punt he had planned would have gone south, this could have said something to John, there were always little lessons there in front of him, but he never took any notice.

Wednesday arrived and he went into the bank and asked for the balance of £550. Why did he need all that though? why not a small amount?

But the cashier replied,
"maximum withdrawal of £300 per day on the wall, £800 at this counter if you have any ID," he didn't have anything with him, "is there any chance I can have more, I don't have my PIN yet," he did, of course, he was just trying to pull a fast one, "call the number on here," she said handing John a leaflet, "or come back with ID", he then went outside and took £300 out on the ATM, then things went a little crazy.

He walked up to the betting shop on James Reckitt avenue for a haircut at the barbershop called Johns, nothing unusual except the timing of this was very similar to when I briefly worked for Boss-John at the haulage firm across the road, although we can't corroborate exact dates, there is a strange parallel to his story and mine, anyway, he had £300 in his backside pocket and his idea of being sensible with the money was to wait until a horse he fancied in a later race was running, and have a shave and a trim first.

This he did, and the dishy female barber Josie, who we mentioned earlier, was on hand to give him what he wanted, well maybe not that, but he came out cleanly shaven and a short back and sides up top.

Josie was dressed a little more conservative with it being the middle of winter, long red leather trousers and she only had half her cleavage showing. John never forgot her, funny that he couldn't recall what the other guy who used to cut his hair looked like.

He then bumped into a friend in the betting shop and the two of them chatted and soon went across the road to the Punchbowl pub for a few drinks, while they were there, John kept an eye on the time and left to pop into the bookies to have a bet on his horse, it was a non-runner so instead of waiting for something else he put some money on a greyhound, which lost, followed by £50 on two-further horses plus a tenner double, with betting tax he handed over £121, and both were running at the same time, knowing if just one of them won, he was in profit, however, if both of them came in, he would be a couple of hundred pounds in front after all expenses, including haircut and beers.

John knew if they lost he would be chasing, for that reason he didn't want to know the results till later, so he crossed the road and back to the pub leaving the hope in the shop, relaxing because what he didn't know, wouldn't affect his afternoon bevvies with his pal.

Back inside the Punchbowl pub, he sank a few more jars and with hardly any time left he went back to the bookies, this time his mate came with him, but that happiness wasn't going to last long.

Both his horses finished second, despite being intoxicated and wanting to continue, he put half the money in his pocket on a horse at slightly longer odds and watched the race, it ran terrible and never looked like winning, he stayed in the shop for over an hour and it was nearly time for it to close, and he needed more money but the bank would now be closed, his mate had a bad day too and was unable to lend John anything, he accepted his losses whereas John never did.

They parted company and john was now on the long walk home, the temperature had plummeted, and his face felt cold after a session with Josie's scissors and cutthroat razor.

Had he been a normal bloke, it would have been a good day, but arguing with a bank clerk, walking miles to get a haircut and going for an afternoon in the pub that culminated in him spending the full £300, of course, he would have spent under £40 if he hadn't gone in the bookies, so it turned out to be a bad day and with nothing left and the freezing cold weather, at least the worse part of the day was over or was it? not today, unfortunately.

As he arrived at his flat at around 8.30 pm and proceeded to open his door, he felt no keys in his pocket, he then checked for his bank card, that was missing too, had he left them in the pub?

He turned around, as he couldn't get into his flat, and attempted to re-trace his footsteps in case he had dropped them somewhere.

He was now out on Beverley road again walking back the same route he had taken to get home, but in reverse, and with a frost settling onto the ground, he walked partly on the road to avoid slipping, and after checking the pavement looking for his card and keys with no joy, he eventually arrived back at the Punchbowl, he then asked the staff if anyone had handed in his lost items, nobody had, it turned out to be a wasted trip.

John could have saved time and done this over the phone if he had even 20p left, only he didn't as two hours previous, he'd carefully counted out everything he had, to put it all on the last race of the day, and this was the yet another knock-on effect.

As the access to his home wasn't a choice, other options also appeared limited too, it was too late now to walk to

Hessle to his Dad's house, his mates lived miles away, but what choice did he have?

He decided to venture to the nearest of these, from his current location this was Bransholme estate, so he set off walking again.

It took him an hour to get there and he knocked on his mate's door, no answer, he wasn't in. There was nothing left for him to do as it was nearing midnight, except finding a place to sleep, and it wasn't long before he stumbled upon the local shopping centre, where he managed to find a secure bus shelter, and laid down for the night, in deep thought about everything that had happened, worried about his keys and his card, but eventually, he drifted off to sleep.

Bransholme was a rough area in those days, and not the wisest place to settle your head and sleep in a bus shelter in the middle of winter, but he woke up a few hours later to the noise of a screeching vehicle, probably someone joyriding. His ears felt like blocks of ice, he also found himself shivering as he stood up feeling dazed, realised where he was and set off to town, it was now 5.15 am.

He gazed around for anything he could swipe to eat or drink, like milk on doorstep's but found nothing, all he could do was walk in a straight line to town, looking in windows to find the time, as his journey eventually passed and he arrived in the city centre.

It was now 6.30 am and he saw the MacDonald's branch close to his bank, but as people where entering he found himself asking them if they could spare him some change, he was a proud person and here he was acting like someone who was homeless, but there were charitable people around and eventually he had enough to rustle up a breakfast and a coffee.

He thought his luck was in when he found a copy of that day's newspaper left on another table, he picked this up, and as if he had learnt nothing from the day he'd just had, went to the sport at the back first, turned four pages in and looked at the days racing to see what was running.

Once 8.00 am came, he felt he was on the home run, and counted the minutes for the next hour, then headed to the bank.

He believed it opened at 9.00 am every day, it did, except Today, a notice displayed on the window stated it would be open for business at 9.30 am.

At least this half an hour was easier to bear as he was able to walk around the local WH smiths to help pass the time quicker, eventually, his bank opened, and he was in almost as quick as the door was unlocked.

He raced to the nearest cashier and told them of his story, hoping they would give him some money without the card or any ID, but they didn't, instead, they advised him to report it as lost or stolen, he declined for the time being and set off to the Police station to see if anything was handed in, there was no sign of anyone taking these items there but was told he could pop back later, so his last stop was back to James Reckitt avenue, and the betting shop, and as he passed John's barbershop, he wasn't even in the mood to have a Stare at Josie, but he still did nevertheless, then he went in the bookies to ask if his things had been left there, half expecting the cashier to say no, but she didn't, she asked him some questions i.e the name on his card, and when he clarified this, she handed both this and his house-keys to him.

He gave off a huge sigh of relief and initially was grateful to get them back until he began to think about the previous day's events as they unfolded in his head, he then found that the hardest pill for him to swallow was how he had left them there, he realised that he had temporally put them on the side when he was searching for money, he then remembered going to the men's lavatory for a poo, he came out to find his horse had lost, at that moment he was also intoxicated from the pub, as the two things that stank the most in that shop were his mood and that toilet, as he left without concentrating.

As it had been left on the side, he must have passed the ledge when he left, he would have seen it then surely? So, someone must have handed it in behind the counter during that five-minute period, but there had hardly been anyone in the shop all day and he was stood with his mate, so why didn't the cashier ask him there and then if he had lost anything? he couldn't understand.

I've not gone into the effects of combining betting and alcohol much, certainly mixing them both at the same time could be a recipe for disaster, but the one thing that Choc-Ice-John and Chris Raddings always had in common, alcohol may turn some people into brave or stupid gamblers, whichever way you look at it, but with us, we didn't need a drink of any kind to become this, we were already these things stone-cold sober, the racing paper and the form guide, not a bottle of whisky, was the thing that gave us false hope.

I never mentioned what happened to the remainder of the money in the account, the only thing we know for sure was he was going to bet with it, and if he won, lost, or broke even on the day, he would still end up losing it and the end result was always the same, today, tomorrow or the day after.

If you owned a bookmakers shop, you would just have to hope he paid you a visit on this day in question, as there was £250 of easy money waiting for you, which was the remainder of his Dad's efforts to always pay his insurance policies, but all that work he did for years on end, John was gambling with it, to him it was easy come, easy go, he was zombified and numb inside, consumed by the habit.

Mark and Jackie knew John had lost the money, they weren't idiots, they knew their brother was still gambling, eventually, so did his Dad, after trying to pretend to himself, he too, worked it out in the end.

As John didn't live with any of them anymore and it was only the blood thicker than water way of thinking as to why they didn't wash their hands of him completely, but, they couldn't cope with him beyond the necessities of the family, so they kept him at arm's length, in moderation, there seemed nothing they could do and no longer wanted to try.

This approach worked short term, but It wasn't over for them yet, there were more dealings to come, but as we are going in chronological order, that is for later in the story.

So now we know the beginnings of this legend, as we return to the time after we first met in William Hills on Beverley road as a pair of horse racing enthusiasts, but things are about to change dramatically for the both of us.

CHAPTER SIX

So, as we arrive back to where we were before the flashback, it's 1995 again, except we now know John a bit better and his journey to this time, and a quick reminder before we left this point, we had just spoken to each other for the first time at the William Hill branch on Beverley road.

I still didn't know much about John, but we continued to cross each other's paths, which wasn't that difficult to do when you both spend too much time in the bookies.

It was rare that I spoke to anyone else, except perhaps Harry, the placepot man, who was an open book, unlike John who was shrouded in secrecy and in a strange way this made me feel like I had known him for years, which I know doesn't make sense but I had things hidden about myself too, I soon realised that we were two peas in a pod when it came to covering our tracks because I soon noticed he bent the truth as easily as I did.

What continued to baffle me was how I had been so wrong about him, I had spent months thinking that he was the real deal in the betting shop, and he was instead a mirror version of me, and this goes to show how you can misjudge a book by its cover, in this case, I thought John was Bruce Wayne, instead, he was the Joker, I could not have been more wrong if I tried.

A couple of months later, John repeated the iconic line that he initially said to me that first time he'd spoken, with a few differences, firstly he increased the amount he asked to borrow, secondly, he had got into the habit of saying my name several times, the setting had changed too as we were in the town centre Ladbrokes shop, another location, the same John, "know what Chris, I am having a bad time Chris, Chris, would you mind lending me a fiver till I get paid Chris, sorry to ask Chris."

This would have worked better had he been in a room that contained nothing except guys called Chris, but this was all aimed at me. If you think about it, saying my name five times, this was a quid for every time he said 'Chris', so with that in mind I'm glad he didn't ask me for £100.

I rarely had money spare, which makes it odd as I always seemed to have it when he asked, so I wondered as he wore specs if they were a pair of x-ray glasses that peered into my pocket, as he always caught me at the right time.

We left the shop together in conversation that day and headed down Beverley road, he didn't like to bet in front of anyone, he was very private or sneaky, whichever way the cap fitted and we strolled a mile before we parted, at which time he was still showing me gratitude for lending him the fiver,
"Chris, I am so grateful, Chris, one day I will be able to help you out Chris, really appreciate what you did, see you soon Chris," I can't remember much more about that afternoon but the one thing I never forgot was my name.

John and I also had common ground in the type of bets we'd participate in, both of us were into horse racing first and foremost, but we also punted on other sports occasionally, Football was something we shared a passion for, but whereas he also liked Rugby, I didn't, and it was snooker, golf and tennis as my other areas.

We may have had similar comfort zones, but changes were ahead, and not just in the bookmaking industry either, other forms of gambling too, and like most things that bite you on the backside, it is slow and subtle at first and before you know where you are, a monster is created that's out of control.

The betting industry decided it was time to distance themselves from the image they had of smoke-filled backstreet bookies and ripped up slips and tab ends all over the floors, and in a revolutionary change that made the evening news and the national press, the main bookmakers, who were called the big-three in those days, consisting of Corals, Ladbrokes and Hill's, decided to make their shops more modern and friendly.

They didn't hang around, work began straight away on bringing in tables and chairs, extra screens, coffee went on sale behind the counter, you could also buy canned drinks, crisps and chocolate. No shops were exempted, and on a trip to my local branch on Beverley road, Harry the placepot man was sat down picking out his horses when I went in, I couldn't believe that a shop that small could hold any additional furniture but somehow it did, and it worked.

They didn't go as far as to fit carpets, wallpaper or put up chandeliers as part of the new décor, there was only so far they could go to make the betting shops look plush, besides, imagine the combination of someone flicking their cigarette ash on an Axminster moorland tweed rug, instead, there remained a smooth floor and a cleaner's mop at the end of the evening, some things didn't need to change.

The technology kept on increasing as well, all races could now be watched on the screens, as audio-only became a thing of the past, everything could now be beamed live into the shops.

Even away from the shops, gambling went into overdrive, the National Lottery was launched and became an instant hit with just about everyone, and nobody thought of it as anything but fun and fantasy, simply pick 6 numbers from 49, pay £1 and have the chance to become a millionaire if they all come out, with smaller prizes right down to a tenner for predicting three.

It was exciting watching the numbered balls come out randomly from the machine as it was happening on television on Saturday night, add to this the good causes from the profits and the mass advertising and hysteria in the press, famously naming winners that had chosen to remain anonymous, it showed everyone liked a chance to win big money, but the odds of becoming a millionaire with a single ticket was very slim, in the millions to one chance of matching them all.

Before the lottery, the football-pools were the most popular bet as far as the similarity goes, and this was about predicting eight score draws on Saturday afternoon matches. This had a slightly higher chance of winning a small fortune.

Despite better odds, and the fact that it had been running for years, the football pools suffered and couldn't compete, and soon lost popularity, but even at its peak, far more people did the lottery than they ever did the pools.

The lottery became a national craze, everyone in the family put tickets on. I never took it that seriously although I did put on a couple of lines each week, Choc-Ice-John never did, he had no interest in it at all, he was still a strict horse racing only punter.

The bookies were not prepared to lose ground to this and still had expansion plans, and the amusement arcades were not far behind, and while they couldn't stop it or currently compete to that level, they could try to take advantage.

The big-three wanted to run odds on the outcome of the National lottery draw in their high street betting shops, but because a hefty amount of the revenue from the profits from the Saturday night draws was paid out to good causes and charities, as well as prize money, they were denied permission by the government and the regulators, believing it would be conflicting.

They were still determined to cash in, and instead, they began to run their own numbers-game, identical right down to the number of balls, they even called it 'the 49s', as they strived to make it just as appealing.

The 49s was launched as a daily draw, unlike the main national lottery at once per week, and it wouldn't be some boring bloke reading the numbers out either, as we now had animated graphics and music playing across the screens in each shop, as the draws took place at tea-time just before the end of the afternoon racing fixtures, but unlike the lottery, you could bet on just a single number, and this paid 7-1, the true odds from six-balls drawn, and throwing the gauntlet down further they claimed better odds and value all the way across the board.

The bookie's poster campaign reminded us that we'd get a tenner if three-picked numbers came out on the lottery, but we would win £500 if the equivalent was achieved in the betting shops.

I don't know how many people fell for this but we're talking about 'just' three selected balls to win with what the bookies claimed was better and fairer odds, but the National-lottery allowed you three-numbers out of six for that £10.

To make this equal with the same matching outlay, we'd have to treat the balls drawn as if we were doing multiple bets, this would work out at twenty trebles at a 5p stake, to make it come to the same £1.

This meant any three numbers from six would net £25, still better odds than the National-lottery, but four trebles would come in if an extra ball came out, again each paid out at £25, so a total of a hundred quid would be handed out from the betting shop counter for this feat.

Four balls on the National lottery was random depending on the number of winners up and down the country but generally was better than the 49s fixed amount that the big-three offered.

If we were lucky enough to net five balls in the betting shop for the same £1, it would simply be settled as ten winning trebles out of the six balls and a pay-out of £250.

For a full house (and a huge missed opportunity), again only trebles were valid, in this case twenty of them, but unfortunately, we were not even allowed to bet on a six-number outcome in the bookies at accumulated odds.

Of course, I have worked this out to keep it to the same stake and create equal chances while comparing to the betting shop real-odds to that of the National lottery, you could pay for more bets such as four-timers, but it would mean a substantially bigger outlay or cutting the unit stakes down even further to keep it on level terms.

My point is that on paper things may look better, but often they are just there as advertisements, which are not always what they appear to be.

I didn't do all the maths and stats with this and unless any of us are sitting our A-levels in arithmetic's, it would be pointless as it would go on forever and I didn't want to get our heads in a whirl, but it's simple to work out that the bookies couldn't match the outcome for a greater amount of numbered balls when compared to the main lottery.

It goes back to what it was all about, the fun and fantasy of why we all took part, the dream of being a millionaire for a quid.

Here is a good time to mention again my theory, that the National lottery was the ignition to the slow fuse that led to the gambling explosion and the governments relaxing of the rules, although this was still the beginning of what was ahead.

The betting shops continued to upscale their jazzy posters in the windows of their branches more than ever, advertising any new games they devised, but never with promotions, it's rare that the betting shops gave anything away, unlike the arcades, who were not going to be left out in the cold.

With many more amusement arcades appearing in the city of Hull, they went a step further than the bookmakers and allowed us to use the lottery tickets from the main Saturday draw, as they began to put their own six numbers up on the walls of their shops, an hour after the National version had revealed theirs on the telly.

How this worked was simple, you walk into the arcades after checking to see if you have won anything on the National lottery and if your ticket is a loser, you get another chance, as you could then check the same slip against the arcades six different displayed numbers, obviously, the prizes were not the same either, these were paid out in free play tokens.

In the arcades, comparing the losing tickets to their draw was done this way, if we didn't match any number then it could be exchanged for a £1 token, the same applied if there was just one.

Match two and you've won £2 of free plays, three balls meant a fiver, four would net you £25 and five was £100, all to be played in the machines, except if you were lucky enough to have all six the same as theirs, in which case you would then get a 'grand in your hand' as they called it. Of course, any winnings from the machines were paid in cash.

Teddys were the first to pioneer this across their many shops, and a couple of other arcades followed suit, for the punter such as myself, it was the first time we had free promotions with no risk.

It got better, as I discovered that we could do this daily in the arcades at the ratio of one per customer per day, I began to realise the potential of this as an opportunity and needed to take full advantage.

The first idea was to take Sally around the branches with me, this doubled up the number of plays I could participate in, but this meant I needed more losing lottery tickets, but if I bought them all myself I would be defeating the object.

I put pen to paper and estimated how many tickets I believed that I could purchase before it stopped being cost-effective.

I concluded that a ratio of ten tickets per week was about right, you could put several lines on one slip, but as you handed the whole ticket to the arcades, several would then be lost, so I had to place them all individually, ten draws equalled ten separate printouts.

The next step was to ask my family members not to throw their tickets away and keep them for me, this meant another five of them were at my disposal, next, with a little imagination I was able to get more.

When people put their National lottery tickets on in the shops, they often brought their losing slips with them to write the same numbers out again, they would then throw them in a bin that was handy at the side, this might seem a bit grotty but

Sally and I both scraped around several of these to pick out losing tickets, with the difference that she wasn't as discreet as I was, and was told off by a couple of the newsagents, but that was the only obstacle as we had no problem in finding many extra tickets per day, and each one meant free plays.

All this equalled easy money with little effort, apart from showing myself up by going through waste-bins that is.

I had my bike, Sally had her unlimited-ride bus ticket as we travelled all over the city collecting and playing the tokens, often coming home with more money than when we left the house.

For the first time, I felt like a professional gambler, which was what I'd always wanted, it was all about making profit, and I was turning over a decent amount, between £20 to £50 a week on average, not a fortune, but my impulse to gamble on the horses seemed more manageable, and this may be because playing the fruit machines was giving me another form of a fix in the gambling world.

It's worth noting that this was before the 'good times' (as we called it in the first book) that was to follow in the future in the arcades.

Sally and I were probably the first of a select number of individuals that were to be dubbed 'the travellers' later down the line, for now, we didn't see many others doing what we were doing, one or two, but it hadn't caught on just yet.

Shortly after I was in full swing, I didn't want everyone stealing my thunder and kept it under wraps, but there was one person that I wanted to know about it, and that was Choc-Ice-John.

I hadn't been able to find him for a few weeks, but when I finally did, I eagerly told him the full story of the promotions and what I had been doing to coin it in.

I suggested he got on board with the free-plays, I even offered to take him with me to show him how it was done, but he promptly declined, explaining to me that the lottery didn't appeal to him, he was strictly horses and betting shops, and didn't want to mix this with arcades, he was happy with what he was doing.

I also learnt from the conversation, that when the arcades had begun these promotions, John knew about them from the start, and after one more offer, I didn't ask him again and even admired him for his convictions and knowing what he wanted.

Sally and I were soon active participants, which meant that we got to know some of the regulars in each branch as well as the staff, but it was the arcades area manager that we learnt to be wary of, he could pop in any shop at any time, and would ban individuals for the least little thing, this big boss as the staff called him, was re-named Mr Muscles by us punters, I never knew his real name, It was probably Arnold Strong or something like that if appearances are anything to go by.

It was hard not to notice how well-built and defined he was, his shirt looked as if the buttons were going to ping off and fly at you, it wasn't a stretch of the imagination to picture him being able to win any physique contest he entered.

Whilst bodybuilders have different cycles, before and after competing in a show, the off-season would see them lift heavy weights, bulk up and pile on a few extra pounds, and pre-season would have more focus on diet and cardio to get to a zero bodyfat before getting on a stage, this guy looked in top shape all year round, he never altered, with a very thin tapered waist and a chest that was like a barrel, with thick muscular thighs that looked like they had squatted 500 kilos before a raw egg breakfast.

Mr Muscles also liked to command the stage at work and everything he said went, you never argue with him as he liked to let everyone know he was the boss, with biceps like coconuts, he didn't need to convince anyone who was in charge.

So did I do everything right and find a stricter, more driven me? to a large degree things were better, but the addiction was stronger on some days than others, and I would find myself betting on the horses again and chasing losses as I always did, but I could re-set myself faster than I was used to over the next day or two once I got back to winning ways with the promotions.

The binges felt like a different feel to my much-needed fix, I didn't crave them as often because of the activity in another form of betting, but the addiction, in a strange way, seemed to tell me when I needed to slip off the new path, and the blowouts would then occur. Despite this It was still a much better place than before.

All this was going as well as it could, especially with my crazy past and tendencies to throw good things away, it was the closest to sustainability I had felt at any time with my gambling and I was happier than I had been for a while, but while I was coasting along, was there going to be a twist in this story too?

Whilst enjoying a new-found calmness within this situation, the insanity that had followed me around for years, which at present seemed to be behaving, was about to rear its head again.

The chances of scooping all six numbers on the lottery were just under 14,000,000 to 1, 13,983,816 to be precise, but if you don't put a ticket on, then you don't even have those odds, and as I've already mentioned, it was the dream of winning big for a quid that made it fun.

My own odds were not improved by much, even with ten chances out of that colossus amount each week because I constantly had that same number of tickets for each Saturday draw, but when there is a fun element, you don't think like this.

You'd be less inclined to bet on a horserace that had a mega amount of runners if all of them appeared to have the same chance of winning, but this doesn't happen, as even in a large field of forty starters such as the grand national, there will always be a favourite or the selection with the best recent form.

With the lottery, I would never have put as many tickets on without the arcade promotions, but although we always recouped the £10 outlay, we did have ten chances at the main national draw too, so how did that work out?

Some weeks, I would find that three numbers came out on the National lottery, but I never managed to get any more than this. The promotions ran for two years, and in that time I would estimate I only picked up the three-ball prize on eight occasions. It wasn't a bad thing when it happened, it instantly paid for my outlay and it was then straight into profit with nine tickets rather than ten to start my week off.

Nothing changed, until late into the second of the two years when I was getting ready to journey to my Mums to collect her losing tickets, I received a phone call just as I was about to leave the house,

"Chris I can't let you have my lottery ticket this week," said my Mum who was on the other end of the line,

"why not?" I asked before she replied excitedly

"because I have five numbers on it," I was stunned and all I could say was,

"wow, that's about two grand or thereabouts,"

"It's not that much surely," said my Mum, but I was too excited and still dashed round to the house, and I wanted to be there when the dividend was announced, the gambler in me was always up to date with the sums, even though I was realistic about the whole thing.

I asked for the tv remote upon arrival and put on the Teletext to check they were right with the numbers, and there they were in front of me, my Mums ticket displayed 10,11,24,29,32 and 40, of which all matched except 24, the number 33 came out instead, it was still five out of six though.

We had to wait for the announcement of prize monies longer than usual that night, and it seemed to take forever, none of us had ever had more than three numbers and we were always happy for the tenner, but then as we were on our second cup of tea, they were finally ready to reveal the amounts, we eagerly turned up the volume on the TV, as the voice said,

"there is only one jackpot winner, who will receive £8,000,000," remember we were one-number off, then we heard the pay-out for five and the bonus ball before ours came through,
"and five numbers pays £2,792.00,"
"blimey," all three of us said at the same time, or words to that effect.

    I was still in shock, my Mum had stuck to the same number's week-in and week-out and never even got close, she even considered changing them but she daren't as she knew what they were, and would have hated to have seen them come in and she didn't have them.

    Basic maths tells simple truths, and when you pick five numbers out of six, there is one that doesn't come in.

    Like a lot of people, my Mum picked numbers that meant something to her, and to break this down, this is what they were, 10 was the house number my parents lived in, 32 and 40 where past address's, 11 was my Mums birthday and 29 was Jeff's, this leaves one number that didn't come in, and that was 24, guess who was born on this day?

    In case you haven't guessed, 24 was my birthday and this was the ball that let her down for around £8,000,000.

    I even realised that if I had been born eight days earlier, the number 16 was the bonus ball, this would have netted a very healthy £300,000 that week. Ironically, Sally's birthday was on the 16th.

    The £300 that was given to me, with an identical amount posted to Jeff, was welcome, although this took a week to do because my parents never had a bank account and there was only one way around this.

    On Monday morning we had to pretend that I had won it instead, so the cheque could be presented in my name and I could clear it through the bank. Several of the staff were giving me financial advice and suggesting ways to invest it, I didn't want to explain that it wasn't mine, back in those days, it was a lot of money, nowadays it wouldn't even get noticed.

It took just under a week to withdraw it all from the bank with the limits, I never minded doing it, but what made it hard was knowing it was the date that I was born that was the single number that would have made a difference, and it made the whole thing feel drawn out.

Nobody in the family blamed me, they only mentioned it in jokey terms, but it didn't stop me carrying my own weight in guilt as well as a huge 'if only', so near, so easy, but so far.

The promotions wrapped up and I went back to one ticket per week, I looked back thinking of my ten weekly tickets for the two years, and it meant I had put over a thousand lines on the lottery draw for my eight - tenner's.

A point of interest, my aunt and two cousins each placed one lottery ticket a week during that same time, and all three of them individually achieved roughly the same number of wins that I did, mostly consisting of the small prize of a tenner, but on a single occasion, one of them manage to get four winning balls out.

Combine their three weekly tickets in that same period, they managed three times my success with a third of the outlay, as sometimes science and maths do not always make the odds happen the way you imagine they should, I could see even then that the rule book may as well be thrown away when it came to gambling with slim odds such as the lottery, the laws of probability don't seem to apply here.

That being said, there is a phrase that is used a lot, 'you have to be in it to win it', but when the odds are stacked against you, buying more tickets, perhaps isn't the answer, as my Mum's example showed, it only takes one ticket to win the jackpot as she almost proved.

Shortly after it had all finished, I ran into Choc-Ice-John while I was coming out of a town centre museum, the last place I expected to bump into him, I had only seen him a few times during the previous two years, after initially bumping into him every week for what seemed like ages, to almost forgetting he existed. I still went to betting shops, but our paths didn't cross much while I was participating in the promotions.

Whilst we were catching up with each other, he explained that he had taken part in offers in arcades before, but only when the cashiers stood outside the branches giving leaflets away, for free spins, he also partook on the odd occasion when Teddys placed cut-out vouchers for tokens in the Hull Daily Mail, but he didn't show any interest in it from this latest angle, he refused point-blank to put a lottery ticket on, and wouldn't budge, he was also fighting the urge to become embroiled in any electronic form of gambling, whereas I went down this avenue almost immediately.

This may have been a chance meeting, I realised that I hadn't seen him for ten months, but the gap between seeing him now, and the last time we met, would never be that long again, he was back, and he was here to stay.

As we approached the latter part of the 20th Century, the whole betting industry continued to grow, successive governments allowed it to develop at an alarming rate, I knew the damage the addiction could cause when in the hands of the wrong person, and you know how it was for John and me, and this was in the old days, then it was a small shrub, now it was growing into an oak tree, and we had the worst to come.

Most new legislation was focused on tobacco, who were to have their rights to advertise limited, followed by measures to hit alcohol and substance-abuse, whilst gambling was thriving. Cigarettes were taxed to the hilt, a pint of beer was hit with duty too while betting tax was abolished altogether, it was clear to see where this was heading.

The lottery was soon twice per week, with other numbered games being invented, they also brought out a range of scratch-cards, which every newsagent would stock, with rapidly increasing jackpots.

The betting shops own 49s went from one daily draw to four times per day, and like the lottery, other games were invented.

The bookies incorporated the Irish lottery too, with only 42-balls initially, which increased with time, as did the number of draws, which went from one per week to eight over the space of a couple of years, a nightmare if you follow numbers, you don't know which to leave out, fearing they will come in if you do.

There was a time when there was a huge debate suggesting £20,000,000 jackpots were too high, then along came the Euro-millions, were the first prize was sometimes five-times this amount, and everyone soon took it in their stride as attitudes were changing as we verged on being a gambling nation.

The bookies didn't need to worry about the National lottery anymore, as they continued their own rapid growth, and soon fruit machines were allowed in their high street shops, with token pay-outs replaced with higher all-cash jackpots.

Things soon went a step further as changes in the law meant one in each betting shop became two, then four fruit machines, all with flashing lights and features.

They went even further to capitalise, as the opening times of each branch changed from 10.15 am to 9.00 am and they would close even later in the evening.

Cartoon horse races were also introduced, with a virtual track, and these had to be seen to be believed, no horses fell, no photo finishes, no bad jockeyship and the odds never changed, the results, starting prices and forecast odds flashed on the screen the second the race was over.

Virtual dog racing soon followed as well, and these also began to run from the moment the shop opened, as you could bet on something every minute throughout the day.

Online betting was hot on the heels and this meant you could gamble even when the shops were closed, and this too was developed at a fast pace and quickly went into overdrive, and you could play the same games that you did in the shops, and lots others too, on the many bookmakers website, and if you couldn't remember what they were called, turn a few pages of a newspaper and look for a full-page ad, or turn on the telly and wait for the commercials, where jazzy advertisements of the websites where shown, or you might watch the Jeremy Kyle Show, and see his team helping a gambling addict, but then you would notice that the program was sponsored by an online bingo company, as hypocrisy hit new heights everywhere.

Even large sporting events had tobacco advertising withdrawn by the government, only to be replaced with a gambling sponsorship instead, displaying all the type of bets you could lay with them and how to access them online.

The arcade stopped the Lottery promotion and trialled a new loyalty card system; this was only a temporary measure while they re-grouped, but we knew that they would be back with a vengeance too.

To my way of thinking, John was right to want to be left alone when it came to changes, he didn't succumb to the new ways of betting, I always had this impulsive urge to tinker with new things, whereas John liked betting on the horses and despised other forms of gambling, such as the lottery as we mentioned earlier, as well as fruit machines and online activities, and one afternoon while we were walking back from the bookies we had a chat about it,
"tell you something John, I can't believe the way the betting shops have changed, it looks like something from Star-Trek with all those flashing machines,"
"Chris, I preferred it the way it was, and I can't be bothered with it all, I know horse racing is boring and the commentary goes over the top, but I have a fondness for it."

I then mentioned the new system in the arcades where a lottery ticket wasn't needed, where it was just a simple matter of registering and receiving a card and a membership number, but he repeated what he had told me already,
"as I said Chris, I don't like crossing the two, I am not interested, and I will never sign up for anything that wants my name and address."

I chuckled when he said this, it was me that should have feared giving out my private details, John was mild-mannered for the vast majority of the time, I had a temper when I was losing and had already been warned for swearing in a few of the betting shops, if they had my name and address though, maybe I would have behaved, who knows? but he convinced me that the newer forms of gambling would never draw him in.

I believed John was sincere with what he said, but he may not have been looking for differentials in his routine, but his daily lifestyle was gambling until he lost everything, unless of course, he won.

John came across as a man of principle, but then I remembered that he never had two-half-pennies to rub together anyway, but he wasn't going to look a gift horse in the mouth, and soon everything changed again.

While John was in the bookies, he rarely had enough money for a bet so half the day was spent watching races, but because the machines were now in the shops, there was no getting away from them, and although he was determined to have nothing to do with this form of gambling, he couldn't help but stare at the sounds and flashing lights and slowly became drawn to the machines, and while he hadn't partaken, as each day passed, he spent more time watching the punters who actively played them.

Around this very time, John was about to be tested, It wasn't a conspiracy to channel him to change his ways for the worse, or manipulate him into becoming someone else, but you would struggle to believe otherwise as Teddy's amusements began to place cut-out coupons in the paper again.

While John had done these before around four years earlier, it was a different environment then, the current crop of machines were no longer the same as before, and as John scraped together his last few pence to buy a paper and turned the pages straight to the ad, he then slowly ripped around the part he needed and threw the rest in the nearest bin.

When he walked into the city centre branch of teddys for his £3 worth of tokens, he was amazed to see the arcade was full of machines of which he had seen in the various betting shops he occupied during the day, they had features and could be tricky to negotiate for the inexperienced, except John knew how to play them from his time watching others in William Hills and Ladbrokes, so he went straight onto one of these for the first time.

He won a fiver with no risk, again nothing new, except he had played the basic bar-x machines on that previous occasion that I referred to four years earlier, which he found boring, but now he was playing a feature machine for the first time.

In his heart, he still didn't want to mix the betting shops with arcades, but whereas he wouldn't place lottery tickets for the previous promotion, this was right up his street, the way he looked at it, why pay a pound for one of those tickets just to receive the same amount in plays? this was a lot more generous, and he only had to purchase newspapers, and as the £5 he won in Teddy's was soon lost in the bookies, this was the next problem, how to get them.

He began to think strategically about the papers he needed, he knew people who bought them, and you could read them for free at the BBC centre, the library and the Hull Daily Mail office, so he went into these buildings, pretended to read the paper and discreetly ripped out the coupon.

It also appeared in the now-defunct Hull Star newspaper, which was free, so while he was at the main Hull Daily Mail office, he mentioned to the staff there that his whole street didn't get a copy delivered, and could he take a few, the clerk behind a desk pointed to a skip outside, saying they were surplice, and he could take as many as he liked, which he did, he took a large bundle home with him to cut them out, problem sorted.

I wasn't as clever as John, I was buying the papers as I was actively running all over Hull as I had before, hoping that it would keep going and not dry up as the lottery promotion did, but hoping doesn't make wishes come true, and the ads stopped appearing, but not before three months had elapsed.

John, unfortunately, did little more than transfer his winnings as everything he won went straight to the bookies, with me it helped make some much-needed credit card repayments although I too had moments where I also lost it in the betting shops, but whereas I had already tinkered and played the machines in the shops, John hadn't but was soon going to change.

Gambling is a slow killer, even if you have the best will in the world, it keeps at you, taking its time to wear you down and weaken your defences, and it wasn't long before John would put his usual horse racing bets on, but all it took was a loser, a close finish, a selection falling when leading at the last fence, and these machines, that John had now already played in Teddy's arcades, where stood in front of him in the bookmakers shop, looking more tempting as he became despondent at his chosen and preferred pastime, and he began to step up and drop coins into the machines, every day a little more regular.

The fruit machines were bad enough, but these were soon replaced with new and sophisticated fixed-odds betting terminals (FOBTs).

Being able to bet on roulette on the FOBTs at £100 per every twenty seconds was a gold-mine for the bookies, but as they were only able to have four playing at once, they opened more shops all over cities throughout the country, but in Hull, they increased to the degree were everywhere we ventured, there were bookmakers within yards of each other, all with the maximum number of these machines.

John was soon playing these new terminals too; he had already crossed the line as he mixed horses and machines in the betting shops, all starting with the combination of promotions, new software and changes that invaded his comfort zone – the bookies, it was never going to take long for the transformation to FOBTs.

From a determined man that was going to resist any temptation to come into the electronic world, he was now contemplating a faster and more dangerous form of gambling, unlike anything anyone had seen before, unbeknown at the time, John was only going in one direction, and that was to become engulfed in this new obsession, as the madness and insanity were about to be ramped up.

CHAPTER SEVEN

After covering Johns journey up to the day we met and the first few years afterwards, we know how he tried to resist the temptation to take the step onto the larger platform, before it overcame him and he succumbed to the beast, and in many ways, this is where the parallel line running between us joined up, as we both entered this scary place, the nightmare world of Fixed-odds betting terminals and electronic roulette.

We pick things up in the early part of the new century, the year 2002, and John and I were so fixated with this new problem, we were even less like our old selves, and more like two protagonists from that George Romero classic 'Dawn of the dead' as we walked around aimlessly, zombies taken over by the will of the betting terminals, whereas I was running credit card debt up, signing up for more of them when I reached the limits, with the occasional bank loan thrown in, while John was betting everything he had in them, and for the both of us, almost every penny was destined to end up on the spin of a wheel.

Unlike me, John was limited to what he could get his hands on, as with no employment or credit history there wasn't much choice, but something happened that put everything into perspective, as Johns Father sadly passed away.

John didn't tell me this initially when we bumped into each other a few days after the tragic news had been broken to him, instead he asked if he could borrow a small amount of money, and as I had just left the betting shop after a decent run of the right numbers coming in, I was on the crest of a wave, heavily in profit with a smile from ear to ear, still unaware of what had happened.

I then asked him if he fancied a couple of beers, which would be my treat, we were soon strolling through Queen's gardens in the city centre, and onto the Rugby Tavern pub.

As we entered, fond memories came flooding back from my younger years, it used to be a regular of mine when I was younger and barely the legal age to drink, and I remembered the place having a heavy metal music theme, full of leather jackets, long hair and the sound of motorbike engines roaring as they parked up.

   I didn't expect this pub to have any significant changes as I entered, but I was taken aback when I saw it was now full of much older gents, and none of them looked like ex-bikers, I was further shocked to see the place was living up to its name, as it was now a rugby supporters pub, it felt like an alternate reality, I was half expecting to hear Iron Maiden blasting from the music box, instead it was playing bridge over troubled water, which in many ways reflected Johns position with his family.

   I bought two pints, a Tenants lager for John and a Worthington's bitter for me, which hadn't been pulled right as the frothy head filled a third of the glass, I would have been within my rights to ask for a chocolate flake to stick in it.

   We sat down and I began the chat by telling him about my finances spiralling out of control, oddly enough he was the only person I ever confided in, everyone else, including Sally and my parents, believed I was debt-free, but I was far from it, but John was another gambler and someone who knew the score, he seemed like the only person in the world that would.

   It was soon after this that John told me about his Dad, which came as a shock, I offered my condolences while apologising for moaning and then stated that my problems couldn't be compared to this.

   He spoke kindly and asked me not to feel bad, we then continued to talk, although I was trying to take this in, as I already knew Johns family had completely disowned him over his compulsive gambling and had made many attempts to encourage him to stop and in the end, they just had less and less to do with him because of the problems that came with his addiction.

   I found out that the funeral was in a couple of weeks, and then the will-reading the following evening.

This was when John would find out the outcome with regard to the property, savings and belongings, and while he didn't have a clue what was going to be left to him, it was suggested there would be something and he knew he was going to be due a few quid, but I felt a need to express my concerns on what I could see happening.

Despite my own problems I felt I had to try to help him, I knew his family had all tried to figure out why he gambled, but it wasn't them speaking to him right now, it was me, I was another gambler and a mirror version of him, I was talking to him as addict to addict, a guy who knew what rock bottom felt like, a person who knew the fluctuation between pain and suffering and the elation and joyous feeling of winning, I had his experience, I was a zombie just like him, I'd lied, cheated and manipulated people just as he had.

None of his family knew any of these feelings, but I had experienced them all just like him, so, maybe I was the guy who could reach him? I was, perhaps, the only person that knew what they were talking about when discussing the habit and the mindset.

I also believed my own twenty years of gambling qualified me to have more than an educated guess at what I could see happening next, so despite the occasion, I had to say to him, "please get help before you receive any money, you know this could end badly and it'll all go in those betting terminals," he nodded his head, but was he serious? I was determined to keep on trying.

"John you know your Dad loved you and would have wanted you to look after yourself with anything that he leaves you," he then showed me he wasn't listening with his bog-standard reply,

"I know I need to sort myself out Chris," but there was no passion in his voice, I knew it was a lost cause, but the part of me that hated what I was doing to myself didn't want to see him go down that road any further, "gambling has changed you John and stole who you once were, this is the time to get the real person you are back again, the good guy that the addiction took away from your family."

That is all I could do for the moment, I then changed the subject and we talked about other things because I felt a small dose of medicine would do more good than the full bottle, he knew what I said came from a good place, but he didn't want a full-on lecture and was more likely to listen if I didn't go on too long, again the gambler in me knew this.

I didn't have the right to push it any further and after another drink and some regular conversation, we went our separate ways, and as I walked away I was hoping I had reached a part of him.

My perspective was that when we met up, there was a reason that I opened up to him about my debts caused through my addiction because he felt like the only person that knew why I was doing what I was doing, it was me crying out for answers to someone that knew the feeling of being overwhelmed with the cravings to bet, so in reverse, I thought he might listen to me, I didn't know if anything I said to him resonated, the mind of a gambler is complex, I didn't even know who I was anymore so how could I fully know what went on in his head.

Two weeks passed and it was here, the funeral had a larger than expected turn out and then there was a small wake afterwards in the Granby pub in Hessle square, here everyone shared stories and had a drink to John's Father, with both Mark and Jackie putting a tab behind the bar.

The next evening was the part that John wanted behind him, meeting his siblings to decide the destination of their Dads belongings.

As expected, Mark was the person that was sorting out his late Father's affairs, and he arranged for the family to get together for the reading of the will, which was done at their Dad's house, John was relieved it wasn't in Hessle as he didn't have a crumb to his name, he hoped that somehow he would leave with some money, but the way they felt about him, would there be anything in this for him? he knew this wasn't guaranteed, but why would they ask him to go?

On the way there he thought about the last few years, of how he tried to hide his gambling addiction from them, but someone would always see him going into a betting shop and report back to the family.

Another tell-tale sign was that he was often destitute when he visited his Dad's house, but they were past caring and couldn't be bothered anymore and just let him get on with it, Mark tried to help him with tough love, and that didn't get him anywhere.

He was paranoid about getting nothing as he arrived at the house and decided to counteract this by looking as miserable and remorseful as he could when he met up with the family, hoping for some sympathy and most of all, some cash.

Moments before things began John took Mark to one side and tried to convince him he was a changed man, and attempted to pull Marks heartstrings, but without much success,
"Mark, all this has taught me a lesson, I'm different now and if I get nothing I won't complain, I don't deserve it, but if I get something I will put it to good use,"
Mark then replied in his normal sarcastic manner,
"is there a horse running called good use,"
"I mean every word, Mark,"
"John, the only truth you said is that you don't deserve anything, it's out of my hands but don't try to con me by pretending that you're suddenly a changed man, you only care about gambling,"
"that's not true Mark," at this point, Johns brother walked away shaking his head, he knew it wasn't going too well.

John had intended to pick his moment and ask Mark for an advance, but he didn't fancy his chances now, so he then thought that maybe the feminine touch would be better to

home-in on, as he decided he was going to ask his sister to help him instead, but that would come later, for now, it was about the will reading.
   This was being prepared to be read out, but there was a twist when Jackie refused to be in the same room as John, so Mark asked him to wait outside, she was angry at the way he had let his family down and saw him as someone who was selfish and made no effort.
   You could defend John here and say that nobody really understands a gambler and what the addiction does to a person, but it's also easy to see her point of view too, as this was a low moment and everyone felt grief, on top of this it was hard for Jackie to contain her anger that John had never wanted to stop gambling while their Dad was here, she didn't believe he would be any different now, and even if he was, it was too late as far as she was concerned.
Should she have given him a chance? if he was going to address his problem, this would be it, he still had his chat with me not long previous, who did understand him, but what did John want?
   Johns Auntie Cheryl came to the house later that evening to offer support, she wasn't in the will but tried to be impartial in the whole thing and had a soft spot for John.
   The will-reading revealed that their Dad wanted John, Mark and Jackie to have a third each, but Johns share was to be held by Mark, who could be trusted, and because he was worried about the potent mix of John and gambling, he wanted John to have bi-annual instalments whatever the cash and house sale came too, spread over a five-year period, hoping he would change in that time.
   Mark already owned part of their Dad's house; he gathered some of his savings and planned to take out a small mortgage to complete buying the rest of the property, so this could be done quickly, he had already agreed on the terms with Jackie, as John was given no say in the matter.
   He later let John know of his disdain for him,

"it sticks in my throat that you're getting part of all this, you're a scourge on this family but I respect Dads wishes," John remained silent while his brother let his thoughts be known.

At the very end of the evening, John was given a sheet of paper to sign, followed by another with information that had been neatly typed out, stating what he would be receiving, there were signatures on the bottom of which John didn't recognise which led him to believe it had all been witnessed and processed with the aid of a legal team.

His family obviously believed John would keep coming for money after the settlement, the word 'final' appeared more than once on the statement, but it was the figures that John was interested in.

The maths had been calculated prior to that evening and it culminated in John receiving £800 twice per year, every February and August, for the five years as requested, to total £8,000 by the time he received his tenth payment.

John had a nerve, which showed as he approached Jackie and started a sentence,
"I don't suppose," of which he stopped at that point when he saw the look on her face, which told him everything before he continued again,
"I don't have my fare home" she then gave him a different look like she couldn't be bothered,
"how much is your bus fare John," he told her how much he would need, of which she then reached for her purse and gave him the exact amount, John then started again but once more only reaching mid-sentence,
"I don't suppose you could also," after yet another look, he paused before he went on again,
"I understand Jackie," she then walked out of the room, John then went to see Mark who was stood in the corner,
"Mark, when do I get my money,"
"It's on the paper John, can't you read?, February and August," it was the first of these months in two weeks,
"what date in February Mark?"

"31st ok?" of course, he was being sarcastic, we know it has 28 days,
"please, Mark," begged John, before his brother replied in one long rant,
"the first of the month you can have it, ok remember that - the first, I couldn't face a full month of you at me about it, so the first," he paused and then continued,
"that is now three times I have told you so don't forget and don't ask again, or I will make it the last day of the month," Mark then turned away to walk into another room but a few seconds later he came back and attempted once more to wrap the evening up,
"it would be easier if you left now John, ok? I will sort this out if you give me some space."

John left with Cheryl and offered to help her get home, which was not something you normally say to someone that has a car and you don't, but it was small talk, to build up to what he wanted, he knew he could rely on her to lend him some cash and she was happy to oblige.

Cheryl knew there was friction between the brothers, so when Mark asked her the following day if John had approached her for money, she knew that she needed to tell a little white lie to protect her nephew.

John didn't understand why they invited him when it had been decided already, the reason of course as he had the right of contesting and they didn't want him to have any room to suggest they were ripping him off.

It was obvious what they thought of him, and it wasn't sibling rivalry, they were appalled with what he had become and how it had gone on for so long.

It was the same week that I saw John again, I didn't learn the outcome at that time as he was still secretive, he didn't make it out he was receiving nothing, but he was coy and I knew it would take time for him to give me the full facts.

My friendship with John fluctuated since I had first met him, it felt like we lived in an alternate universe when he came to me to borrow money after I had been to everyone else to lend it, I never looked down on him or felt I was better than him in any way, but it was almost like he was on a run of the ladder lower than me when it came to finances, I mean, who would want to depend on me for money?

We had almost come to blows on a couple of occasions, when I was in a bad mood after losing in the bookies, and shouted or snapped at him when he tried to tap me for a couple of quid, but we always made up the next time we met and none of us mentioned it again, there was something about the double act of Chris and Choc-Ice-John, but we were far from being Butch Cassidy and the Sundance kid, more like the Chuckle brothers of gambling.

Something always happened which kept us on speaking terms, there was other stuff going on in my life and in comparison he wasn't near the top on my list of priorities, I was always changing jobs, living at home with Sally was difficult, she always seemed to have a bee in her bonnet more than ever to the degree that I was living on my nerves, I hardly had any money and was getting over my head with credit card debt, and I knew that very soon there would be no way out and I couldn't stop it happening as I felt powerless to control the addiction, it was stronger than me, and nobody except John knew all this, so in many ways, he was a distraction and the one person that I could relate too.

If things had always been one-way traffic like it was most of the time, I would have felt as if I was being used, but when he had it, John was generous, there is nothing more giving than a man that wins money he didn't expect when he was used to walking the streets penniless, and as February was a few days away, of which the first inheritance payment was due, John was confident enough to borrow more than ever while at the same time remain secretive.

He turned up as I was leaving work, waiting outside the front doors of Kingston-Communications, where I was employed at the time,

"Chris I need a big favour,"
"how much?" I replied knowing it was about money,
"a tenner Chris, but I have money to come at the end of the week, a guy owes me, and he has just got a tax rebate and waiting for the cheque to clear."

   I didn't believe a single word, it sounded like a Mickey Mouse excuse to me, why didn't he just tell me the truth instead of fabricating a story?

   I decided to give him the benefit of the doubt, and I reached in my pocket and handed it to him with a condition, on Thursday, the day his imaginary story was happening, I wanted him to meet me near the Amy Johnson statue outside Prospect centre.

   This iconic Hull figure may have done the first solo flight across the globe, but I knew the guy in front of me was sending me on a journey himself, down the garden path, yet I still did it, and I tried to figure it out, I needed to know, why?

   It didn't make sense, I could have been chasing him forever for that money, why did I give myself this hassle? then I realised my reasoning when it came to this man.

   Deep down, part of me saw John as a case study as his actions unfolded in front of me as if I was watching a soap opera and I needed to know what was going to happen next, I knew my own life verged on craziness, watching him made me feel like I wasn't the only person affected with the insanity of gambling, I knew others that were, I'd heard stories from gamblers that were so amazing that you would question if what they said was real, but I knew that this mental addiction made the silly things happen, John had allowed it to grow and morally corrupt him, he didn't know the truth from reality and would do anything to get money for his next bet.

   Thursday came, and there was just myself and Amy Johnson stood outside Prospect centre, he was a no-show and I cursed myself for trusting him, and I didn't view him in the same light as I had a few days earlier, now I was wondering why he fascinated me so much, why did it matter to me what he was going to do next?

I knew I was playing a silly game and allowing myself to be a guinea pig in the middle of it.

To me, he was just a liar who ripped people off and I needed to pull myself together because as far as I was concerned, I was done with him, nothing interesting about that, but this was the anger talking because I was left standing in the cold.

Nine days passed and during this time, I looked everywhere but no sign of him, it was almost as if he had been abducted by aliens, but after a week and a half, I didn't care anymore, as far as I was concerned, ten-quid was a small price to pay to get shut of him.

Saturday afternoon came and it was my usual 'shut out the week I've just had' time, as my weekly ritual kicked in. Out came my bike and a plastic carrier bag containing a litre bottle of Russian Standard, it was my favourite day of the week as I set off to Karl's in time for the Saturday afternoon live football score programme on the BBC, all set to down a few vodka and oranges as the goals came in, we'd shout at the screen when decisions went the wrong way, this was an afternoon of release after a week that generally consisted of problems at work and home, not to mention gambling.

I always rode there the same way, which was through town, up to the top of the steep bridge on Anlaby road before free-wheeling down the other side, then a straight line for two-miles till I arrived at his street, but today, I went a different route.

I de-toured for no reason and went the long way around via Spring bank west, probably because I felt like varying the route for a change of scenery, but as I got to the point where I would turn off, on the horizon like a water fountain in the desert, I spotted the 'Tote' betting shop, and I found it hard to ride past, next thing I knew I was locking my bike outside, almost uncontrollably. I only had a £20 note and the bottle of alcohol in my Tesco carrier bag, but I had the urge to play roulette, it was binge time for me.

As I entered the shop, who should I see playing on the machine I had intended to go on myself, none other than Choc-Ice-John! He was quid's in as I looked across at the right-hand corner of the screen and saw the sum of £300 sitting in his win-bank, he first looked shocked to see me but then he readjusted and replaced the awkwardness with a friendly chat,
"I'm glad I've bumped into you, Chris,"
"Yeah John, that's why you're in a bookies shop mile's from anywhere."
   He then cashed in his winnings and handed me £40,
"that squares us up Chris with the tenner I owe you and something extra which I don't want back, it's a treat, I wish I could give you more, but I owe a lot out," my whole tone towards him then changed,
"thanks, I appreciate it John," at this point I was wondering if I was beginning to sound like him, I hoped not, but everything seemed to go around in circles.
   Karl lived about a mile away from my current geological position, John stated that he was going to a mate's house who lived in the same area, so I decided to push my bike so we could walk together.
   John didn't like anyone around when he was winning, but what made this harder for him was one simple fact, he couldn't walk past a betting shop and each time we approached one he had to go in, and he remained on a roll, he loaded some money into the terminals and selected his favourite version of roulette, and proceeded to cover high and low numbers but left the middle section out, as he always did.
   After starting with a few spins that alternated between wins and losses, he hit his best number, which was red-seven, followed by another decent one coming in, and he was another £70 up in no time.
   He cashed this in and gave me another twenty-pound note followed by the words,

"you've always helped me Chris; this is a treat and I don't want it back," I had heard him say the same thing twenty minutes earlier.

Soon after this we were in yet another betting shop further down the road and he won again, handing me another tenner, this meant I had my original £10 back plus an additional £60 on top, money that wasn't a loan, it was a gift, I was now feeling guilty after the fuss I made over a measly ten-pound note.

When he counted-up, he had won around £500, but he didn't carry a wallet, it was all stuffed in his jacket pocket. We parted ways but not before I said the words I knew was a waste of time
"John, that's your money now, please go home with it and treat yourself to something nice, by a DVD or something,
"I don't have a telly Chris or a DVD player," I didn't know what to make of this, but doesn't everyone have a telly?

I then went to Karl's with my bottle of vodka and we sank them like a pair of alcoholics locked in a whisky factory while watching final score, I couldn't help but think how easy it was for Choc-Ice-John to win all that money, but I knew the guy deserved a break and I refused to be anything but happy for him.

Unbeknown to me, John had received his first inheritance payment, this had been due in his account on the first of February, but Mark didn't put it in for a few days afterwards, which John believed he did on purpose.

John had lost most of the £800 he was paid, but when he was down to his last £50 things changed, his fortunes turned around and he began to peg things back when a run of decent numbers on the roulette machine came in, that was when I turned up.

Although he was still down from where he started, the recent streak made him feel like a winner, it's funny how psychology has an influence on the mind of a gambler.

48 hours later came the end of my least favourite day of the week, Monday. It was 5.00 pm and I had just finished a particularly long and pulsating day on the phones in the call centre, and after listening to consumers moan that their internet wouldn't connect for eight long hours, I could not get out of the place quick enough, and I ran down the stairs from the tenth floor that had felt like my prison and out the entrance for some much-needed fresh-air, all very welcoming except what I saw waiting for me, as there was John, fixated on my employers front door, or to be more accurate, yours truly, making sure he caught me as I left work.
   He looked like Michael Myers from the Halloween movies when he was waiting and gazing at me, he knew my patterns and worked out my sub-routines when he wanted to find me, but was like a camouflaged-chameleon when I searched for him, which showed how predictable I had become, but there he was, bold as brass as he was waving for me to come to him, remember he had won a stack of cash when I saw him two evenings earlier, so I wasn't sure what he wanted, but I soon found out as he got straight to the point,
"Chris I have a bill and I can't pay it; I need £60," I was stunned,
"John, you gave me that money and said it was a treat, you didn't want it back, you can't just expect me to find money just like that, I have spent what you gave me,"
"I need it, I am in trouble Chris,"
"what happened to the money you had John?" I then waited for some excuse to come out of his mouth, but a half-truth left his lips,
"I paid a few things out and got some shopping and lost most of it back", but I wasn't having this crap,
"tell me the truth, you lost all of it didn't you?" he then nodded, but I already knew as much.
   I had no choice and arranged to meet him later at Macdonald's on Beverley road as I didn't have it on me.

When the time came, I arrived early but he was already there, they say sarcasm is the lowest form of wit, but the way I felt as I saw him stood as if he had done nothing wrong, it was all I had as I walked up to him,

"you're on time, good of you to be here promptly, oh, I forgot, I am giving you money so you arrive early, funny how you can't do it when you owe me," I then had to stop myself from throwing the money at him as I handed it over and stormed away.

It felt as if he wasn't there in any other humanly form except a fixation for the money, and oblivious to the effect on me or anyone else, he just wanted the 'treat' back, as once he lost, it turned into a loan and as far as he was concerned it was only my money while he was winning.

He tried to talk to me when I was a few yards away, but I shouted the words
"not interested," with my back turned to him.

I didn't see him for a couple of days, then he turned up while I was on a fixed-odds betting terminal on Princes avenue, I rarely saw him down that road but no surprise, he always bumped into me when I was winning, which I was doing on this occasion and my mood was high, it shouldn't have been, I had a debt consolidation loan of £12k with monthly repayments I couldn't afford and hadn't started paying yet, I had paid off all my credit cards with it, so sensible at first, but it was short-lived.

Each creditor put the limit up to what I could borrow after I had settled up, and here I was having a successful run of luck, but the previous two days weren't that good, as I had withdrawn and lost £300 in cash on each of my five-cards, that's £3000 of lost money that I had to pay back with interest, but I couldn't see consequences, instead I was in a good mood as my best number, which was black, evens and high twenty, came in for the second time in four spins and added to my already fruitful spoils, as my bank showed £600 for the £40 I had put into the machine an hour earlier.

Credit cards charge withdrawal fee's for cash advances and interest on the outstanding balance if not paid off straight away, but what we can work out was things were not as lucrative as the first glance at the top right-hand corner of my screen suggested, but, of course, the balance on display was the thing that got John's attention.

He began by apologising for the previous time we met before telling me how I was the only person that helped him and how wonderful I was, he then watched me play the machine further, prompting me to cash it in and walk away while in front.

I lost half of the balance back as some bad numbers came in before I got another streak of better ones and returned to the same point of profit again, I then pressed the collect button and cashed it in at the shop counter, once I had the winnings in my hand, I handed him a twenty-pound note, saying, "here is a treat, unlike you I won't be waiting around every corner for it back next time I lose."

I needed to say this, I also had an urge to calm things down and walk away from the FOBT's, as I had spent most of the last two and a half days on them, and going to the Linnet and lark pub across the road was just the tonic, and I decided to buy John a drink.

It was here that I asked him how the funeral had gone, we hadn't discussed it since, and after a couple more pints followed by a neat Southern comfort with ice, he told me about the payment plan his brother had set up, he wasn't specific, he was a gambler with secrets, just like me, but I worked out where he had gotten the money from a couple of weeks prior, and how he had lost the first instalment, just like I had predicted, although the way I was losing money in a different way, it showed something scary, I realised that if I was in his situation, I would have done exactly the same as he did, I knew what the illness did to him as it was doing the same to me, we were in the zone and out of control, morals and principles where out of the window, it was about cash to gamble with, it didn't matter where it came from.

2003 turned out to be one of the most insane years of my life since the day I had my first bet, and both John and I encountered what was the best period for gambling that the city of Hull had ever produced, called 'the good times' by us punters.

I covered the story of this in the first Insanity of Gambling book, and none of us like sequels that are remakes of the originals so I will briefly recap.

This fruitful period lasted two and a half years and happened when all the amusement arcades began to offer double your money promotions on their fruit machines, with the maximum being between £5 and £10, depending on the day or the week or in some cases, the location.

The arcades also upped the number of feature machines, whereas they had previously had the old fashioned bar-x slots, and with these newer and more sophisticated all-cash bandits, came several games or 'features', of which you were given bonuses, money offers, high or low gambles and lots more.

They were also programmed to pay out a minimum of 72%, this meant if you put in £1000 over a period of time, you should get three-quarters of that amount back at the very least, in theory, depending on what the previous players had done.

The double-up offer meant us punters could put our cash in, and they would match it, and if I put in a total of £5, the cashiers would put this same amount in, all I had to do was then collect the wins and I could average a few pounds profit.

For one person spread over fifteen arcades offering this twice daily, and you're talking about up to £150 per day of free spins, of course, we had to put this amount in, but it was only done at a fiver to a tenner at a time so I didn't need to leave the house with this much money, but in a full week that is just over one-thousand-pounds of free plays.

I took Sally with me to get plays for her too which doubled the above stats, however, it was hard to get to every promotion with time restraints, but we managed more than two-thirds of them.

You could be even more astute by watching the previous player on the machines and if it had paid for them, then you could avoid, however, if they made a loss, you knew it was ready, with a little integrity you could figure out which ones were riper to produce than others.

Teddy's and the other arcades pushed the promotion for their own way of advertising, creating new machine players, expanding, and of course, it didn't cost them too much as promotions don't have the same taxation as profits, so while it was generous to us punters, they were still a business looking for long term growth.

Whatever their motives, the generosity also meant opportunity, and while I have already made comparisons between John and me when it came to these promotions, we couldn't have been more different in what we wanted from them.

I didn't stop gambling like a zombie in the zone until I had maxed all my cards out, it's only when I couldn't get any more cash to gamble that I could face the problem, and there I was, rock bottom and on the verge of defaulting on my first loan payment, with debts over £28k and not enough income coming into the house, I was in deep trouble, and ended up having to beg the banks to freeze the interest after making an offer of a monthly payment to each one for a six month period while I sorted myself out, but this made no difference, I was still over my head.

I found out about the promotions during the same week as receiving my first response from one of my five credit card companies, who accepted my offer but demanded the first instalment immediately.

I was a desperate man as I nervously took part in the first double-money promotion, but the prosperity that followed helped to not only stem the tide, but it also gave me surplice money and allowed me to pay additional funds onto the debts and reduce them further.

As I changed my job from the call centre to three-night shifts at the hospital in the medical records library, I had time on my hands during the day and as well as being paid for my overnights, I was earning a wage from the arcades too, I averaged between £100 to £250 a week profit, but occasionally won even more than this.

That is what the 'good times' meant to me, a way to undo the mistakes I had made and balance the books on my sinking ship, what did they mean to John?

He won a healthy amount too during this time, but almost every penny of profit he made in the arcades, was instantly taken with him to the betting shop and played on roulette.

The effect of this meant he would finish each day broke, without a penny to his name, and often he wasn't even buying food or amenities despite having extra revenue at his disposal.

The down-side of this was that when he had no money to start the day, he couldn't take part in the promotions, but he had a way around this, and that was to borrow the outlay to start the process, and he would find me at 9.00 am and ask to lend the first fiver, after a couple of arcades he would then give me this layout stake back, and after all the double-money offers right through to the early afternoon, he'd walk away quid's-in, usually £20 to £30 in front.

John would usually then lose all this profit on roulette in the bookies, and then find me in the evening to borrow again, of which he would once more make a few pounds for himself, pay me back yet again, then back to the betting shop once more with the second wave of profit for that day.

Repeat this whole cycle starting again the next morning and throughout the day, and this was what the 'good times' were to John, a way of funding his need to play electronic roulette.

This went on almost every single day and span over the entire three years, he was the same zombie in the zone that I was when running my debts to the credit limits.

The only days I got a break from this ritual was when he won on the Roulette machines, but this didn't seem to happen very often.

He didn't always manage to pay me back if the machines weren't paying, he sometimes ran up losses, or ask for a tab of which he owed me, which I'd get back when he won in the betting shop, or maybe February and August when he received his inheritance payments, and that would only happen if I could catch him before he went to the bookies with it.

He didn't put any thought processing behind it, he just got out of bed and his function appeared to be getting funds to play roulette.

It was during this time of course, as mentioned in the first book, that he earned his nickname of Choc-Ice-John, on an occasion when he muscled in uninvited as a third player in a branch of Teddy's down Hessle road where Sally and I were waiting for the cashier to come to us to sign the board and receive the match-up, which, on this day, was a six-for-six offer, done for us both, totalling £12 with the same amount matched.

John appeared from nowhere, out of breath as if he had been running, and asked to team up with us on the match to make it a total of £18 for the same in tokens, he then asked me to put his share in as he was skint, I reluctantly did, I then began to play the £36 in the machine and found it was streaking, two jackpots and several other cash wins later, I finished and found I had won just under £90 in profit after my outlay was taken back.

He then asked me for a third, this was the day I regretted not telling him to clear off while throwing two-pound coins at him.

It was also the day he went straight to the supermarket and bought a full box of choc-ices and ate them in front of me.

He then left me, and I didn't see him again until the evening sessions, where having lost the money he conned out of us in the afternoon on roulette, he then asked to borrow another outlay for the evening promotions.

Before the good times stopped altogether, they began to wind-down bit by bit, inch by inch, first with new clauses, then with stricter rules, followed by limits to the number of branches you could use, but this is where we could reflect on the chance we had.

Despite several binges during this time on roulette myself, most of the money was used to reduce my debts and I paid a couple of thousand pounds from the cards total, and as they were suspended, the money I transferred was one way.

I also spent surplice monies by having several tattoos etched onto me and put on a stone in weight by visiting the takeaways on Beverley road, which became almost daily.

I often look back at the time and reflect on what I could have done if I hadn't run the credit cards up during that crazy period, like an all-inclusive-family holiday, but instead, I suffered a knock-on effect from it, and apart from reducing my overall debt, I had nothing to show for it, apart from taking the impending bankruptcy option off the table for a while.

John had even less to show from this lucrative period, he spent the whole three-years winning in the arcades and feeding it straight into the fixed-odds betting terminals in the betting shops, so William Hills and Ladbrokes were the real winners, as these were his regular haunts.

It's hard to estimate how many thousands John earned for the bookmaking industry, but their shareholders would be happy at his service to them, a wasted opportunity because of the insanity of the gambling addiction.

If we think about that time before all this happened, prior to the gambling explosion, John tried to resist everything that wasn't horse racing, and it took a while to get his attention, but it was under his nose and eventually watching became playing, then it consumed him, he was a different animal and he became everything he was determined to avoid, going down the roads and avenues he was determined not too.

The compulsive gambling addiction was a lot stronger than him, as well as everyone else, and as it changed its ways, it was going to drag the unaware punters with it.

The promotions may have been shrinking, but the madness that was all around John wasn't diminishing and was going to continue to grow, little did he know what was ahead, but even then it may not have stopped him.

CHAPTER EIGHT

"John, I can't believe the good times are over," I said on a warm afternoon during the middle of 2005, referring to the incredible run the two of us had at the arcades, at least while it lasted, he then paused for a second and replied,
"know what Chris, I wish they had never started in the first place, I don't like mixing the two."

I wish I had a pound coin for every time he had said that same sentence about 'mixing the two', but he knew what he wanted and never changed his mind.

It was difficult to understand why he never budged on his opinion, especially after I'd witnessed him rinsing the arcades, even if he literally transferred it to the bookies, so I tried to remind him of his prosperity,
"you did ok out of it surely?" in an odd way I was looking to hear some gratitude from him, I knew I had been lucky myself, and the good-times had prevented me from going bankrupt, but I couldn't understand why he threw away his golden goose, and I could tell the way he was complaining that if he could go back in time to the beginning of this lucrative opportunity, he would do the same again,
"Chris, I resent them, I never wanted to get into it, I just want to play roulette."

I strangely found this annoying even though I should have allowed him to form his own judgment, but I hated the betting terminals and it was as if he was defending them,
"you seem ungrateful John, you have won loads in the arcades, you're probably the biggest winner in there," I could feel at this stage that I was venting at him,
"you never lost a penny back as you always went straight to the bookies, you might like playing those awful terminals, but I lost twenty-grand in three months on them and I'm still being punished for that today," then he said it again,
"I don't like mixing Chris, simple as that, it puts me in a place where I don't want to be."

I didn't know how to answer this, what on Earth did that last sentence mean? answers on a postcard because I still can't work it out, was the word 'place' he referred to a physical structure such as Teddy's, or a metaphor for something psychological?

We don't need to remind ourselves of Johns status with gambling, and we have also asked whether this stretched to the thrill that came with it, did leaving the house destitute, no food, can't pay for his gas, did he enjoy being in this position so that when he dug his way out he felt a different type of high?

Did he enjoy any of the insanity of which I highlight in the story at every opportunity, because what happened next took place in the space of a week, or to be more specific – seven days of pure madness.

Before we get to day one, a couple of points that connect to this story, John began turning up at my workplace more frequently, not every day, but it was more often than before.

Typically, I would leave at 5.00 pm and I'd spot him standing outside waiting for me, he'd then proceed to make small talk, tell me how he was going to get his act together, and then he would ask to borrow money.

It was rare I'd get it back until he won, sometimes I had to wait for weeks, on other occasions I didn't, he was unpredictable, but I was at the end of my tether with him as it had totted up in dribs and drabs to seventy-quid that I was out of pocket.

As well as this and despite being warned by his brother to keep away, he turned up on Marks doorstep on two occasions with the best excuses he could think of, and to him, it was worth the insults if he left with money.

The last time he went in person, he asked for a couple of hundred pounds as a loan but was given half that amount, which finished with a threat and a promise from Mark that he wouldn't get any more money of any kind if he ever asks for it again, being reminded a deal is a deal, but John did ring his brother one more time after this when he was desperate, which ended badly with Mark banging the phone down and telling John he was now 'done' with him.

John hoped this was an empty threat, but to leave nothing to chance, he kept his distance as the next few weeks passed.

Now that's out of the way, let's zoom to the first day of this Choc-Ice-John version of the Solomon Grundy week.

It began on August 1st, 2005, and you don't need to look at your calendar, I can tell you now this was a Monday, and you may have also worked out that this was the day Johns Inheritance payment was due to go into the bank.

John woke up excited but anxious that morning, while he knew what day it was, the last communication with Mark was at the forefront of his mind, and even if that hadn't happened, it had still been fraught over the years, Mark had lost his temper countless times when it came to John, even to the point where you wonder what his landline phone was made from when you think of the number of times he had slammed it down when he had finished talking to his brother.

This left John wondering if the money was going to go in his account at all, remembering the last time they spoke, Mark had told John he was 'done' with him, but there was only one way to find out, and he was soon out of the house, heading for town.

He had nothing to worry about, even though he expected Mark to keep him hanging around for it half of the day like he usually did, which he was certain from his perspective was done to make him sweat or to teach him a lesson but not today, additional funds were sat there on display a few seconds after he pressed the 'balance' button on the ATM.

With the worrying now behind him, he was soon regrouped, and the next thing was the amount that was paid in.

John never had to do much arithmetic when he got any monies credited to his account, he usually had pence rather than pounds occupying the balance icon on the screen.

It was always small change available to view because even if he had as little as a single pound in his account, he would take thisced out at the counter, even if he had to stand in a large queue to do so, this is why he knew the amount was less than he expected, it showed a balance of £700.02 – yes John had a couple of pence in there the previous evening before he went to bed.

It was £100 less than he expected, this was the amount that Mark let him have a few weeks earlier, and he deducted it, of which John spoke aloud, although there was nobody around, "he is so greedy, he could have let me off with it, he's got more than me."

How quickly John's demeanour changed, because when he first saw the money had gone in, he felt a huge sense of relief, less than a minute later he was feeling peeved that Mark had taken money back that John owed him.

John couldn't even speak to anyone about this, and we know the reason why, he didn't share this type of thing with anyone, when he had money he kept it to himself and would proceed to render himself as hard to find as the invisible man.

He was still disappointed about the lower amount even though it was him that borrowed and lost it, but he wasn't deterred and was determined that he was going to use the money wisely and learn from his past mistakes.

John had never won on the day that he received any of the payments dating back four years, was that going to continue? he had this on his mind from the offset, but this time was going to be different, but he didn't know that.

The first thing he did was head for the barbers, and he needed it because at this point John was beginning to resemble Robinson Crusoe after being on a barren run with no success, so he arrived and sat in the barber's chair, it wasn't at Josie's shop who we mentioned earlier, his regular place for a tidy-up was now the 'Strand hair-cut-inn', situated on Beverley road near the Brunswick avenue fish and chip shop, the same guy who used to cut my hair when I was growing up for another parallel, here he had his usual shave and everything off on top, which was the main tell-tale sign for me not to run in the opposite direction when I saw him.

This felt like the perfect start to the day for him, spending money before he went in the betting shop, and getting a smart groom before playing on risky cartoon roulette wheels was somehow classed as a way of being sensible in his warped logic as a gambler.

He then walked to Anlaby road with his total wealth coming to the sum of £692, oh, and don't forget the two-pence.

The next stop was you know where, and Johns first bet was a loser, it was for the sum of £20 and was put on a horse.

There is often a tendency with most people to start modest, before, unfortunately, it gets out of hand, I am sure most gamblers feel like 'today' they can control themselves, certainly while they are winning it's easier to do this, but even then it's not guaranteed, it can be hard to walk away from something when the mind is in the zone.

He was soon reaching for another twenty-pound note, this time it was for the roulette machine, he made an effort not to rush into this, but the time from him walking into the shop, placing the bet on the horse and watching the race was less than ten minutes, so although he felt like he was pacing himself, the truth is that the FOBTs tended to have the same effect on him as a steel-can does to a magnet, it was just under a quarter of an hour before he was playing on the terminals, but by his standards it was an improvement.

So, the first spin landed on black twenty-two in the middle block, and he had nothing on it, he wasn't panicking yet though.

I teased earlier that Johns luck was going to change on this day that he received his bi-annual instalment, you've had the spoiler already so you know he doesn't lose, he did get slightly further behind but all that it took for him to find himself in profit was a string of the good numbers coming in, and the ball began landing in the right high and low sections, middles may have started well, but soon they weren't coming in at all.

Although his best number was red-seven, the ball didn't land on this once, and he was only playing half of the maximum, a reserved £50 a spin, but this didn't stop his balance in the top right-hand corner steadily growing to a healthy £440, and he had laid out less than fifty quid on the day, including a haircut.

This profit was more than the £100 that he felt his bank payment was light, he had this money back and surplice cash into the bargain, and after weeks of misery, he was thinking the words 'about time too.'

He pressed the collect button, took his slip to the counter and was paid the money out, he knew that it wouldn't be long before he was on them again but with him being out of touch with the feeling of winning, it left him wanting to savour the moment while he could.

Gamblers often feel that while they are on a winning streak, they are never going to lose again, but the one thing John had was gumption, he knew the bigger picture, so he set himself up for the next gloomy period.

All of his friends were gamblers, he knew who would help him when he was destitute, and who to avoid, you could say that he knew them better than they knew themselves, so when he got the chance he slipped a couple of the right people a small treat, maybe a twenty-pound note, remember I had been on the receiving end myself and he was straight back at me as if he had only lent me the money, and this was no different as his generosity was a way of feathering his own nest when the gifts turned into loans when the losing days came.

He was soon back on the animated roulette table again, and even when he had a couple of bad numbers coming in, the good ones were not far behind and most of the day was about winning modest and cashing in, he then did something else out of character, he put a decent amount of credit on his gas and electricity token meters, before a couple of other friends received yet more treats from him.

He was relishing the feeling of being on the crest of a wave, and you can argue that he deserved it, although you have to say it was with money from an inheritance, and this sprang to his mind, as his sister's reactions to him resonated with him.

The last time he saw Jackie was when she shunned him when the family met up to sort out the estate, she had muttered that John was a lost cause and he had made no effort to prove her wrong, because she was right, and this was the last time he had seen or heard from her.

It's funny how he thought of that at this time, but it made no difference as he was soon back on the machine, chipping his favourite numbers again and pressing the button to send the silver ball flying around the edge of the wheel, hoping it lands in his chosen areas, listening to the losing chips clinking as they were being dragged off and the noise of his bank increasing if it landed on a fruitful section of the board.

By the time 6.00 pm came, he had an additional £700 stuffed in his pocket that he didn't have in the morning, and this was after his expenses, he had given some money out to a couple of his betting shop buddies, paid some bills and had a haircut, but who was his real friend? me, and that's where he went next, to the library.

I was on the free internet, and I only saw the silhouette of him approaching from the entrance door, I gave off a massive sigh as he came up to me, then he said, to my surprise, "don't worry Chris, I'm not after money, meet me outside when you have finished, you will like what I have to say."

I then looked up and saw his smooth chin, I should have done this first as that was still the best tell-tale sign that he had won, but I then replied,
"I don't need to stay on the computer John, I'll leave with you now, I am going to the internet café later anyway."

This was because I was writing to some lady in Finland of all places and she was a pen friend, she was called Lis-Brit or something like that, I'd known her for years online, but we hadn't ever met, she didn't live near Helsinki or I may have chanced a flight, but she was at the other end of the country so it never happened.

Lis-Brit was an ex competitive bodybuilder and now ran a bar, alcohol seemed the last thing you would advocate if you seek the body-beautiful, but people are interesting in their variety, but back to the here and now and the most 'beautiful thing right now was the fact that I expected to be handing out cash and instead I was going to be given something from him, for a welcome change.

We walked down the stairs and left the building, John reached in his pocket, he often kept his money, which consisted of small change, in a plastic see-through bag, the same ones that the banks use to take coins in, but not today, as he produced a thick wad of twenty-pound notes, and he handed a ready-counted amount out to me,
"here Chris, this is £80, and I don't want it back, you have been good to me when others haven't, and I wanted to give you a treat," I didn't know what to say, obviously I thanked him.

We then walked down Beverley road, and the further we got, the more I noticed that his whole personality had changed, after the initial niceties, it was almost as if I was beneath him now, he wasn't saying my name every other word and didn't even look at me when he was talking.

I had seen this before, there is nothing like having a few quid to make a person change, not this quick though surely. I began to question who was the real John, was it the guy who will say anything to get what he wants, no confidence, subdued and desperate, or was it this cock-sure, arrogant and stand-offish guy who looked at you like you were no longer in the same class as him?

If John had never gambled I would know the actual person he was, for now, though I knew gambling could steal a person's personality like it had mine, I didn't know who I was at this point, I could only remember who I used to be in the distant past before I placed my first bet, but I had seen glimpses of this during attempts to quit gambling, so how could I know the real him when he had never tried to stop.

Whoever John really was, I still liked the pleasant and likeable person I knew, he must have felt worthless for the majority of the time and it may have created issues with him, it was likely to be coming out when he didn't need anything from anyone, but he must have known it was temporary as he left me to jump on a bus heading for Bransholme, I heard him ask for a weekly bus ticket so another rarity, he usually walked everywhere.

He was going to pay his mate called Kevin, who lived in that part of Hull, a visit. His plan was to pay this guy some money back that he owed and to give him a treat too, which, no doubt also meant lining him up for future needs.

With the bus taking off and John sat on it, he was out of sight which meant I could cross the road and enter my premises, returning to my flat without the danger of him knowing where I lived, for now.

Johns winning streak continued into the next two days, and it was Wednesday when I saw him again, I like to think it was by accident but I knew that I had a strong fascination about him, and walked near to the shops that he might be in, true to form, as I passed the town centre branch of William Hills, there he was.

When you think that he had unlimited travel on buses around the city, you couldn't normally find him when he had funds of any kind, yet here he was, this surprised me.

The moment I walked towards him, he was playing – and winning, however as soon as I got too near, he saw me and hurriedly cashed in his ticket, he didn't want me to see the money in his bank at first but he could soon see that I was happy for him and that I didn't want any of it, I enjoyed seeing him win.

Soon he left the shop and asked if I needed anything, but I said I didn't, he knew I was going to say no though, he wasn't daft.

He was soon relaxed enough with me to put the cash he had just drawn from the counter with the rest that he had, I'd never seen him with so much paper money, the wad was at least double what he had at the library, and he put the lot away in his tracksuit trouser pocket, good job it had a zip, as there must have been at least two-grand, a big jump from the two pence he had a couple of days before.

It was incredible to think that he had all that money despite giving around three-hundred-quid away to mates, but the way he was going he didn't miss any of it. I then tried to give him the usual friendly advice, begging him to spend some of it on himself, I suggested among other things that he purchased some much-needed items for his flat, or tickets for the next few rugby games, all the usual stuff to try to get him to have some quality of life out of the money.

I stated that if he spent £500, then the bookies couldn't get this off him. Then came my usual example from my days of gambling, as to why I was tattooed all over my chest and back, that's one of the things I did when I was winning, so the bookies couldn't get it back. Again, I said all this as a guy who had been where he was, a friend who understood everything he had been through.

We then parted and I went home, and I didn't know where he was going, or maybe I did.

The following morning was a normal Thursday, but to him, very different to all the others in the calendar year, because the previous evening, just before he went to bed, he spread the money all over the floor and stared at it for a lengthy time, and this was the first thing he saw when he woke up, it looked as if he had just robbed a bank.

Now, what would a normal person think or do when they stared at a small fortune? Would they go out and buy a new garden shed? a bigger and better telly? maybe a meal in a fancy restaurant that they couldn't afford before? perhaps even an all-inclusive holiday for 14 nights on the coast of Spain?

Anyone would have thoughts like these, Choc-Ice-John didn't even own a television, he could sure afford any in the shop right now though, but none of that crossed his mind as he continued to look at the floor, and all he saw was gambling money.

When I said it wasn't a normal Thursday, the money was one thing, yes, but it wasn't going to be just that, this was destined to be a day that he would never forget, one that he would talk about for years to come, as the insanity of gambling was about to live up to its name yet again.

John had the giddy feeling that came with the winning run he was on, and his wealth was accumulating, and he was soon up and had his normal bowl of cereal covered in sugar for his sweet tooth, there was a chocolate orange in the fridge too which had his attention.

He looked at the time, it wasn't quite 7.00 am, and the bookies didn't open until 9.30 am, so what could he do to kill the time?

He impulsively decided that he was going to take a trip to Scarborough on the east coast, so he grabbed all the money, yes every note, not half of it, or £500, but the full £2000 and squeezed it into his pocket, he then grabbed his keys and the chocolate orange and set off to the train station.

It was only a twenty-minute stroll to get there, and upon arriving he looked at the screens, and he couldn't have timed it much better if he had tried, the train was due to depart in ten minutes, and a very short queue to get the tickets.

Hull's Paragon station doesn't usually mean running to find your platform, the reason being that despite being a major city, there are only eight railway tracks' in and out, it's small in comparison with some of the other stations around the country.

John boarded the train heading to Scarborough, it was an old carriage and was a proper boneshaker in comparison to some of the others, but he didn't care, he was used to walking everywhere, this felt like a luxury.

As the train left, it soon speeded up once it had gone through the towns consisting of Beverley, Driffield and Nafferton, he knew it was close when he arrived at the first of three seaside towns, which was Bridlington, then shortly afterwards there was Filey until he reached the final stop on the journey – Scarborough, where the train terminated before setting off on the return journey to Hull.

The east coast gets more beautiful the further up north you go, and this seaside town is one that surprises you, when you see how picturesque it is.

He walked towards the promenade, but he already saw the most beautiful sight he could imagine before he even got there, a Corals betting shop, it was 10.00 am so it was open for business.

John was soon on the terminals and loaded up his favourite roulette game, and his winning streak wasn't finished, it continued here too, he wasn't on the machine long though as punters began gathering around to watch him, so he cashed in with an additional forty-quid to add to his tally.

He didn't have to walk far to the next shop as there was a Ladbrokes just around the corner, upon entering he found it was less occupied and he could do what he wanted in peace without an audience, if he had wanted a crowd, he could have stayed in Hull.

One of the plus points of going to the seaside was solitude from other peering punters that not only observed, but because they knew him, his success or failure could soon be gossiped about and spread around the city, and people who John owed money too may have come looking for him.

Because he was winning, he had more self-control and calmness about him and found it easier to regroup, he took time out to buy a can of coke at the betting shop counter and had a look at what was running in the afternoon race meetings.

His thoughts were as positive as a man who couldn't stop winning could have, and he was thinking of the fish and chip dinner that had his name on it waiting for him in another couple of hours'.

A quarter of an hour later he was slotting a couple of twenty-pound notes into the FOBT, and he wasn't starting small as he had previously, and he slowly chipped the numbers he wanted with his finger before the first press of the button that sent the ball ricocheting for his initial £40 spin, but things here were different, as soon his luck began to run out and it was only a half-hour later that he was betting the maximum of £100 while at the same time finding himself £700 down.

Before he could bury himself any further he spotted a greyhound race and without looking at the form, he wrote £150 on trap-six to win on a betting slip and took it to the counter, this was currently priced at 7-2 on the screen. The bookie was reluctant to take the bet but as he had enough cash in the shop, he stood it.

John looked at the state of the race as the dogs approached the traps and thought he had made a mistake when his selection drifted to 5-1 in the market and seemed unfancied, but it was too late as the hare came running around the edge of the track and the greyhounds flew out of their boxes.

He regretted the bet at this point as he stared at a potential loss of £850, but his dog led at the first bend as all the other greyhounds collided and went spiralling over each other, as his choice romped home for a pay-out of £900, which was yet another £50 of further profit, only he had to work a lot harder in this second shop, the day was already proving an adequate thrill and it was only 11.15 am.

Already questions appear, does winning every day becomes stale and boring if it doesn't spike the adrenaline?

Are the fluctuations in fortunes something that the punter gets accustomed too and craves without knowing it?

It's hard to weigh up the exact science behind the mind of a gambler, I doubt anyone knows, John seemed to want to get into trouble and pull his way out, but in the unpredictability of things, he never visualised that everything would depend on a four-legged canine, I doubt even he wanted this much excitement.

It was too early for dinner, so the next stop was a bakery for a snack and more junk food, this time a sticky bun with pink icing was just what he needed.

After a stroll along the beach, he headed towards the amusement arcades, where he could hear the noise of a thud as a guy was punching a boxing bag, the harder you hit, the more points you earn and you could put your name on the hall of fame if you appeared in the top five best scores for the day, but hit it wrong and it's a sprained wrist and humiliation in front of your mates.

He then heard the sound of a bingo caller, as players were sat marking numbers in a circular seated area, with prizes galore on display, depending on how many winning tickets you get, there was everything from a toilet brush to a small telly and lots of other prizes in between, the bigger stuff would probably cost more to win then it would to buy in the shops over the time it would take to get enough full-houses, but people enjoyed this, again not Johns scene.

He could hear some more clattering as a couple of young lads began playing air hockey, vigorously hitting the puck to score at the opposite end,
"you cheated" bellowed the moans from one sore loser.

Of more interest to him was the coin-slider, a standard seaside arcade machine, with moving compartments as you attempt to push ten pence-pieces over the edge, this was more him, not conventional gambling but the first time he ever used a stake in an attempt to win money, this was it, nostalgia stared at him in the face.

In his mind he couldn't do much damage on this machine, it was a long way from the dangers of electronic roulette, and more fun if you take away the excitement that came with the other, but it wasn't long before he realised he had changed enough notes into coins to warrant being £60 down. He also didn't realise how long he had been in there, over two hours!

He left but didn't come away empty-handed as he managed to win a watch, which came colliding down with several coins as he had thrown everything to get it onto the tipping point of the slider, but when he tried it on it didn't fit, the strap was so big that he may as well have put it around his ankle, you could tell it was cheap and cheerful.
     The last time he had a watch in his possession it was for his sister Jackie all them years ago, when he lost the money in the bookies on the way that day too, he thought about this but not for too long, he would have been shocked to realise that was thirty-five years ago and he was still just as bad, if not worse.
     By now he had enough time away from the FOBTs to think a tad clearer, he had lost money in the amusements but it could have been far worse, it was scary to think what would have happened if that greyhound hadn't won, it made him appreciate where he was now, although at the front of his thoughts, he wanted that sixty-quid back.
     For the next hour, he walked on the beach again and dipped in and out of the arcades, playing the fruit machines this time, which were mostly low jackpots with features that had been around for years, this didn't help though as he was soon a further £37 down, he had lost just under a hundred quid on this trip down memory lane across the sea-front.
     It had been three hours since he was last in a betting shop and the pining to play on the roulette machine was growing stronger, and as time went on it felt as if he would be ill if he resisted, and up to now he had enjoyed the day as a whole, but the craving was almost in his gut, he felt like he was going to keel over if he didn't hear the sound of that ball soon.
     It wasn't long before he was where he wanted to be, a further branch of Corals for his next venture, and here he recouped his losses as his numbers came in, and best of all, was the red-seven on a couple of occasions, he totted everything up, he soon counted that he had two-hundred pounds more than he had on his floor in the morning, which

meant he had won back the cost of his train tickets, the arcade visits, and even his sticky bun was free, plus around eighty-quid on top of all this, his trip to Scarborough had been free and he even had the bonus of a watch that would fit around his leg.

He set off for the station and as he approached he could see the train was just arriving, he was soon in his seat as it set off back, and for him, he was thinking how days don't get much better than this, but it wasn't over yet.

When John was only ten minutes into his journey, he reflected on how close he came to losing, one dog had become a turning point, he knew he was lucky but he still felt invincible, when your winning, it doesn't matter how you get that success, you feel like losses are a thing of the past, right now he was sat with a handful of people in his carriage, he didn't join in any conversations, good job really, because his cockiness was even higher than before.

The train arrived in Filey and remained still on the platform for a few minutes, and then left this first stop of the return journey, it was currently 4.30 pm as John looked at his watch, the one that fitted on his wrist that is, not the huge monstrosity he won at the amusement arcade, that probably wouldn't tell the time anyway.

John then decided that he would get off at the next stop, Bridlington, another seaside town that he hadn't been too for years, why come back when he must go through it anyway?

His thoughts were that he may as well make a real day of it, and catch a later train, all now planned out. Going from Scarborough to here would at least shorten the journey he had to make later.

It then dawned on him, he hadn't even had fish and chips yet, you can't go home without that when you're at the seaside surely? he was going to put this right, as he stood up to get off the train as it came to a halt at Bridlington.

Like Scarborough, it has a beach, and as he headed there he soon stopped, as it wasn't much different to earlier that day, where he spotted a betting shop and had an urge to play roulette again.

Upon putting his money into the FOBT, and starting conservatively in his stakes, he was up and down for a large amount of time as different and inconsistent numbers came in, at one point he was £210 down, but turned it around when he finally got a streak of very high numbers coming in, but as he was in a trance as he pressed the repeat bet button constantly, he had lost all track of time, but he was still on this amazing winning run, and although he had put £280 into the machine, the bank was an awesome £790, and a further £500 up.

He was worried about the last train, he didn't even know what time it left, so he nervously looked at the clock on the wall, it was 7.15 pm.

He left the shop with over £2,700 stuffed into the same bulging pocket, he would have been a muggers dream if he had been walking on some dark and dreary depressed estate, but this town was full of retired older people, he would have been unlucky if he had been robbed, although you could say the bookies are usually the ones that did that too him, with his permission, but not so far this week.

If I have described already about him feeling on the top of the world, he was even higher now, it was like being on a drug, one that doesn't wear off, and had lasted four days so far.

When he arrived at the station, there were two trains left that went to Hull and he was going to get the penultimate of these.

His thoughts were of a restaurant that he liked for when he got home later, an Indian he once visited and enjoyed, so with this in mind he pictured the main course, followed by a sweet for dessert, and this would make up for the fish and chips he never had on this day, but he didn't care about that anymore, the way he was now looking at it, Hull was full of chip shops, he could get that any time.

As for the present, it was a 35-minute wait before the train came, he thought about buying something to read to pass the time till he got home and maybe a snack, something that wouldn't ruin his appetite before his planned meal.

He crossed the overhead bridge to the other side to look for a newsagent, but what did he see instead? a William Hill's betting shop!

With a half-hour till the train, he felt there was just enough time for a last punt of the day before he took the sixty-minute journey back, so off he trotted and into the shop.

Things started well and he was so confident with all the ammunition in his pocket to back him up, even though he only set out to have a small bet, he switched quickly once he was on the machine, he wasn't sure if it was a flutter or excitement that he pined for.

After four spins of the roulette wheel he was a further £15 up, not a fortune when you are minted like he was, but a lot of money if you don't have anything. John intended to play until ten minutes before the train was due to arrive and this was good on paper, but then a few losing spins struck, he increased his stakes and it wasn't long before he was hitting £50 every spin, sometimes as quick as twenty seconds between, as he kept pressing repeat spin, as the numbers that had been coming in, may as well have been taken off the wheel, he never changed his formula all day and was still backing both high and low numbers, leaving the middle section out.

When this wasn't working, he tried to mix things up and put numbers elsewhere across the table, but he couldn't seem to do anything right as his stakes increased to recoup his losses.

He looked at the clock, his head was working like a calculator when he realised he was £800 down, he didn't have to increase far to reach the £100 for what he intended to be his last spin if he got any profit, if not he would spin again, which is what happened when Red-sixteen came in with nothing on it, he repeated, so did the number sixteen.

The next spin was a loser and as if by magic, the ball landed on red-sixteen for the third time in four spins. If it had been red-seven instead of this number coming in by that same ratio, John would have had the option of coming away with close to his money back from this shop.

As he looked at the clock again it was time for him to leave, but after slotting another five twenty-pound notes and spinning yet again, he knew there was another train in a further hour, so he decided to stay and see if his luck in this shop would change – but it didn't.

Soon he was betting faster and was too anxious to even count-up, he had no idea how he was doing and when he did finally get his head together and looked at what he had left, the wad of notes in his pocket felt much skinnier even though there was still £700 remaining.

This was the same amount of the instalment on his inheritance money that he received, he thought he had lost the lot till he realised that he still had £600 in his account, this was profit, more if you count his expenses, so he was still in a good position, although it's hard to call it that.

He wasn't about to cut and run though, and eleven spins later with only two profitable numbers coming in, the lot was gone, all lost, but, he had remembered about the money in the account, and he went to the manager working behind the counter,
"where is the nearest cashpoint mate?" this is when the bookie should have asked John if he could afford to lose any more and perhaps refuse to let him continue, instead he replied, "there is a machine just around the corner," pointing left.

John was soon there and withdrew the maximum of £300 and ran back to the shop, feeling sick as he loaded £100 into the FOBT.

The first two spins where winners, followed by a loser, another decent return followed before four bad numbers out of the next five spins left him distraught, he had put the full amount from the hole in the wall in the machine by this point and he put the last £11 remaining on a single number, of which red-thirty-four came in, one of his best numbers normally, unfortunately, he had all his chips on black-seventeen, which was one he never chose, this is how confused he was.

He was now too far down to make any difference, but he asked the bookie if he could bet with his card, which he had never done before, of which the guy said
"you can if you know your pin."

John put this into the card reader,
"how much do you want," said the bookie,
"three-hundred" replied John.

This was declined before John said,
"try it again with £290", this then worked and was loaded onto the machine.

After starting with another loser, John put £12 on eight red numbers, he picked the right colour but, one of the others came in that he didn't chip, this was followed by black-fifteen and the final spin he had was all his money on the first six numbers, and red-sixteen came in again to rub salt into the wounds, the number that had done a lot of damage on this day.

John walked to the door resembling a man whose heart had been crushed, feeling sad and close to tears, and although he was normally a cool customer that didn't show emotion, he said to the guy as he left,
"I wish I had not seen your shop when I was at the station," the bookie then shrugged his shoulders, he didn't care.

John didn't like his attitude, so after walking a few yards, he turned around with the intention of going back to tell the guy what he thought of him, only to find the door was now locked, and upon looking through the glass door, John could see him emptying the machine and counting all the money, which was just over £3000 with the cash withdrawal and let's not forget the further funds from his debit card, as he looked at the huge wad which took the guy ages to count up, there were even a few coins of which John had slotted into the terminal, all that he had was gone, as he felt his empty pocket, knowing all that money was zipped away safely ninety minutes ago.

Did I say ninety minutes? remember John had a thirty-minute wait for the train and the last of the night was an hour later, add this up and that's ninety minutes, right? he then realised he had lost track of the time.

He sprinted back to the station, but he missed it, only just though, as he could see it when he looked up the track. If it had been a few minutes late he would have been ok, but that didn't help.

Right now, he was hungry, thirsty, stressed, upset and angry. He had suffered the rollercoaster of emotions that go with gambling, up to the highest of highs, and suddenly down to the lowest of lows, as bad as a drug, the feeling of the life being ripped out of his body, he now had to suffer further because he was stranded.

As if things couldn't get any worse, he then realised that his train ticket was only a cheap day return, so it was invalid for the next morning, but he had to get on it whatever.

This may have been the first time John had won initially when it came to the inheritance pay-outs, but he felt that he may as well have lost it the day he got it rather than suffer all this.

He strolled to the pier, the beach was out of bounds as the tide had come in, nothing much else to do, but the evening was lovely, he looked at the sea as it glistened and wondered why he couldn't have just come and enjoyed this, he didn't need to bet any more once he had won as much as he had, but that was now past tense.

You couldn't think of anything for him to be grateful for at this time, but he got his inheritance February and August, at least this was the warm month out of them if you are forced to sleep rough, it might have been snowing if it had been six months earlier.

He contemplated walking home, but he knew it would take too long, and he felt too undernourished for such a journey.

Only one thing left for him to do once it got late, he headed for a pub, to pop to the loo and have a drink from the cold-water tap, desperate and still in disbelief after what had happened, then it was back to the station where he would wait for the first train in the morning.

He laid on a bench and closed his eyes, wanting to cry, in possibly his lowest moment ever.

John took a while to fall asleep, but once he did he slept well with all things considered, but when he woke, the realisation came flooding back to what he had done the day before, the sick feeling in his stomach of what had happened.

It was hard to think of the previous morning when he woke up with £2000 in full view on his floor, today he was miles away, in another town with no money and sleeping in a train station on a bench, how he had fallen because of his gambling addiction.

He looked at the clock and it was 5.15 am, he already knew the first train came at 6.45 am, so he walked around for a while and it seemed like the longest ninety minutes ever, but eventually it got to the time where he could finally leave Bridlington.

He felt a huge relief as he stepped off the platform and onto the rear carriage, it was like the end of a nightmare for him, although the relief was tarnished because of the prior evening, he was still pleased to be on his way home all the same.

Now for the next problem he had caused himself, he had no ticket for this day's travel, he sat at the back and as soon as he saw the conductor coming down the middle of the train, he went in the toilet to avoid inspection.

He stayed there for a while and was rather unlucky that the guy came passed just as he was coming out of the loo, because a few seconds longer and John might have missed him.

He then asked to see the ticket, John showed him the one from the day before, but the conductor, unfortunately, was a jobsworth,
"this ticket is for yesterday," he said, but John had his story ready,
"I'm sorry, I told them I was coming back the day after, it was the mistake of the guy who sold it to me," but the man wasn't buying this,
"it's your job to check it and I can't let you carry on without a ticket," but John hadn't finished with the excuses,
"I did check it, but the last train didn't come last night," which may have worked but the chap came back at John,
"yes, it did, I was working on it," this was the response John didn't want to hear, he was now desperate,
"please, I bought a ticket, I just want to get home," but it wasn't getting him anywhere, John kept on pleading to the conductor's better nature, if he had one,
"I don't have any money," but John was wasting his time as he soon found out what his only options were, as the guy was not going to budge,
"you can talk to the Police in Driffield, or you can get off at the next stop," this left John with two choices, one of them was to leave where the conductor was going to kick him off and try all this again on the next train, the other option is what he did,
"I might have just under a tenner left in my card account, can I buy a ticket with this," as he took this out of his tracksuit trouser pocket.
   Johns current account card must have felt very lonely in his pocket, as its £2,700 worth of paper buddies had all deserted it, but the conductor nodded and he told John this would come to just over £9, although he did have some money, he didn't even know if there was enough to cover this, so it was a relief when the sale went through and the guys machine spat the valid ticket out, but he was now truly skint.
   He sat down on the train, he didn't need to hide anymore, but all the stress had made him thirsty and he began to look

around to see if anyone had left any half bottles of water, he had no luck there either.

He then realised he was heading to a home that had no food except a quarter of a box of cornflakes, but he didn't have any milk in the empty fridge, and the only thing he had eaten all day was a sticky bun from the bakery in Scarborough as gambling had mesmerised him.

With both the fish and chip dinner and the evening meal at the fancy Indian restaurant both escaping in, it was all now like ancient history, except the past had messed up the future that he saw in front of him.

He was kicking himself because he never even did a food shop when he had the money, but he was quick to remember all the people he had treated a couple of days earlier, and he never gave them money because he felt charitable, he strategically headhunted specific personalities, again not as a reward, but because he knew what just happened was potentially on the cards, and now it was a reality, he was in a stronger position to call in the favours.

Choc-Ice-John had lured us all into a false sense of security with his familiar catchphrase, each time saying,
"this is a treat and I don't want it back", now famous last words, remember, he gave me eighty-quid too earlier that week.

He was finally back to where he was exactly a day ago, Paragon station, and he walked home slowly knowing he was again in another predicament because of his gambling, the pain and inconvenience etched on his face, he could not even comprehend what he was doing to himself right now, his mind was zombified with his habit.

He went home to eat, with a meal consisting of cereals and water, and it was the bottom of the box with the dust and broken corn flakes, but he was hungry so he couldn't be picky right now.

He then went to bed for a nap, and woke up two hours later, looked across and saw an empty floor, compared with the day before when he had enough £20 notes to wallpaper his bedroom with, now it was a distant memory, I should be saying what a difference twenty-four hours can make, but in reality, it was a crazy ninety minutes and £3,290 on a cartoon roulette wheel, and from everything going so well, and some heavy-duty chasing later, it's all a mudslide.

Shortly afterwards as it hit mid-day, he put on his coat and locked his front door, and left his flat with the intention of calling in favours, although his points of call were all people that had done more for John over the years than he had done for them.

Right now, as far as he was concerned, he was the one that recently handed out the lolly, so he felt he was the one in the position to call upon these people that he called mates. With friends like him who needs enemies.

He first headed to Bransholme estate to his fellow gambler Kevin's house, this was about five-miles on the bus but you could cut half a mile out on foot if you took the cycle track near Cleveland street and as he had no bus fare, walking this way was his only choice.

John had no idea if Kevin was even going to be in, because like most of Johns mates, he liked a bet, although to be fair, he did ration it out better than our friend.

When Choc-Ice-John got there it took Kevin a few minutes to get to the door but for a moment John thought he was going to have to cover more ground on foot to search for him in the local area's betting shops, and knowing if that failed he would have to walk to one of his other mates who he also treated a couple of days ago, lucky for him it wasn't necessary.

Once John was in the house, he was soon pleading poverty and telling hard-luck stories. It was hard for Kevin to take in as the last time he saw him, John had a swagger and his pockets looked like they belonged to Baron Roth-Charles, but in the here and now he was in the position he was, the money was gone and wasn't coming back.

There was one small mistake John had made here, he relied on a gambler for money and Kevin didn't have any, but that didn't stop John asking,
"Steve are you sure you can't do me something,"
"no John I am broke, otherwise I would help you, I had a bad day yesterday and I don't get paid till next week," so John now had to go for the next best,
"could I bother you for something to eat Kev, I haven't got any grub in my flat,"
"of course, John, get your backside sat down in there and I will make you a drink too" as he pointed to his lounge,
"I'd rather take some teabags and milk home than have a drink if you have a spare bottle to put some in," said John cheekily.

He was often like this when it came to someone offering him something, he always thought ahead when it came to survival, but he didn't do the maths that told him that money equals food, but a logical type of thought processing wasn't the norm now.

Kevin went in the cupboard, put some bread in the toaster, opened a tin of beans and fried an egg, giving John a share of what he had left for himself, survival till payday food, at least he thought ahead and filled his cupboard before he went to the bookies.

John ate this but still wasn't finished, remember, to his mind Kevin still owed him,
"do you have any biscuits or chocolate Kev? I have a sugar rush and need something sweet," Kevin then proceeded to bring in the cookie jar to reveal a couple of custard creams and a broken rich tea biscuit that looked like it had been in there for weeks,
"thanks," said John as he finished them off,
"I better get off as I need to try to get some money from somewhere," and he then walked out to start a new journey.

He walked back the longer route and called in at another friend's house on Beverley road, but, as expected this one wasn't home, but by now, he looked at the time and it was perfect, he had just under an hour to get to Hull Royal Infirmary to find a certain clerical personnel leaving work, you've guessed it, me!

He arrived outside my workplace, this is where I was like clockwork, every evening I left at 5.00 pm, I never changed my hours or daily schedule and he knew this.

The £80 he gave me was not enough to change my life, but it felt like a lot of money in the situation I was in, put it this way, I was grateful for it and although I wasn't there yet, I was growing tired of the devastating effect gambling was having on me, and problems that stemmed from this over the years, I had reduced money that I owed and tried to keep busy, but problems I caused through betting seemed everywhere and although I was still gambling, I was in a transitional period contemplating getting help. I didn't have a lot of surplice cash, so the money he gave me went a long way.

I left work and there he was, I was surprised to see him and thought he must be there to try and give me more money, another treat, but I was determined to refuse it, this at least, was how my mind was working upon witnessing his presence.

The last time I had seen him, he was loaded, I had never seen him with so much money, it dwarfed the previous times by far, and that was only two days earlier, I did not know the story of Scarborough and Bridlington, or that he had even more cash at one point, I just saw a man with two grand in his pocket a couple of days earlier, so I didn't expect the words that came out of his mouth, with a ready thought out excuse, "Chris, I need £80 as I have the chance of a holiday and without it, I can't go,"
"John, please no, I mean it please don't do this to me, I am in a really bad situation and you gave me that money, please don't ask for it back,"
"sorry but I need it Chris," I couldn't believe it, so I tried to put it into perspective,

"let's get this straight John, once again, you need the precise amount of money that you gave me and didn't want back, do you remember?"
"it's not like that at all Chris, I did give you it, but I need this much for my trip,"
"ok John" I said,
"where are you going on this holiday?" I knew he would struggle for an answer, and after a long silence he replied,
"I am going to stay with a cousin who has invited me down for a few days, but I need to get a ticket, and some spends if we go out," but I was not letting him off easy,
"your family don't talk to you and you've never mentioned any cousins,"
"it's one I haven't told you about Chris,"
"yeah right," I said as I showed my frustration to him.

Trying to explain that I was in a bad situation, I asked him if £30 would do but he kept insisting he needed £80, as he continued to tell me that it was nothing to do with it being the same amount he had given me.

I knew he was lying, and I was within my rights to refuse, but I didn't, and I dug £40 out of my pocket and handed it to him and withdrew the rest from the ATM and said,
"here, that is everything I have, now I am in a worse situation than you and you have done me over once again."

I had always made sure he was alright over the longer period, he was only generous to me when he had won a shedload of cash, whereas I was consistently bailing him out, but I emphasised that by taking all this now I would no longer help him, or ever trust him again, but his reply put me off him even more,
"I've been let down myself Chris, I treated Kevin and I went to his house because I was hungry, and all he gave me was bloody beans on toast."

I saw just how ungrateful he was right at this point, and it showed in my reply, "so, John, you gave him a few quid, so he has got to feed you with Royal Oscietra Caviar and Dom Perignon vintage Champagne?"

"no, no it's not like that but I wanted better than beans on toast, it was even cheap bread that I don't like," this coming from a man who had nothing after emptying his pockets into a FOBT, talk about beggars being choosers.

He then took the money and walked away. I went home and back out again on my bike, riding past betting shops in the area even though I knew it was pointless, but I eventually rode past a Fred Done bookmakers on Princes avenue and saw him playing roulette on the FOBTs with the money he just took off me.

I was strongly tempted to confront him, but I thought it best to walk away a wiser person and to put it behind me.

This saw me becoming even more determined that I was never going to have anything to do with him again despite an ever-lingering hold he had over me, as a fellow compulsive gambler, he was still fascinating and it felt like a hole in my life if I didn't know what he was going to do next, but even then I knew I hadn't seen him for the last time.

So, this was only five days and I said it was an insane week? Saturday was another walk to Kevin's on Bransholme for some more baked beans on toast, despite what he had said to me.

Sunday was a much quieter and less eventful day compared to the previous six, which was more than you could say for the next day that followed.

Remember the train journey when his debit card gave him that ticket? On Monday morning he received a letter from the bank telling him he had been fined for going into an unauthorised overdraft, albeit by a single pound, the transaction on the train went through but he didn't have enough in his account to cover it, and when he went to the ATM the £35 bank charge had already been taken out, a knock-on effect as his balance was now showing minus-£36, a lot less healthy than a week earlier when the amount of 2p was showing, as this week of madness concludes.

What can you say about that seven days John experienced? There were a few pinnacle moments during that mad week, sadly one thing remained consistent with all the other occasions, John lost and the bookies got his money, and you feel that if it hadn't have happened the way it did on the east coast, it would have still had the same conclusion, he unwittingly glossed up the story by travelling to Scarborough and Bridlington, rather than walk to his local betting shop.

Why do things like this happen to the compulsive gambler? Again, it's hard to talk about the science behind a betting addict, I've heard theories, but do we know?

As a none-expert in brain heightening, I can only talk from experience and the feelings that I had when amid the addiction, and I know there is a reason we call it 'the Insanity of Gambling' with the strong tendency to be pro-active in lying, cheating and stealing to raise revenue to bet with, it somehow creates a low-boredom threshold when the gambler runs out of funds that perhaps wouldn't exist in a normal world, leading to intensity and a loss of mental stability all at the same time, and crazy things unfold around them.

John and I reacted different in the better moments, when we were fruitful on our punts, I tried to spend as much money as I could during these times so I couldn't lose it back, this could mean taking the family out, having a native American in full tribal headgear tattooed on my chest, or buying a takeaway for everyone, anything to stop the bookies getting it from me because I knew I was powerless.

John also knew what was around the corner when things were prosperous and tended to give money away like a modern-day Robin Hood, except that fabled outlaw didn't ask the peasants for his contributions back when he fell on hard times.

Gambling had corrupted this man, but he was happy to stay this way and not escape from it, he was in the only place he'd known for years, with that in mind it was highly likely that days like the trip to Scarborough would happen again because he was making concessions to make sure they did by not seeking help.

Incredibly, another insane event was soon to follow on the east coast yet again only a few weeks after that reckless visit to a Bridlington betting shop, but in the unpredictability of gambling, a very different story and outcome were on the cards.

CHAPTER NINE

After that insane and memorable first week in August, John was quickly back to his old ways as if it had never happened, but he may not have felt different once the dust had settled, but changes were ahead, and not just for him, for both of us and they were not the ones we would necessarily have picked if we had been given a choice, unfortunately, we hadn't.

My gambling debts had been coming down slowly due to the promotions, but while these may have stopped me going to court for bankruptcy, the outstanding amount that I still owed wasn't a few quid, it was several thousand, at one point I'd lost enough money to have bought a house, but currently at around £20k, I knew when Teddys started to wrap things up, I was heading for trouble again.

I always knew that unless the good times had carried on for the next ten years, then it was only a short term measure that allowed me to temporarily brush my money problems under the carpet, I could only live in the hope that they would start up again, but that wasn't going to happen, and we were soon left with no doubt.

The talk of the new card and link up system was still going around, but when there was constantly no sign of it happening, I began to believe it was a red herring, a way of playing mind games with the punters, I mean, surely a programme that links arcades up doesn't take this long to design? we are talking about Teddys amusements, NASA could have built a space program in less time, so I would believe it when I saw it.

What I did see each time I entered a branch of Teddys was a mood of change that was sent down from the management, with the staff asking every punter if they had been to any other arcade that day.

One afternoon things were stepped up and as I approached the Newland avenue shop, the man himself was standing outside, ripped as always, Mr Muscles was there and he was a prominent figure as he was catching punters entering the shop, in particular the ones he dubbed the 'travellers', which was what he called those who did multiple promotions in various branches in one day, reiterating that it's one offer per customer per day at one site if you wanted to participate in anything they were doing.

The first time Mr Muscles caught me as I was going in, it was as if no other punter existed as he moved towards me menacingly,
"Chris, I know you have the tendency to go all over, but it's not allowed, if you get caught in any other shop doing a promotion, you will be barred and won't be allowed to join the new link-up card system," I looked at him, this is not how I expected a customer to be spoken too but I simply replied, "ok, not a problem," he then set his sights on looking for others so that he could give them the same warning.

A few days later, I was about to enter a different shop, this time it was Teddys on Holderness road and there he was again, Mr Muscles was stood outside of another entrance, it was clear that he was rotating to catch as many as he could, and as I approached, I overheard him telling some guy that all signatures were going to be checked for cheats, but as he hadn't seen me I didn't go into the shop.

It wasn't long before he was gone, I was sure that anyone with a physique like his would be due a steak and broccoli snack before too long.

As soon as I saw him leaving, I entered the arcade, and to my amazement, the feature machines had been taken out and replaced with the old fashioned bar-x bandits, these were shocking, boring and a waste of my time as I never enjoyed playing them in the first place.

Soon I was witnessing the other branches wheeling out the good machines as more of the bad ones where being set up to play.

In many ways, I was happy to see this happening, as much as I wanted the good times to go on forever, if they had to come to an end then I didn't want to be teased, half in and half out, dipping in my little toe and fighting against hope, I wanted decisiveness, not doubts, it was a good day for me as far as having my way forward made clearer, I could accept the generous promotions were finally over because I had no choice, and that chapter of my life could be put to bed, it would force me into another plan, hopefully, something long term.

   A couple of weeks passed and finally, it happened, the card-link system was being set up in the shop, it was a small machine with a barcode scanner, an engineer was there with a laptop feeding some data into it, now I knew it was real and they were telling the truth, but why did it take so long?

   I asked the guy who was fixing it to explain how the system worked as I knew Teddys owned several branches around Yorkshire, and he went on to tell me that it worked in their Hull arcades only, it didn't link up to their other branches in Withernsea, Leeds and Doncaster, which was a good job as to what was going to happen in the very near future to our friend Choc-Ice-John.

   John may have criticised the good times, but it was always prosperous for him, and he was still doing the dregs, or whatever was on offer and there remained a £3 cash match at the Golden-Touch arcade on Holderness road.

   There were so many gambling facilities down this area that Las Vegas would be envious, to me it was a great place for a night out, with pubs everywhere plus enough kebab shops to keep an army of junk food eaters happy, but for betting purposes, it just didn't work for me for some reason, although it didn't stop me venturing there, it just lacked a certain atmosphere for me as a punter.

   One evening around this time, nothing new or unusual, John wanted to do the cash match on Holderness road, he didn't have the money to participate with the offer, but that didn't stop him taking an hour to walk there, he was looking for someone to lend him his stake, but what he was going to find was another chain of events that would lead him to more insanity.

If I had been around, he'd have known because he would have found a lamppost or railing that had my bike chained to it, this was still his best tell-tale sign that I was in the vicinity, however, I wasn't the only person that left clues for John to decipher, Sherlock Holmes could have learnt a thing or two from our buddy.

As he arrived onto Holderness road, he looked in the distance at his destination, and he could see that there was a Pharmacy van parked outside Golden-Touch, so he knew who he would find when he walked into the shop, none other than our mutual acquaintance, Brian the Alchemist.

It's funny how Brian had this nickname and ended up as a delivery driver for an actual chemist, and although he didn't try to do what his nickname suggested and attempt to turn metal into gold, he was always trying other ways to make money one way or another within the gambling world, looking for the dead cert, insider tips, hidden cheats on fruit machines, you name it, he tried it.

Brian had attended night school with me at Hull college when I was studying IT, but he was seen by everyone as a know-all and that is why we nicknamed him the Alchemist.

The group of us became friends in the classroom and this extended to us all socialising out of the college too, we would all meet on the last Friday of every month, which started in 1997, and Brian was the brunt of some of our humour, and one of our friends, Paddy, said of him on one occasion,
"he thinks he knows everything, watch this," and he signalled Brian over,
"Brian, do you know anything about haemorrhoids? I think I might have one," we were giggling inside but daren't laugh out loud, but of course, Brian knew all about them and divulged this to us, in what seemed to go on for ages, he explained the full history and root causes, plus treatments, he thought he was impressing us with his knowledge, little did he know we

were taking the mickey out of him, but that is what he was known for, being an expert on everything.

Brian soon stopped coming out with us because of money problems and slowly others did the same, one by one, people weren't turning up, and a year after we left the course, I went along for the final time and nobody was there, I never tried again once the following month came around, that was that.

We were a solid bunch of friends and I thought it would have gone on for longer than it did, but no WhatsApp groups in those days or even mobile phones, this meant we simply made arrangements to meet and couldn't get in touch if anyone didn't turn up, so we reluctantly went our separate ways, and you wonder what happened to everyone and what they've been up to, until you bump into them one day when you least expect.

Now I knew why Brian was always skint when I knew him, he was a gambler and a qualifying member of Choc-Ice-Johns band of mates.

John saw Brian playing on a fruit machine when he went into the arcade, sorry for stating the obvious there, as if you couldn't work it out, and approached him,
"hi Brian, good to see you, man," wait for it,
"don't suppose you could do me anything? I don't have any money," luckily for John, he was in the right place at the right time,
"well John, I don't have anything, but I have a bill that needs paying and I am going to Withernsea tomorrow to do the arcades, if we win I will make sure you're ok, come to my house in the morning."

What is it about gamblers and their bills? we have been through something like this earlier when Choc-Ice-John didn't pay his Dads electric bill, there were stories too in the first book about me not paying them when I should, and gambling the money instead, and here was another gambler – with a similar problem, can't pay what he owes and wants to win the money.

Withernsea, where Brian planned to go, is on the east coast, south of Scarborough, Bridlington and Hornsea, and we know what happened only a few weeks earlier when John was last on this coastline, but there was no hesitation in his voice, just a big fat 'yes' while arranging a time to meet at the house.

Remember, Teddy's amusements were originally called 'Teddys of Withernsea' when they first came to Hull, they owned literally the whole of the seafront with most of the arcades there.

I always had a soft spot for this town, as we had a caravan at trailer park when I was growing up, with no gas or electricity (which would have solved Brian's bill problem) and a communal outside toilet that was literally miles away, and around three pubs of which the 'Spread Eagle' was the most famous.

We always ventured towards the sea and onto the beach that had so many Sharpe stones, you'd stand up after an hours' worth of sunbathing looking like you'd been laying on a bed of nails, but it was nostalgic for me, but for John and Brian, it was all about the gambling, and Brian had an agenda, he needed money desperately.

Teddys may not have allowed us punters 'the good times' in Hull anymore, but there was plenty of double money offers still happening at Withernsea, and as mentioned a short while ago, these arcades were not part of the link-up system that now runs through our local branches back home.

John went home thinking that whatever was going to happen the next day, Brian was laying out the monies for them both and was responsible for feeding and watering him, it was a no-lose situation, what could possibly go wrong?

Upon waking up to a pleasant and warm September morning, John was soon up and dressed as he set off early to enjoy a brisk walk to Brian's house, he knew this would take him less than an hour.

He arrived a solid ten minutes early, he was always punctual if there was something in it for him, and despite the focus being on Brian's bill, he was looking forward to a day at the coast and a catch up with his friend, just the two of them, or so he thought, as he knocked on the door and waited.

Brian was warm in welcoming John into the house, "sit yourself down in the front room," John planned to do exactly that, but as he went in, expecting only Brian to be there, he was staggered to find four other people had arrived before him, watching a cartoon on the TV, and with Brian waving his gas bill around and saying he needed to win enough to pay it, everything felt surreal, it was as if the loony toons on the telly was becoming reality in front of him.

When he managed to get Brian on his own, John said with a disappointed tone in his voice,
"I thought it was going to be just us Brian, that lot can't be coming with us surely,"
"John, I have a bill to pay, so everyone is helping me then I am going to reward all of you later," but he did not say this in a reassuring way, more about his own needs above all else.

A short time later Brian was briefing them all on what he needed, yes, going on about that bill, the six of them that he had gathered together were all gamblers, and like John, none of them had a penny to their name, even me in my heyday wouldn't have got involved with this lot.

They then discussed seating arrangements, and soon after this, the gang walked to the car.

It's not a long drive to Withernsea, but it seemed longer with two at the front and Brian driving, and three sat on the back seat of his Nissan Datsun, and one laid across the floor out of sight in case the Police came whizzing by, and it was our friend John that had the task of laying across three pairs of feet, at least on the way there.

There was a time when just about everyone drove down Hedon Road to go to Withernsea, and it took about an hour, and only a handful of people knew about the country-lane route, through the villages and hey presto, your there a little quicker, now more people travel this way too, and with Brian being a professional driver, he knew this shortcut.

They arrived after 55 minutes and parked up and got out of the car before Brian mentioned something that he had said around ten times already so why not make it eleven,
"I have a bill; I need to win the money to pay this first", Brian was the only one with money, so he could call the shots.

Normally, If you have to rely on gambling to pay the bills then you really are going to be living in the dark and eating out of tin cans, but with the promotions at their peak, you wouldn't even need a gang of punters you would just need a pocket full of coins and a bus ticket.

Here there were four promotions in the arcades done twice per day at the weekend, it already seemed like a distant memory to the time when Hull was doing this every day of the week in over ten arcades and we were coining it in.

For the maths, six guys on a £6 cash match done twice in a day added up to £72 worth of free plays in a single arcade, spread over four shops was £288, some serious money could be won. It's hard to understand why I never came here myself

John had been to this town before with Brian, but it didn't always go the way he planned or liked, as Brian wasn't a split down the middle merchant, if they only won a small amount like £20, he would say,
"I need to take a tenner for my petrol and a couple of quid for the lunch I bought you."

John could be walking away with just three or four quid for a full day and if he looked away or went to the loo, Brian had a tendency to pick up coins from the tray and put them in his pocket before the count up and he still took his expenses, and John couldn't negotiate because he never had his own stake to put into the machine, which meant full control to Brian.

The day started well with Brian putting in everyone's money as planned, over four machines for the cash match but insisting he played them all and pooled all the money into his own pocket as the other five skint gamblers could only watch, insisting the splits would come later.

With an early spin, he hit a £25 jackpot, a perfect start, and by the time he came off the machine, he was already £47 in profit.

Next, it was onto the other three arcades and by the time he had played all the credits, the combined winnings were an additional £28, and Brian felt rather disappointed, but it was still an overall profit of £75.

The reason it wasn't more was that two of the machines hardly paid out, nevertheless, Brian now told his five buddies exactly what the score was,
"If I take £65, which is the amount I need for my bill, plus a tenner for the petrol, then I have the expenses I need covering, anything we win from now is our profit and we can share it out later," as five jaws hit the floor.

Everyone was thinking to themselves as to why they were doing this, as all of the winnings were sat in Brian's pocket and nothing for anyone else - yet, and they did not even get any entertainment value either, as Brian played every credit on each machine himself.

While they were waiting for the evening sessions to begin, Brian could hear his belly rumbling,
"I'm sure everyone is hungry, let's get some dinner, we can square up later," and they all walked to the nearest chippy,
"how much is a bag of chips Luv," he said to the woman who was working there making sure he didn't spend too much on his gang,
"65p" was the answer so Brian ordered,
"five bags of chips please, Luv," he then asked each individual if they wanted salt and vinegar, then he ordered for himself,
"Luv, can I have fish and chips with mushy peas please? and can I have a breadcake buttered as well? cheers darling."

As far as Brian was concerned, none of them had money, if they did they could have put the extra cash down and had the same as him.

As his meal was given to him, Brian then said, in front of everyone,
"can I have two sachets of tomato ketchup please; I hate dry chips."

Choc-Ice-John approached Brian after they had all eaten and asked for a small amount of money to buy something from the paper shop,
"I have a sweet tooth and need some sugar," what you don't ask for you don't get and Brian obliged, and John came out a few minutes later with a chocolate wagon-wheel and some sherbet lemons, he felt he deserved it after laying on the floor during the journey, but everyone else was beginning to feel used and was just hoping the evening turned out profitable so they could go home with some money, up to now it was all about one guy.

They walked along the beach, everyone took turns in doing what people from Hull do at Withernsea, reminisce on childhood memories of the place, back in the days when coming here was a luxury to look forward too.

Soon the pleasantries were over, and it was back to the task at hand, as they ventured back into the arcades for the second wave of promotions, but they were doing it in the reverse order from the afternoon, going into the place they finished to start proceedings and arrived a quarter of an hour early.

Everyone was thirsty and as they were there before things began, they all asked for a drink, which was always free to machine players, they can refuse you if you're not actively playing credits off, but the cashier wasn't a typical worker who acted like it came out of her own pocket, and poured out the beverages, Brian shouldn't have needed a drink as he bought himself a can of Pepsi on the way there but decided to have a coffee too as it was going begging.

Soon, the Alchemist, Choc-Ice-John and the posse were ready to begin again, but it was Brian who was still leading the way, "same as before, I play so I can collect the wins as I know how to do this, don't forget lads, we are now on profit-sharing so let's finished the day off in style."

Once the cashier had matched the cash for tokens, Brian played off the credits in the same bandits that had let him down a few hours before, and for the £36 he put in for £72 worth of spins, came a return of only £15, which was another chunk gone when you consider he had put more than twice this in, Brian was livid, but when they aren't paying, you can't do anything, soon he was digging in his pocket and into his afternoon winnings,

"I'm back into the bill money now," he said as he fruitlessly tried to salvage something but with time running out on the promotions he walked away and stormed off to the next arcades, where he ended up winning the loss back and a small profit of £11 on top, so this meant there was finally a split,

"that's £1.75 each if my maths is correct, but I still think that machine that skanked me has to pay out," as he marched back to the same slots that had let him down all day.

He proceeded to slot a couple of quid into the machine that frustrated him, but he got nothing back, the loss was followed with him dropping another nugget into it, then another, and another, and another but the machine just didn't want to pay and he was soon losing ground on the days profit once again, Brian was soon expressing himself to the gang,

"I needed that money for the bill," was this now twenty times they had heard this? they were all pig-sick of him constantly repeating what he needed it for.

Soon he lost all the afternoon winnings and some of his own when he finally hit a £25 jackpot while down to his last few spins, it's amazing the feeling of warmth a win can give, even if your losing.

Machines that are paying-out are said to be 'streaking' while it's happening and he thought this could be the start of one of those runs, but it wasn't, and it simply went straight back into 'money eating' mode and he lost it all back again, to make it worse, he made a trip to the cashpoint outside and began playing the more expensive and lethal £500 jackpot machines in a vain attempt to win his money back.

He then went to the hole in the wall for the second time and came back with a hundred quid, and one of the chaps turned to John and whispered to him,
"why didn't he use that money in his cash-card for his bloody bill, he had enough all along but wanted us to come with him, so he could win it and not fork it out of his own pocket," the word 'greedy' was mentioned a few times in that conversation.

By the end of the night he was broke, and when you think that at one point he had his precious bill paid, a free fish and chip dinner and some chump change for his mates, but it wasn't enough, and he paid the price for chasing on a bad machine, which was probably going to come good for someone else after Brian had filled it up.

He should have been going home with a healthy profit, a few quid for his mates but he was left surmising how much they could have won if those two bandits had behaved themselves and coughed up.

Choc Ice John and the lads got a day of watching their mate play fruit machines for hours and a greasy bag of chips, but the guy who should have been the real winner turned into the heaviest loser, and as it was 10.00 pm, the arcade was closing.

From Johns point of view, he was teased that he may go home richer than when he came, after all, he left his flat penniless, but it was less painful than the previous time he went to the seaside, this day was entertainment at its best, especially when its someone else doing the chasing, so he was philosophical about what had happened.

John may have had a laid back approach, but there were no mixed feelings from the other four guys, and when Brian mentioned his bill again, and how he couldn't pay it, they wanted to take it off him and shove it where the sun doesn't shine.

It was now the task of sorting out the seating positions in the car, if they were drawing short straws, it would have been everyone except two of them, Brian was driving and John laid across the floor when they were coming, so it was agreed unanimously that he should be in the front seat this time, so it was between the other four.

If they had left on time, one of them could have caught the last bus back while the others had a seat in the car, that wasn't an option anymore in what was another knock-on effect from Brian chasing, they should have set off back a couple of hours before they did.

How many times do we come across a person that claims to have a bad back? it could be at work, or moving home, and they expect to be exempt from doing any heavy lifting, while some mug ends up doing the donkey work.

If you question whether they are legit or not, and it turns out that they are genuine, you come across as mean spirited and unsympathetic.

It was no different with these four guys who were arguing about who should lay across the floor, and instantly the bad back came into the conversation from one of them, and to make matters worse, he was the shortest person there and would have fitted across the floor, he was around five foot and seven inches, eventually it was settled and a guy over six-feet tall ended up taking this uncomfortable position, crazy or what?

Once this was sorted and they took their positions, Brian turned on the engine and switched his headlights on, he then moved off and despite how things were, at least they were on the way home, nothing else can happen surely?

There should be a major difference between driving to Withernsea in the morning light and coming back late at night after it gets dark, you drive more carefully on the return journey, am I correct? not according to Brian, whom after travelling through the first strip of road and onto the country lanes said excitedly,

"I love the part of the road that we are about to come onto, it's the best drive in the world," what could he possibly mean by that? and this was the question that five-minds almost in synchronisation all thought at the same time.

What Brian was referring too was an area that consisted of winding, bendy roads where you could see for miles ahead with nothing but a few trees that were sufficiently spaced out, and oncoming traffic was especially easier to spot in the dark because of headlights.

During the day, you would struggle to spot a car coming in the opposite direction, but as it was pitch black, Brian looked ahead and saw nothing but the dark and he couldn't contain himself,

"here goes" he yelled, as he pushed the play button on his car's CD, and turned the volume to full, the music sounded like something from a rave in Ibiza while at the same time pressing down on the accelerator, and the 40mph speed limit was soon broken as he flew at the bend while driving on the opposite side of the road, confident that nothing was coming, although he soon had to slow down to negotiate a sharp corner, of which everyone breathed a sigh of relief, but this was short-lived as Brian leaned forward to look up the road to see if the coast was clear before he shot away again, but this time exceeded 110mph, every one of his passengers was bricking it, shouting for Brian to stop, but this couldn't be heard as the beat from the music drowned out all there screams, as he continued to drive at an even more excessive speed.

He speeded into a corner and it appeared that he temporally lost control as the vehicle skidded and it felt like the car was going to either fly into a ditch or tip over.

Brian was a lot of things, but driving was his forte, but they didn't feel safe as the speeding seemed to last forever.

It's easy to imagine what was going on in everyone else's mind, remember an hour earlier, they had witnessed him losing all his winnings, then his own money and he followed this up with two withdrawals from his cash-card account.

He wasn't just in a bad mood when he left the arcades, he was genuinely distressed, and here they were, all together in one place, sharing a car with him, and he suddenly drives like a lunatic, for all they knew he may have been trying to kill himself and everyone else, as it happened, Brian does this type of driving on this road often, but they didn't know this and he didn't tell them.

Soon he had to decelerate as he approached the first of several villages on the outskirts of Hull but by now everyone was as white as a sheet, and you have to feel sorry for poor Choc-Ice-John, sitting at the front on the way back during Brian's speed-fest, after laying on the floor coming, nothing goes right for our poor friend.

The current guy who was taking his turn to lay across the floor wouldn't have had a clue what was going on as all he heard was men screaming to a loud disco beat above him, at least he was already in a crash position, and the short chap with the bad back was now wishing he had laid along everyone's feet, a touch of Karma there perhaps.

Everyone felt safe again as the rest of the journey was in normal communal built-up areas, complete with speed cameras, but John said to Brian,
"what if someone had been coming from the opposite direction with no lights on, or they were riding a bike," Brian then replied,
"well, that would just be unlucky," and this is all he had to say!

As they all parted, Brian's mood had lifted since the thrill-ride, John was dropped off on the corner of Beverley road where he walked home thinking about the day's events.

The way he saw it made him realise Brian was not the friend he thought he was, he was out for number one and at its best, it was a day that saw Brian wasting everyone's time, he would have let them all spend their full days financing his utility bills.

Apart from Brian, everyone went with nothing and came back with the same, but at least Choc-Ice-John had another memorable day on the east coast.

John could relate to Brian's behaviour with regards to chasing his losses, he could even go some way to understanding the adrenaline rush from the speeding, John had played maximum stake cartoon roulette at a breakneck pace himself and felt excitement while doing so, there was something in his DNA that was like Brian in some ways.

John saw one of the guys from the trip a few days later, and he made it clear that none of them would go on any more journeys with Brian, but John knew that he would go back to the same place again if Brian was to ask him because he rarely had money of his own, he would take any chance to go anywhere if there was even a small opportunity of making something, even a few quid, and the hope would be that the next time would be the day that everything went smooth, but the line for things going wrong with gambling was always paper-thin.

After all the excitement, a few more weeks passed and we were staring at a new year as 2006 was on the horizon, and it looked bleak for John, there were only two payments left to come from Mark, he no longer felt he knew who his true friends were, and with opportunities thin on the ground, it wasn't looking great, but even reaching rock bottom didn't faze John as it was a place he had been many times.

CHAPTER TEN

2006 was soon upon us and John and I started the new year with different mindsets, he was still caught up in the addiction but with only two inheritance payments remaining, it felt like the last chance saloon for him.

On the other hand, things were seemingly changing for the better for me, although I was still gambling, luck was everywhere around me in that I hated the new formats that were being introduced, and it unwittingly seemed as if it was having a positive effect and weaning me away from the addiction, was this even possible?

For starters, the process of changing from horse racing to FOBTs resulted in things getting so bad at one point that I found myself barred from every betting shop within a two-mile radius, caused by me kicking off when I lost at each branch individually.

The feature style fruit machines that I found myself thinking about day and night with a constant craving to play were almost gone from the arcades, which helped me massively, and with bar-x slots now everywhere, which I hated, it was easier to find the control to keep away from Teddy's amusements.

Even the pubs started introducing new machines that were unlike anything I'd seen before, with higher jackpots but double the price to play, and I purposely kept away from these, I didn't watch punters who went on them so I couldn't learn anything about them.

In many ways, this was reaching my inner self, the part of me that wanted to quit gambling for good, I felt safer in the short term but knew I wasn't out of the woods, the one resonating fact that was in front of me as plain as day, was that I still hadn't stopped altogether, the addiction and compulsive urges remained stronger than I was, even with everything that was going on to seemingly help me, so what I felt that I needed was a fix that I could control.

By doing things this way I felt that I had a decent shot at adopting that normal life I wanted while keeping the addict in me satisfied at the same time, and I knew how I was going to do it.

The answer that I could see in front of me was the one promotion that still existed, the solitary £3 cash match on Holderness road, this branch kept some of the decent features, although not many, they were the old fashioned ten pence plays with five-pound jackpots, it wasn't about money, it was about temporarily dipping into the danger zone in a controlled fashion to feed my cravings and then coming out again, and I believed that it could work.

Since my gambling appeared to be more under control for the first time in years, clear thoughts were beginning to emerge out of the thick fog that had clouded my head, and my career ambitions took a more centre stage, I had more energy and focus and wanted to drive myself into finding a better job.

With my computer qualifications, experience in administration work and an urge to get things going in my career, I went online and applied for positions that would push me up the ladder.

Although I tried to stay as close as possible to what I was used too, I did tinker outside of my area of expertise, and it was to my surprise when this looked like it had paid off, as I received a letter in the post inviting me to attend an interview for the role of a pharmacy assistant.

This had prospects and learning opportunities written all over it, I never expected to hear from this particular application that I'd submitted, but now I had a chance as suddenly, there was only one barrier between me and getting the position, and that was convincing whoever was to interview me that I was the right person, easier said than done.

My allotted slot for the interview was in a weeks' time from when I opened the letter, Thursday at 11.00 am, the only problem I saw was that I was on a nightshift the evening before and didn't finish until 8.00 am on the day in question. I needed to be there and be at my best, but I would only have three hours.

All the options that I looked for to make this easier hit dead-ends, I had no holidays left to take in my current position and I knew it wouldn't look good if I asked for the time and date to be changed for the interview, talk about bad timing, so how was I going to do this?

There was no magic solution, I had to go without sleep that morning, simple as, and it wasn't long before the Wednesday evening came, I attempted to have a nap before I went to work but I tried too hard, my mind was active and I found myself lying awake until it was time to leave the house.

It was a busy night and I was on the phones; I couldn't have had a nap if I'd wanted, I never slept on nightshifts, not even for a short while, I simply couldn't.

It eventually reached 8.00 am, and when I arrived at my front gate a half-hour later, I was so tired walking down the garden path that I could have slept on the clothesline.

I felt my chance had gone and the prospect of a change in career was scuppered, I didn't even know if I could stay awake, but I wasn't giving up without a fight.

I looked at the letter again, and then I saw that I had made a mistake, the interview wasn't on Anlaby road, where I thought it was being held, but at Cottingham which was miles away from where I was and I didn't have any spare money, I didn't know how to get there on a bus and there was only one solution, my bike.

First things first, I drank three black coffees on the bounce, I then tried to watch the telly but felt myself drifting off to sleep, so to prevent this and keep myself awake, I went upstairs, and after a quick bath I put on my best shirt, my brown suit and matching tie and went back downstairs, ready for the challenge.

I popped back into the front room and looked at the clock, it was 9.45 am and time to compose my thoughts, so I sat down with the notes I had been making about what the job entailed.

The next thing I knew, Sally came in the front door and woke me up, it was only then that I realised I had fallen asleep, and in a panic, I looked at the clock again and it was now showing 10.20 am, not good as its at least a forty-five-minute bike ride, I felt worse now, I was groggy but tried mustering up some energy.
    I pulled on my shoes and went into the shed to drag my bike out; I was soon sat on the saddle peddling for all I was worth heading for Cottingham.
    I went through every red light and even jumped on the pavement to avoid traffic, the last half of a mile was uphill and it was tiresome as my old fashioned bike didn't like gear changes, and as I tried to do this the chain came off, quick as a flash I put it back on and set off again, but my hands where now covered in oil.
    I continued up the hill and turned into entrance-two, as per the directions on the map they'd sent me of the grounds, I then saw a bike rack and locked it up. Within seconds, I was running down a long corridor and saw the sign for the Pharmacy, I looked at the clock upon arrival, it was exactly 11.00 am.
    I was told to sit in a room but asked where the toilet was, as much as I wanted to be sick, I had the problem of getting the oil off my hands and used the soap and hand gels while scrubbing vigorously with a paper towel, I was a few minutes there and despite looking better, my hands were a lighter shade of black, but the bathroom itself, which looked immaculately clean when I walked in, now looked like a team of mechanics had just used the facilities, the sinks where full of oil, the paper towels in the bin were black, and the basins were now mucky, but it wasn't confined to just there, some of the filthy water had splashed onto the floor but I had no choice but to leave it.
    I timed it well, and as soon as I walked out of the loo, I was then asked to come into a room, where I was told that I would be doing an aptitude test upstairs before the actual interview.

Once I had climbed the stairs, I was asked to sit in front of a computer which had a pre-loaded test on the screen, I was advised that after completing this there was a further exam sheet to do on the adjacent table, which was laid face down with a pen at the side for me to complete, and I was allowed half an hour to finish both of them.

I didn't find any of the tests difficult, the computer contained a memory program where I was asked to state images that were shown earlier, and the written exam was basic maths and English questions.

I finished in half the allotted time, and as I looked up the hallway, it was as if the world was aligning itself around me as there was alcohol gel on the wall next to a packet of antiseptic wipes, and further ahead I could see another set of toilets.

It couldn't have worked better as a couple of squirts, wipes and elbow grease with a paper towel later, my hands looked clean again, but then there was another problem, some of the oil had gotten itself onto the bottom of my shirt sleeve.

It may have been the tiredness spiking my brain, but I didn't panic and was able to think quick, I rolled my sleeves up to my elbow and put my jacket back on, and it wasn't coming off again.

Soon it was onto the interview itself, I entered a small room where I was asked to sit down, facing me were four people sat at a desk who took turns asking me questions, again, I didn't find them hard but I tried to use my current working experience in a health profession to the maximum, I was then asked to describe myself in three words, I should have said, liar, gambler, untrustworthy, but instead the words, "reliable, empathic, ethical," came out.

I shook hands with the panel, left the building and despite everything going wrong that morning, I enjoyed the experience but didn't think I would be successful and be offered the position, but that wasn't my problem right now, tiredness was setting in and I had a long journey home, it was made worse as my pupils were dilating because of the lack of sleep, and this made the light from the sky seem a lot brighter, but I persevered and despite all this, I seemed to do the return trip a lot quicker.

I went to bed but put my ringtone on loud, and three hours later it woke me up, as the lead for the interview, a pleasant lady called Jeannine, called to off me the job, I wasn't expecting it and I was amazed, excited, bewildered and shocked all at the same time, but in a good way, I didn't hesitate to accept the position.

I had already been advised that the start date would be in eight weeks' time, they enrolled every year, I was further told three positions were offered to this many candidates, of which I was one of them, so I hadn't beaten all the other applicants, myself and three others had instead finished joint first, but as I didn't have any previous experience in pharmacy work to develop an ego as far as this went, but I had grown one in another way.

A few days passed and the upcoming position at the Pharmacy had been constantly on my mind, as were the dreams again, but they were new ones, I had already planned the next few years in my head and all my thoughts were prosperous, it was different from when I fantasised about being a professional gambler, this was real, black and white, a generous income with a pension, working towards having the credit to obtain a mortgage and buy my own home, even if it was just my council house.

I didn't dream about a detached four-bedroom home and a yearly cruise to St Lucia that came with the gambling, my bike was good enough for me and maybe a small car one day, not the sports vehicle speeding to the racetracks as per previously, what I enjoyed was feeling like it was in front of me, and not just achievable but probable, if I did things the way I foresaw.

Choc-Ice-John came into the library on Saturday morning while I was there, I told him of the new job and that I wanted to limit my gambling, that I felt I now had it under control, all the pain had changed me, plus I wasn't as passionate towards it any more.

I then stared at his long beard and this told me that he didn't have a penny to his name, and to make things worse, all the walking had worn his shoes out and he asked me if I could lend him some, I never allowed him to know where I lived so I arranged to meet him later.

When we met up again in the afternoon, I gave him some spare size-ten trainers plus I also bunged him a fiver, I felt sorry for him, but I also felt something else that
I hadn't before. With me moving away from gambling plus the new fancy job, and with him not wanting to do the same, to carry on as he was, I looked down on him, I saw him as pathetic, not in a bad way but just someone that I didn't want to be as if I was better than him, my life was going uphill while he was flushing his down the toilet and he wouldn't listen to me or anyone else, with the recent changes I felt justified in thinking I was wiser than him but was I right?

The truth would come out in the end, for now, I was lost in the moment, but was I in the good place that I believed I was?

My lessons were to come later, just not yet, for now though, John was about to spiral into another short period of madness, as we were mid-January and Johns penultimate inheritance pay-out was due in two weeks' time.

Fourteen-days isn't a long time for someone to wait if they know that they are going to be receiving a nice amount of money at the end of it, you would think he would plan what he was going to do with it, but that's not how the mind of this guy worked, if he wasn't a betting addict, he wouldn't think the way he did but the cravings were present every day for a flutter of some kind, it may as well have been two-years rather than two-weeks.

On top of everything else, he was desperate, especially as he had just been paid and proceeded to blow all his money, he could borrow off his friends if they had any cash, but they were all gamblers, admitted, most of them didn't have a problem on the scale that he did, but they struggled, none of them won very often, so what could he do?

If Mark had shown more pleasantries' to John when they had previously met up, the option of an advance on the money might have been on the table, but as it was, if he said the wrong thing, Mark threatened to pull payments, and although it was hugely unlikely, there was bound to be a lot of shouting, this meant that approaching Mark was the one avenue he was determined to avoid at all costs.

John had little option but to wait and somehow bite the bullet, having no food in was one thing, he could remedy this by visiting a couple of people that had received 'treats' when he was winning, but he hadn't topped up his gas or electric, it wasn't the heating that was the problem, he sat in the cold like a polar bear in the north pole most evenings already, but he needed lights, cooking facilities, a bath, all the little things that we take for granted unless we spend the day placing chips on numbers that don't come in on an animated roulette wheel of course.

Forget food and amenities, let's get to the real problem, this is a gambling addict we are talking about with no money, and a brain that is fully spiking to support his habit, he would surely think of something? and he did!

His idea wasn't a brainwave, but if he had needed one he would have found it. The plan was to venture to the local employment exchange which was situated in High street in Hull's old town back then, the building he needed was called Oriel house, here he intended to stake a claim for a grant that he wouldn't have to pay back, if unsuccessful he would try for a crisis loan or anything he could muster from the department of social security.

The problem he had was that he already took out a loan three months earlier which was to be paid over six months, so he didn't feel he would qualify if he went down that avenue, but in an emergency, they might help him.

He walked in and grabbed a ticket, it was pink with fifty-seven printed on it, the same number as Heinz varieties, he then had to wait while they called his number, which went in order and they were currently only up to the mid-thirties, and he began to wonder why there were so many people sat in there with cash problems, and why nobody ever left the queues, what he failed to look at was why he was there himself.

He decided to walk around town for a while and go back later rather than sit staring at the clock for a couple of hours.

John felt a degree of anxiety while he was away in case the numbers began to go down quickly or if people decided to give up, all he knew was he wasn't going to be one of them, what he did do, however, was step into the loo in the betting shop and begin to punch himself in the face, this was for his planned story, more on that shortly, he certainly didn't need to do this to himself, there were plenty of people that would have enjoyed doing it for free, but joking aside, this is what he had become, so lost in the addiction that he would do something like this.

When he arrived back the ticket numbers were up to the late forties, once it hit fifty he was in sight.

It took ages to get to this milestone that he set, but he still had seven people in front of him and it was over two hours since he first got there, it was also now 12.30 pm and he had the feeling staff would be going for lunch, and as it appeared to slow down, he was probably right, on the bright side though, it allowed more time for the bruises on his face to show.

1.35 pm came and they finally shouted out his number, a couple of people had left when their allotted tickets were called out, or it would have been longer for John, the queue of people waiting behind him was now a lot bigger than when he first arrived.

He was finally in a booth, where a guy who must have been John's junior by a clear twenty years was waiting for him, dressed in a navy-blue shirt and tie, with immaculately spiked hair and a neatly cut goatee beard.

John had over three hours to think of an excuse as to why he needed money and he still ended up sticking to the originally planned fable that he was mugged, the guy didn't believe him and refused to give him a grant or a crisis loan, John was then wishing that it was this guy's face that was receiving his punches rather than his own, but the young chap did offer John another form of help.

He walked into the back but came out a couple of minutes later with a form for a budgeting loan from the social fund, and he offered this to John instead, explaining that he would be allowed to top his current existing loan up and have the entire total added together and reset over a longer period, still in instalments and interest-free.

Johns reply to the guy behind the counter was the same words he said to his brother Mark when he found out he was getting a share-out from the will,
"when do I get the money."

John was talking as a desperate man and he was hoping there was a quicker way of getting it to him even though he did this every few months, but the chap went on to explained that it would come in the form of a giro-cheque, posted out in two to three days on average after they had received the completed form back, John already knew this, it was words he didn't want to hear, he wanted some cash that day.
"take this home and fill it out," said the young chap, reiterating that this was the only offer that was going to be on the table.

There was one thing that was a certainty, that form was not leaving the building to come back again, John couldn't wait and reached in his pocket and pulled out a pen that he had taken from the betting shop, the man stared at this for a while as if it was telling him the story that John hadn't, then as he walked away to find a space on the table in the waiting area, the pen didn't write, so John approached the security guard, "can you lend me a pen."

Twenty minutes later John had filled out the form and applied for £200 to go with the £100 he currently owed, which he wrote in the additional information section.

John was surprised to receive a quick reply in the mail the next morning, his application was processed that same afternoon and sent out in the last post of the day, but good news for him, he was accepted.

The offer was that he would receive a giro-cheque, but the repayments would be taken out of his fortnightly money at the rate of £11.54 for a year, his next twenty-six payments would have this deducted from his money before it was paid to him.

After the acceptance form was signed, John saw that there was a Freepost return envelope enclosed, but he wasn't going to wait that long as he was soon out the door in a hurry and back to Oriel house again, no queuing today as he simply handed it to the person at the reception and once more asked about the time factor, in this conversation John was told of a recent change that the guy in the booth didn't tell him or didn't know.

They no longer posted Giro's first class, it was now a bank transfer and it would take three further days after the reply had been dealt with.

On his way home again he went into a phone box and rang the centre to see if he could speed things up, but the person on the other end of the line stated that there were other customers to deal with and his loan wasn't classed as urgent and he would have to wait.

He was mortified that it could take a few days longer, but he still went to the bank to check his balance daily just in case but kept leaving disappointed.

To make matters worse, the shoes that I had given him didn't fit very well and were beginning to feel too tight, hence, it was hard walking all over Hull for food at his friends' houses but he had to do this to get fed.

A full week passed since he had sat in Oriel house, and upon checking his balance and preparing for the worse, he found the £200 had been paid in, his imminent reaction to this was instant as he pressed the 'withdraw cash' button.

The date on this day was 30th January, yes, two days before his inheritance was due into his account, he could have paid the loan back as he no longer needed it, but not him with his mindset being what it was.

Instead, he was soon walking around with the full £200 in his pocket, the first thing was a shave and a haircut at the first barbershop he could find, which was in Queen's gardens, from here it was to Whitefriargate to William Hills.

John soon had the roulette game loaded and chipped his usual numbers and started with a moderate stake, but soon the £200 was gone, and now he was going to be £11.54 worse off every payday for the next year

If you went out with a couple of hundred quid in your pocket and came home with just a haircut to show for it, you would think Vidal Sassoon had been the guy with the scissors that gave you the trim.

Losing this quickly heightened his emotions and lowered his mood, and as far as he was concerned the money he was due from Mark the following week already belonged to him, he was desperate and on the spot, he started walking to Hessle, the shoes that were too tight suddenly took a back seat as he set off on the five-mile journey on foot to confront Mark about his money.

John began walking like a man on a mission, peeved about all the messing about he had endured over the past few years, waiting for dates for what was already his, but the nearer to the destination he became, the more he began to calm down out of fear as his hostile attitude turned to anxiety, and by the time he arrived, he had spent a half-hour rehearsing what he was going to say but he was a bag of nerves as he opened Marks garden gate.

'knock-knock' was the sound John made on Marks solid oak wood front door, he then listened for movement and as he was about to go around the other side of the house to peep in the kitchen to see if anyone was home, he heard a stirring sound and knew someone was inside, and a few seconds later, Mark opened the door with a smile, but this soon dropped when he saw John looking at him,

"oh, it's you, what won the last race?" Mark was as sarcastic as ever, but John then said what he had been rehearsing,

"I wouldn't normally come like this but I have the chance of a cheap holiday, I was wondering if I could have my money a couple of days early Mark," this showed that the five-mile walk hadn't helped him to think of anything better than this, but nothing came to him and this was the best he could come up with, but Marks response said it all,

"hahahahahahaha," was Marks reaction in loud thunderous laughter, but after a few more moments it calmed down and he then carried on in a calm voice,

"you don't disappoint me, John, I've got to hear the rest of this, get yourself inside," John looked to see who was at home, but Mark explained,

"everyone has gone out today so I'm in on my own," he then changed the tone back to why John had come,

"I can't wait to hear the rest of this story you have come up with to get money out of me," this prompted John to realise as to why he was nervous coming, there was no excuse he could make up what Mark wouldn't see-through, as he didn't trust him, but this day was at least going well as his brother was being very civil and fetched John a drink and the biscuit jar, before saying,

"tell me again what you need the money for John, you said a holiday so whereabouts are you going?"

"Benidorm", replied John, before it set Mark off again,

"hahahahahahahahaha," in an even louder fashion, this time uncontrollably, again he took a few moments to calm down, and after a brief false sense of security it soon went exactly as John initially expected, as Mark disappeared for a few minutes before coming back in the room with his laptop,

"I am transferring you all of the £1,600 your due John, it's the remainder of your share of the money Dad left you but it comes at a price," John would have settled for anything but he never expected this, and he didn't let Mark finish what he wanted to say,
"thanks, Mark, I will make sure that" but he never finished his sentence as his brother carried on and made himself heard by raising his voice,
"save it, John, it's all of the money you have left, the price like I was saying before you interrupted, is that you never come to my doorstep again, now be on your way, I will do it in the next few minutes, once you're out of sight, not before," once again John tried to thank him whilst making more promises but Mark opened the door, and as John was leaving he said,
"the sooner you blow it the better, have a nice life, John, and try not to put it all on the next favourite,"

As John was halfway down the path, he turned and started talking again,
"I don't know what to say Mark" but for the second time, he didn't get to finish as he heard a familiar noise as the door slammed.

As he reached the street corner, John disappeared around it as quick as he could, he didn't want Mark to change his mind, but walking is thinking time and this should have been the perfect moment to reflect, and thoughts could have led to a feeling of shame, hurting his family and friends and letting everyone down, knowing too that he had so many rounds in the last chance saloon, where does it all stop?

It wouldn't have mattered if either of Johns heart or mind had been in control, because both of them were owned by his gambling addiction, and all he could focus on was the money he was getting, he should have felt bad, but he was overcome with excitement.

The cash may have felt like a gift, but John knew it wasn't, this was February and August's payments together with nothing else to come, not ever.

The previous £6,400 he had received in the last four years was gone, all gambled away, every penny, and the money he was due was all that was left out of eight-grand, but he couldn't comprehend it, the loan from the social security that he had lost that very morning seemed like a distant memory now.

He checked at the first ATM machine he saw and £1,600.67 was there, Mark didn't mess him about as he wanted John out of the family fold while he was doing what he was doing, there was always a reason for John to see his brother over the years, even though things were bad but now for the first time, it was over, finale, John had officially lost his place in the family because of the addiction.

He didn't think about Mark, Jackie or anyone else and right at this moment, John didn't care, he had the money, which was supposed to last him until the end of the year, but it wasn't even time for Februarys payment yet and there it was in hard cash.

A few split-seconds after he stood staring at his balance, the whirling noise where the notes were counted for a quick withdrawal was happening as £300 popped out and it was a straight choice between grocery shopping or the bright red Ladbrokes shop that may as well have been calling his name, it was no contest.

Ok you know the score by now, John always fascinated me and I couldn't put my curiosity to one side, but in the middle of all the chaos, unpredictability and bravado, and the many different permutations to the way he would lose any windfalls he had, the result was always the same.

The money was lost by the end of the following day, with the date being January 31st, 2006, the day before John was due to be paid out with a further transaction six months later, now all gone.

I never knew any of this was happening to John, I was wrapped in my new world, believing I was going places and my view was cemented when I received a call confirming my starting date for the new position of a Pharmacy assistant.

Rarely had I felt nerves as bad as this when I began other jobs over the years, but I had much more at stake now, it felt like my new life depended on me successfully transferring my skills to the pharmaceutical profession and as far as enthusiasm went, I was bursting with it, I just had to match it with hard work.

I turned up on my first day to find the three other new starters that I was told about, and as we all chatted, I settled in quicker than if I had begun on my own.

We were soon shown around and spent the first-morning training in a classroom-type environment, then after lunch, we were placed in the dispensary and given usernames and passwords for the software, things happened quickly, before long we were printing out labels for prescription medication, this was then checked by a qualified Pharmacist before we were all given our permanent rotating shift rotas, of which weekend work and late nights were expected, it didn't matter if this was to my liking, what was important was what I had planned, it was about getting that NVQ and then either staying or leaving but using it to open doors and developing long term aspirations, as well as further opportunities within the career.

Towards the end of the second day, I had been working with one of the other new starters that I'd befriended, when he said to me,
"know what Chris, I think I have made a mistake coming here to work, I wish I had stayed in my other job," while this was how he felt, it affected me as I had been living in denial for my first couple of days, and in responding to him I admitted that I too felt the same, that I was regretting it as well and that I also wished I had stayed working the nightshifts.

This felt like the time for a reset and some adapting as I tried to look at the positives and what I could get out of it in the long run, it was going to be hard though, as I was now openly admitting that I didn't like the job.

The third day went better, I was in the swing of things and it was busier, with a lot of labelling and matching up the medications, it was here that I began to think it may not be as bad as I expected, but there was a shock when one of the senior members of staff who I hadn't had the chance to meet properly came up to me and said,
"Chris, we have had a call, there is a man here asking for you, he said it's very urgent," this sent shivers down my spine and I was wondering what had happened, was it the Police with bad news?

I was told to go and see what it was and let them know if I needed anything, which made me feel warm in the knowledge that the place I was working for fully supported their staff, and as I nervously went to the front of the building, I saw who it was, standing there was Choc-Ice-John!

He had scruffy greasy hair and a face that hadn't seen a razor for at least three weeks, and I knew what was coming next,
"Chris I won't bother you again, but I don't have any gas or Electric, can you lend me a tenner," I was both stunned and furious in equal measures,
"John, you drag me from work to ask me for money, try asking William Hills or Ladbrokes for it, that's where you put it".

I soon relented and lent him the money but made it clear I wanted it back on his payday, he then told me when he was due to be paid and where he would meet me, but I knew this was phoney, it was a different day of the week from the last time when I had all this palaver, and once I walked away I instantly regretted it, I would have followed him to see where he went next, but I had to go back to work again.

Upon arriving back, I told my boss that a relative had locked themselves out of the house and I had a spare key while apologising and promising that it wouldn't happen again, but they were not bothered, I was only gone a couple of minutes, and it cost me a fiver for each of them.

John, did, of course, take notes from the place I came from and it had the opening times outside, this is how he began working out my new pattern.

When I went to meet him for the money, he didn't show up, I shrugged my shoulders and couldn't be bothered, I had bigger fish to concentrate on.

What I did believe, was that John and me had this connection, that we were similar up to a point but now I was going in a different direction, the ego I had developed was still growing, seeing him on that day and him letting me down kept my feet feeling like they were on the ground, that I was above him.

As the next few weeks passed, the odd good day kept me going, but on the whole, all I could think about was getting the qualification and leaving, this wasn't for me but I wasn't going to give in, I needed to stick it out.

I didn't know at the time but It wasn't going to be plain sailing, I knew my maturing as an adult had been hindered because years of gambling had effected my social skills and the sobering from a teen to an adult, but how thick-skinned could I be if I was tested? I was soon going to find out.

Part of the NVQ modules was about gaining experience and aptitude at different areas within the Pharmaceutical industry, and I was given a three-month stint at the other branch as I was set to work at the main stores and logistic Pharmacy warehouse, this was a huge building with depots, loading bays and storage units.

Along with me on this venture, the management sent three others, a guy who was around ten years my senior, and two that were much younger, aged 19 and 21.

The warehouse manager was called Benny and he used to give everyone a sharp talking-too about timekeeping and what he expected as soon as they arrived, this didn't go down too well but again, it was about the bigger picture for me.

On my second day at the depot, I was placed in the stores main loading bay, to count stock and help with the deliveries, and as the first lorry came in, I was told to stack boxes onto a wheeled-trolley and take them to the storeroom.

I wasn't happy at doing this job, the last time I worked in a warehouse was at the packaging place when I was younger, where I drove a forklift truck, it was a disaster and when I left, I promised myself I would never do it again, except this time I had to handle things manually instead, without a lifting vehicle.

Soon I was loading eight boxes onto my trolley and could only just see over the top of these when Benny came up to me and insisted that I was wasting time,
"you only have eight boxes, you can fit ten on there," and he soon demonstrated this, but he couldn't see in front of himself as they were stacked too high which I thought was ludicrous, if he had run into someone, he would be liable, I didn't see the point of doing it his way, but he was the boss, as he told me what I needed to do,
"I want to see you do it like this from now on," he said as he walked away.

I did as I was asked but during that first week, I took longer than if I had done it the way I wanted, I had to walk slower as I had no idea what I would bang into, the boxes all fell over at one point, which meant picking them all up again, but on the whole, I felt that I could have made more trips in a quicker time if I had been transporting less.

Benny gave me a few similar tellings-off at a few opportunities that he could but it was something else that shocked me, it was while I was making the trips down the corridor with my stacked-high trolley that I kept noticing something, the two youngsters I mentioned, were always sat at a computer with a small handgun like the ones you see in a supermarket, and they were scanning sheets 'beep beep', then manually entering numbers.

When deliveries had come in, they were imputing the data, but it meant sitting down all day on a computer, as there were thousands of sheets that needed to be input for the whole Pharmacy, which were sent off for analysis.

I went past early morning, midday or late in the afternoon, but the same thing 'beep-beep' from the youngsters, constantly.

I assumed we would swap roles, but after a month I asked Benny how long things would be going on like they are and when we were changing over,
"we are not, you are in the loading bay for the whole time," he said before I replied,
"how am I supposed to learn the whole process doing just one job?" he then upped the attitude,
"it's about evidence and we sign it off if we see fit, but it's more than just your qualification, we are a workplace too, it doesn't revolve around you," as he sounded cock-sure of himself, but I was livid,
"what is evolving around me now?, I am lugging thousands of boxes around at forty-years-old while two twenty-year-olds are sat on their backsides all day, drinking coffee and beep-beeping," he could see I was angry and his attitude changed, "stick with it, we'll get you that NVQ," he said patting me on the shoulder, I was motivated for a few minutes at least until I saw yet another lorry driving up.

Benny wasn't an NVQ assessor, but one was on hand and she took feedback from him and others there and I hadn't exactly done what I set out to do, and that was to keep my head down and get on with things, instead I showed my resentment for the two 'beep-beepers', doing a cushy job while I lugged boxes up and down the corridor all day.

My assessor arranged to meet me, I thought it was to give me a pat on the back for my hard work, instead, it was to advise me that I hadn't done enough to show I understood the stores part of the Pharmacy and couldn't sign me off as a pass, but I could come back for another two weeks at the end of the course and she would take me through it intensely and stay with me.

I was disappointed, I had left work late on a few occasions, sometimes I had been the last in the building and now I had nothing to show for it, but I was in for an even bigger shock, both the young 'beep-beepers' were signed off as a full pass, again I went home angry.

She wanted to make sure I earned the NVQ and knew what I was doing, it wasn't my fault that I had been carrying boxes all the time, but I got the impression she knew it'd been done wrong but couldn't publicly admit it in front of me.

Proof of this was when she stated she would be with me the whole final two weeks; and I wouldn't have to come back to the stores, they would allow me to work at the small outlet at the main Pharmacy, but she tried to motivate me by reminding me that I had not failed, I just hadn't passed yet and I would have the certificate if I stuck to my guns.

I knew deep down that I needed to start accepting my disappointment and see the job through, I could then leave if I wanted, or stranger things could happen, I knew I might get offered somewhere where I liked working, as after the first year it was possible to be in one place, and I wanted to work in the Pharmacy shop on the tills, so if I knuckled down and worked hard the rewards would surely come?

When I left the stores and returned to the dispensary, one of the assistants couldn't wait to take a pop at me, suggestively saying warehouse work was too much for me.

The story that spread around was not my version of what happened, it came across as if I was afraid of hard work and complained because I had to do some. I heard remarks about how I hated grafting and wanted things easy, this was the impression I gave and the one that was on most people's minds.

I wasn't happy at this but I was determined to prove them wrong and win my reputation back, but it was still all about that NVQ and eventually, the truth would come out, that I wasn't afraid of hard work, I didn't like it, but I didn't duck from it either.

With work not going too well, at least things away from the place seemed to be going better for me.

In the work versus professional gambling days when I was younger, this would have made me lean once more towards betting, but I didn't have any confidence in that area anymore, even though I was still visiting an amusement arcade daily for a fix, at the only remaining branch that still did a cash match for £3, I was simply focusing on feeding my need, winning a very tiny amount and walking away for the rest of the day. Sometimes this worked, and sometimes it didn't, but I strongly believed I was working towards eventually quitting the habit for good, even though it was not happening at this time.

I never had much money, my debts were mounting up but the Pharmacy gave me what gambling once had, a dream of a future career, not the one I wanted when I was younger, not as prosperous, but there in front of me and there for the taking, but the whole time I was still learning from every angle, as one night on Holderness road, I had a moment of clarity, as things continued to go wrong for me.

It was time for the double-up and I was eagerly waiting, as was Choc-Ice-John, he had no money as always and I lent him his stake. I never mentioned the tenner he owed me, besides, the way I felt at the time, forgiving him was easy, in a way he was a good distraction from what was happening elsewhere.

The machine I played wouldn't pay, my mood was all over the place as I continued to slot coins into it and in no time at all, I lost twenty-quid over the next half an hour.

John won on his machine, but I began to shift my mood and I not only asked him for my stake back, I wanted his winnings too, even though he only made a couple of quid, but because I had lost, I insisted it was mine, I then played and lost this.

I left with no money and wanted it back, so I peeped in the betting shop window and saw who was working as I was barred, I didn't know them, so I went to the ATM and drew everything out, soon I was playing on the FOBT.

I couldn't win to save my life and I asked John to watch the machine while I went home and got some more money. Upon arriving home, I selfishly emptied my son's money box as he was out with his friends, and I also looked in Sally's purse while she was in another room and took out the only £20 she had and went back to the betting shop, convinced I could still win and pay them both back.

Soon things were going wrong again, and I felt in my pocket and found another ten pounds that I didn't know I had, I placed everything that I had left by putting chips all over the board, saying the words to John,
"I have some good and bad numbers but guaranteed to get something back, whatever I get I will cash it in, some will only win me £3.60 but I will accept the loss, but if red-fourteen comes in I will get £72," John then looked and said,
"you don't have anything on black-thirty-five Chris,"
"oh yeah, I'd have to be unlucky for that to come in John," too late, I had already pressed the button and the ball went around, where did it land?
"no, it can't be, that's impossible, these are rigged," I shouted as black-thirty-five came in.

I cursed and shouted all the way back, then I had to go home and face the music, and as bad as I felt, I was determined to stop gambling at this point, my thoughts seemed clear, as did the realisation.

When the dust settled, I realised that I had looked down my nose at John as if I was better than him when I won the job at the Pharmacy, it seemed a fairy tale the way I got the position.

All I could see was John gambling away his inheritance while I thought I was prospering, but I had a stark reminder that I wasn't better than him, not by one inch, he didn't have kids or anyone at home, he ripped his own family off but so did I, and I'd just stolen from my son, as well as Sally's shopping money.

I knew the negative effect of my compulsive gambling urges, but I couldn't stop, it was stronger than me, but if I couldn't fight for my job at the pharmacy, how could I beat this addiction, which had plagued me for years and was harder to conquer?

John was more honest than me in some ways, he lived the life he wanted whereas I kept mixing things up, bringing misery on myself, he was not only happy to gamble, he embraced it.

The scope I had wasn't great either, with mounting repayments for the debts that I accumulated in the betting shop, how could I think I was better than him? I had little money, this meant my family didn't have the things they deserved, again, why was I more special than John?

I currently had a job I hated, John didn't work so he was the clever one, at least he never change things and knew where he was day to day, year upon year, he wanted to gamble but he knew who he was, at least in that way.

I felt ashamed of myself right across the board, realising that I was lost, but could this low feeling make me stronger, or succumb and accept what I was.

I knew I didn't want to be what I was right now, so this was not an option that I wanted to face, I didn't put the hard work in at the Pharmacy, or anywhere else, I always bailed, but I knew that removing the gambling addiction from my psyche could be the hardest challenge I'd ever had.

There was no room for things to get worse, and it was on my mind at this time more than ever before, and if I could find any degree of abstinence then I was going to try to save John too.

CHAPTER ELEVEN

With four months left until the deadline for gaining my pharmacy qualification, I was doing alright as I had most of the units signed off by my assessor, with the only problems being the time I spent in the warehouse and a hangover effect from what had happened, which left my reputation in tatters.

This sort of situation can build up in any workplace, in this case, it had got to the point where I was working hard while being criticised for being lazy, all because I couldn't keep my mouth shut when things weren't going right, but I was in sight of my goal and that was all that mattered until an opportunity presented itself.

The job that I left to join the Pharmacy was advertised, it transpired that the person who replaced me was leaving to relocate out of town, this was a chance for me to go back to a place where I was happy, but it wasn't that straightforward.

If I already had the qualification that I came to the Pharmacy to achieve, the decision would have been easy, but I didn't have it, in sixteen short weeks though I probably would.

I wasn't guaranteed to pass, nor was I certain to get my old job back but if I was put in this position then it would come down to a straight fight between my heart that wanted to go back to the place I left, or my head that wanted that NVQ certificate, so, in the words of that great band 'The Clash', 'should I stay or should I go?'.

When your unhappy, a week is a long time, and I had sixteen of these staring at me, I couldn't visualise how I could stay for this amount of time, but then I thought of the qualification as I always did when considering options.

Another scenario came into my head, once I had that certificate in my possession, how long would it take me to find alternate employment? and I had the chance to leave standing right in front of me.

After long deliberations, I knew what I wanted to do, and I decided to put my happiness above everything else and made the easy decision to apply for my old job and jump ship if they would take me back again.

It wasn't long before I had filled out my details and submitted the application form online, then it was a matter of waiting.

The next two weeks dragged and because I had made my mind up, working at the pharmacy felt harder with this hanging over me, and after a bad day at work I came home to find a letter on the mat inviting me to attend an interview, this lifted me as now I had hope of getting away from yet another job that didn't suit me.

It was only a few days before I was interviewed, and as nervous as I felt I knew I had to get it right. It wasn't a normal question and answer session as I had to both sell myself and show my regret for leaving in the first place.

Firstly, I explained that I wanted to try things out there and explore potential ambitions, I then admitted that it had been a mistake and an error in judgment and I wanted to come back, once I had said the important stuff it went smoothly. I was offered the job later that day.

I felt very mixed, overjoyed was an understatement, but sad because I had wished this position had come up a few weeks later, so I could have got what I wanted before I left the Pharmacy.

Although I didn't have everything my way, I soon grew happier with my decision, this was cemented later that week when I bumped into one of the 'beep-beepers', who I'd last seen at the stores, I proceeded to tell him that I would be leaving soon and I wouldn't be able to obtain the qualification, his reply then baffled me,

"I was signed off the final unit last week and have already passed mine," I was stunned, to say the least, he had only worked there two weeks longer than me and gained his qualification in a mere eight months.

I had never seen this young lad break into a sweat, never mind lugging boxes about like I did, but he was chatty and friendly and if he was asked to do something, he got on with it and didn't complain as I did.

Personality is an important trait in the workplace and although mine had its highs, it had its lows too and if I was upset, I showed it.

This gave me something to walk away and think about for the future, but for now, I wanted answers for this revelation.

I approached my NVQ assessor and politely asked why the young lad had passed so quick after I was told it took a maximum of a year, she then advised me that you had to pass in the time or you failed, but it could be done quicker if enough promise was shown by an individual.

I wanted to mention how I felt about this and had an urge to state examples of the potential that I too had shown, and occasions where I had used my initiative, and that I was every bit as good at the job as the guy in question, but I didn't, instead I replied,
"good on him, yes he is a real talent and at his age, he soaks knowledge up like a sponge, I'm happy for him," I then walked away knowing I had said the right words, and even though I didn't mean them, I was proud of myself as it said more to me than her, I showed a maturity that I had previously lacked, but above all, I had finally learnt to keep my big trap shut.

It may have been many years too late but as there was no longer a work versus gambling, it was down to me to learn to fit in, and I had to start somewhere.

Even with all this going on, the fact remained that I was leaving, so a part of me didn't care who passed the certificates and who didn't, I was moving on from this and now I could concentrate on my gambling problem.

Despite betting less than I once did I couldn't get the binges out of my mind and the occasions when the cravings got to strong, and this was a problem that scared me, and after the recent blowout where I lost everything of mine and everyone else's in the house, the evening cash-match which I allowed as a fix was another that I wished they would take away. I knew I needed help.

I then looked at what was in front of me and it wasn't a pretty sight, as much as I wanted a fresh start it was going to be hard as my family didn't trust me but how could I expect this when I had this awful addiction.

Even after paying the money back to everyone after my latest binge, it wasn't going to improve things in a hurry, I could see the issues towards me were clear, nobody in the house was impressed with what I did, they loved me, I could feel this but they didn't always like me, I would say that I didn't like myself but I had forgotten who I was to dislike.

I didn't know what was ahead but there were different feelings within me, and each one opened up others, my calmness settled again after the storm and a period once more followed without the full-on gambling, but this made me edgy because I was facing reality, this, in turn, made me anxious, carrying with me a constant fear of what damage I might do when my next binge came along.

My debts were getting harder to pay, my creditors no longer froze the interest, and this meant around £150 was added per month, and this was before charges were slapped on for late payments, or fines that were applied if I went over my limits, which some months added up to an additional £100.

Often all the above meant I often had to fork out £250 of dead money before I could think about reducing the overall debt, my finances were in a bad place again.

Starting back at my old job was a massive help as it always had unlimited overtime, and after a further year had passed which saw me paying extortionate rates to my creditors by working myself into the ground, 2008 came and I was at the end of my tether, so I started the new year with a strong determination that changes were going to happen, and the saying 'it's not how it starts but how it finishes' was going to be my theme of the twelve months ahead, as I tried to figure out what to do.

I was desperate for idea's and the pressure of this alone made it impossible to think straight, I needed to talk to someone who was not judgemental because I couldn't get any kind of plan going, but I ruled out anyone from the family as I didn't want to tell of the extent of my problems or see their mouths open wide when I made more revelations on top of the one's they already knew.

Telling my scenarios to a non-gambler would be difficult too, it was highly likely that they wouldn't relate to the problems that I had, they would question why I created them in the first place, but I had the perfect person on hand, someone who wouldn't judge while at the same time could easily step into my shoes, as I bumped into Choc-Ice-John in the early part of January, and once the opening line of him asking for money was out of the way, I was ready to go.

First I gave him what he asked for despite things being tight for me too, I was glad to see him and fished a tatty fiver out of my pocket, we then walked together for a while, he was the person I needed at that moment, and I hadn't always said that about him.

From his perspective, he was happy with the money, it felt like a lot to him as he had nothing at all, but as far as I was concerned, I was paying for a counselling session, except it was out in the open air, and the leather sofa was replaced with four cheap plastic trainers as we strolled together.

I talked about my debt problems, with real figures and transactions in a way that I couldn't tell anyone else, I had come clean to a degree about my debts with the family but not the amount I owed or the extent of the repayments and interest, but he was the only person who was told everything.

I spoke of my plans to quit gambling for a lengthy period, I even spent some time on the subject of my problems at home and how I wanted to leave Sally because of her mood swings and her ability to never let me forget the wrongs I'd done, I needed a fresh start, as much as I deserved the ridicule, I was no good to anyone if I didn't stop betting, and the bad atmosphere wasn't a help to her or me.

The conversation also helped as I tried to look at the bright side of living in the house and what the alternative would be.

Finally, after what was a decent and unexpected therapy session with John, I changed tact and we reminisced about the good times at the arcades and what we should have done when we had the chance, this led to me asking him if he had signed up for Teddys card-link system and he replied,
"I will never sign up for any card system, I won't ever divulge my details and it doesn't matter what is on offer, I will never, never, never do anything that means I have to carry a plastic card to play," you heard him say that right? and he said 'never' three times, remember this for later.

After we parted, the talking seemed to help me think straight again, and soon after this more ideas came flooding to me like they hadn't before, I now had plans that I needed to put into practice.

The most pressing of my problems were my debts, and I wanted this sorting above all else, and there wasn't exactly a lot of choices on the table, so I reluctantly prepared myself to go back to the Citizens Advice Bureau to begin the procedure of declaring myself bankrupt, as the banks were being merciless with me, there wasn't any other plan that made sense.

The house living situation wasn't something I could do anything about in the short term, this needed to be part of a bigger picture, this wasn't as pressing now.

The biggest problem that I had was gambling, this was the wheel to every other negative thing in my life and I had to quit, and a full stop, no fixes or binges, I needed to find help here, I realised that.

I made an appointment at the CAB office for a week, but the plan changed and I didn't need this in the end, as the next day there was a large poster covering half a page in the paper, advertising the Individual Voluntary Arrangement program, better known as an IVA, the timing could not have been better, just as I was doing something practical about my money problems, this appeared as if by fate.

The IVA was for people with heavy debts that they couldn't manage, and if accepted, offered a single monthly payment for five years and a huge chunk of the outstanding balance written off.

I was never a now person, so I decided to make the call the next day and to spend that evening psyching myself up, I also dug around in the house in an attempt to find any paperwork that I could lay my hands on, payslips, bills, letters, in case they asked me questions, I then made the call.

A polite lady answered the phone, the rest just happened smoothly, they took my details, called me back twice more that day and sent the forms to complete with a list of what they needed.

Within two months, the first IVA payment of £300 left my account, all my cards were then suspended, and I couldn't get anything back from them, but the interest and fines ceased as well.

Although I wasn't happy with the amount I had to pay, I had been hoping to have the extra funds to get the rest of my life back on track, but once the process had begun, it was up and running and I knew I would be debt-free in less than sixty months.

I did, however, feel a large degree of annoyance when I looked at the last few years as a whole, I'd gone to the CAB for help in 2003 and wanted to go down this road then, but was advised to make a flimsy offer to the creditors suggesting a token payment whilst asking them to freeze the interest, why didn't anyone put this option to me then?

It would have been much easier five years prior, especially as the good-times where running, the first couple of years would have been a breeze and I could have pocketed everything I won, rather than use it to pay my debts off as I did, and to make matters worse, had I started back then, I would be completing it now, instead of starting it, the banks could have gotten sixty payments then and I would be debt-free, instead, they were going to get this now, totalling £18,000, but they got all those additional efforts from me too.

I looked for my local GA online but there didn't seem to be the information I sought, it was no longer at the old YPI, but I knew this was an avenue I needed to go down, but as I didn't put in the hard work to find it, I ended up putting it off for the time being and considered it to be something I would do later.

All this planning, as positive as it was, was about my problems, but I wanted to do something selfless, and I had a desire to help Choc-Ice-John, I had only tried to offer him advice up to now, which when you think about it, does any compulsive gambler have the right to lecture another?

I wanted to do something more worthwhile, and while he had helped me to think about my path, my imagination when it came to him was easier, as I was a person on the outside looking in at him.

I didn't see John as a distraction anymore, in the year of changes that included my own mindset, I was attempting to re-invent the wheel and it was hard to look at him and the effect roulette was having on him without wanting to reach out and help him.

I thought of a couple of ideas to get his mind off the FOBTs, both were longshots but worth a try, more of this shortly, but first I had to find him, how would I do this?

It was one of two things with John, if he had money, you couldn't find him if you tried, but if he was skint like he currently was, he would find you, and that's what I was going to do, let him come to me.

The library and the use of the free internet café was a place where he knew I visited regular, so I booked a PC, sat and waited, I knew he would be there, he sussed my routine when he wanted me, except today I was fishing for him.

He didn't let me down as I saw him entering the room, "hello John," I said as he approached my booth,
"How do you fancy going to my first Gamblers Anonymous meeting with me? I'll give you something for your troubles if you come, I don't want to go on my own," this was the first of my two ideas and I would have been naïve if I was surprised at what was coming,
"no thanks Chris, I went there years ago, and there were guys in the room telling me off and still gambling themselves," we know about this as we covered it earlier, but I then tried to be more convincing,
"John that was in the early 80s, G.A is different these days because gambling has changed so much over the years, it's fast, it is everywhere, it's all the time and those FOBTs have upped the ante even more,"
"maybe one day Chris," which to me meant never, but I felt it was worth a shot so no regrets, I didn't even know where the meetings were held anyway, but it would have prompted me to find out had he agreed.

Then he asked me for money, this too was what I was waiting for,
"Chris, can you do me anything, I won't ask again, it's the last time,"
"John I have something to show you and I will make it worth your while, I'll come back to you when you've finished," as he

was about to register his details for the internet, but he then showed he couldn't chance me not coming back,
"I don't need to go on a computer Chris, I only use them to watch films on YouTube when I'm bored," so we left the library together.

This is where my second idea was put into effect and I'll fully reveal my plan, I came up with the notion that he could play roulette for free on a couple of websites that I had found, rather than lose all his money in the betting shop versions, so I led him to the internet café on Spring bank to show him a couple of these, where he could play for virtual money and not his own.

Bet your thinking that you've spotted a plot-hole here and that we had just left the free computers in the library?

That is spot-on, the only difference was that the library PC's had restrictions and firewalls, preventing access to various websites such as gambling, so it was a nonstarter, it had to be the café and soon that is where we were.

The place had around twenty computers but as luck would have it, there was two free, even though they were at the opposite ends of the café.

I set him up by paying for him to have an hour on one of the available PC's and opened up the Ladbrokes website, despite being able to play high stakes games on there, they also had a section where you could do the same for pretend money, and this is what I had brought him here for, to sample this.

I then reached into my inside pocket and took out a sheet of A4 paper and as per the best of Blue Peter, a list I prepared earlier, with other sites neatly written down that offered the same, then came the words I needed to say,
"you have an hour John, and you can play roulette, you could do this for free, have a go and see what you think, this could help give you a distraction from those money-eating versions that they put in the bookies."

I returned to the counter to book myself onto the other computer, thankfully, nobody had come in and sat down to use it while I was showing John or it would have been a dull hour, I wanted him to experiment on his own without me standing over him, telling him what to do, I felt he had more chance of gaining a connection if he didn't have any distractions, just him and free-play roulette.

This was one of the better café's for speed and connection, some of the others were ok, but their computers tended to freeze or crash. I had heard the terms super-fast, fibre, light-stream and broadband many times but I never knew what they meant, but something was used at this place along those lines and it was simple to click an icon on the screen to access reliable internet.

As I considered myself a compulsive gambler to the letter, and the way it was described to me when I first started betting, it all rang true, I never had a car, it was thought punters didn't, so in the modern-day, I evolved to not having a home computer either, and this is more than likely why there isn't a story in here of me sat in my pyjamas with a laptop placed on my knee blowing thousands of pounds without going past the doorstep, I had to get dressed and go to the betting shops to do this instead.

John was sat in the middle of a row of five people, behind him was another set of desks facing the opposite way, on the next row back was where I was sat – looking directly at John's screen from an angle, as I looked at him from the side, I could see he was getting into the free roulette.

This was satisfying, and as it was going the way I intended I went on to do my own thing, I started with the usual stuff, from dating sites to online shopping, I wasn't into social media back then but I did have a couple of friends that I emailed back and forth so it wasn't hard to pass the time.

Looking at John's screen, I could see that he had just lost an imaginary thousand pounds, which was surely better than that day on the east coast when he threw away a larger sum with real money, I was going to pop across and show him how to top his bank up and reset the game again, but he did this himself as I stayed back, impressed with his knowledge of the internet.

A few minutes later, I looked across again, he was still on the roulette site and I began to believe I could reach him, and as the saying goes, 'a thousand-mile walk starts with a single step', but shortly afterwards he closed the game down and I was soon going to learn that the journey I referred to didn't even get to the end of the street.

At first, I didn't take much notice, because as far as I was concerned I had done what I set out to do, remember, I'd also given him the sheet with other sites that offered similar free play, I thought that maybe he was going to look at some of these now.

He removed his glasses to squint at the screen, I didn't read into this as his prescription was over ten years old and he had a history with his eyesight, so maybe he could make words out better without them. I decided with half an hour to go I should concentrate on me not him, and proceeded to look at some holiday websites, as a guy that couldn't even afford to go to the neighbouring town, I don't know why I was teasing myself, but as I looked across at him a few minutes later, I was wishing I was a thousand miles away at the destination that was on my screen, anywhere but that internet cafe at that moment.

John had only searched and clicked onto a hardcore porn video website, and soon he was looking at it the same way that someone in Soho might be watching a peep show. I was stunned.

He was not discreet either, as he enlarged the image so it played on the full screen, the whole café could see this, I was at the other end of the room and I was probably the furthest away and even I could see the site of some woman laid down been gently hit with what looked like my left leg (use your imagination for that one), then there were three bodies on the screen, all stark naked and doing things in positions athletes couldn't get into.

I was amazed that the owner didn't approach him, and I was waiting for someone to tap him on the shoulder and say to him 'do you mind'. I was paranoid because we had walked into the café together, I had been there before and the guy who worked there was beginning to remember me, I didn't want them to know that John was with me.

I was sat in my chair reflecting on my attempts to help John before that evening and realised that even though I hadn't given up on him, and felt I could talk to him as compulsive gambler to compulsive gambler, I was still not seeing what was in front of me, and I don't mean the naked actors on his screen.

Whilst I was determined not to judge him as I once had because when push came to shove, he had a gambling problem just like I did, he had let people down, stole, cheated and lied to get his hands on money, again, snap, but while this was running in my mind, so was reality.

The evidence was in front of me and spoke for itself, us the readers have seen this too, he had lost his family and a cushy job because he didn't want to keep out of the betting shops, all his friends were gamblers, he was the only person that borrowed money from me and that on its own was saying something if you add to this all the times he lined people up for favours while knowing and accepting there was a fall ahead, he had spent his whole life conditioning himself to be a hardcore gambler as well as a hardcore adult entertainment enthusiast.

The maths didn't lie and that was all before this evening in question, where of course I took him to play free roulette and he decided that he would rather watch porn in the hour that I paid for.

So, we know all this, we know my story too, so what's my point? why was I trying to help him?

I saw this as my way of rebelling against gambling, I was still doing it but I felt I was trying to fight the problem, I wasn't succeeding as I now tended to binge because I wasn't cured, I couldn't stop even though I tried because it was stronger than me, but this evening gave me the realism, that John didn't want to stop, I knew this before that evening but felt there may have been a small part of him that did, but I realised there wasn't.

I thought I could get us both away from the addiction, now I had to leave him to what he wanted and go on my fight alone.

This was a moment of clarity for me, I had a few similar occurrences over the years and each one was a learning curve. I knew there were the two co-existing personalities inside me, the addict that took me over and the person I once was before I had that first bet, and these struggled in a tug of war over the direction of my life, at least John had no battle, there was only one person inside him now, the addict, this is the part of him he fed, the old version of him was lost by his choice.

Moments, when realism appears more clearly than others may not cure an addict, and everyone is different, mine was slow lessons and I had them in different places, but I was in the IT café at the time of this one, and my hour was up, and we could finally leave the shop, as John put his glasses back on his head and his jacket around his shoulders, I did the same, only I wanted to put my coat over my head after everyone must have seen what he was watching, they couldn't miss it, at one point there were more people on his screen than Heathrow airport, and I quickly stepped outside, embarrassed because of him.

I didn't mention what had happened, nor did I feel any urge to confront him, I was just relieved that the hour was up. I changed my mind on what would have been my next idea, which was to pay him for taking the time to try the free roulette, instead I took him to the large Tesco's in St. Stephens and told him to get a fiver's worth of shopping, and I would pay for it.

He took his time and it seemed like forever before he came back with his shopping basket, and as always, he bought rubbish, a packet of chocolate biscuits, crisps, a loaf of the most expensive bread and some cuts of the best beef, it came to under a fiver and he asked if he could keep the change.

I reached in my pocket and pulled out another £5 and handed it to him,
"here john, I want you to have this, I don't want it back, unlike you I mean it."

It was easy to understand why Mark was always sarcastic to him, I wasn't that far behind him before John replied,
"thanks, Chris, I really appreciate it," and all the usual pitter-patter, but I stayed quiet.

I processed the whole evening as I went along, from one moment to the next I never knew what I was going to do, like the shopping or the money, spending time with him always confused me and I was thinking about myself more than him but I wanted this charade to unfold, and I still didn't know what was going to happen next or how the evening would end.

We reached Beverley road corner and I asked him what he thought of the free roulette, I appreciated him telling me that it didn't excite him enough, in a weird way I had tried to pretend that it was as good as the real thing but it wasn't, and I knew what he was saying, I had to agree, it was never about the roulette, the free version lacked the thrill, the edginess, the nerves and the relief when the good numbers come, even the despair when the ball landed on the bad ones, it was all part and parcel of the rollercoaster that took the emotions up, down and side to side, shaking them all about and creating an adrenaline rush.

It was not Johns fault and I would have said that I wasted his time, but he did ok on the evening, it was me that was out of pocket and this is what got me thinking as we reached the area where we were due to part.

It was here that I said what I needed,
"I've tried to help you John and it was wrong of me, I am gambling and feel two-faced that I am concentrating on your problem, it's just that you seem full on all the time but I binge, but I have more to lose than you, that's why I fight it."

He was generous in praise for how I had helped him and nobody else had, and how he stuck up for me when other punters had talked about me and some of my behaviours when I lost, but he then reminded me of something,
"Chris you won't remember," (I didn't),
"you once told me that gambling steals a person's identity, it's taken mine," I then replied,
"that is true, it's taken mine as well and I want it back more than ever, but do you ever want to stop gambling?" John then paused for a while before he answered,
"I hope one day that I want to stop," again I appreciated this, underneath everything that happened to him he had been honest, maybe there was hope for us both.

I then reluctantly said what I needed to say,

"you may want to stop one day, mine is here now," I then paused although I knew what was coming, it was hard to find the words,
"I want you to do one thing for me, while I sort myself out, please don't come to me for money anymore, I have given you a small amount to help," he then said a few more nice words to me but I had to further stamp my position,
   "John, I can't be an option anymore, I need to walk away from it, maybe one day we can go for a beer as non-gamblers, I hope you find your place, John."
   My words sounded philosophical, heavy and dramatic, but I still didn't know what was ahead of me despite the clarity.
   So, was this the end of the Choc-Ice-John story? Not a chance, and as we fast forward a few years he did keep seeking me out, albeit a lot less frequent, I'd give him a couple of quid or so, but it was more friendly in that time, but I never allowed him to bung me 'treats', although he wasn't in the position to do this very often, maybe once or twice per year on average, I always answered with the same sarcasm,
"sorry John, I can't afford your interest rates when the gift becomes a loan."
   I left Sally in 2010 and moved in with Natalie, whom I met at work, who I initially thought would give me a reason to address my gambling problem, but a new relationship didn't stop me, it felt like nothing could, and constant arguments with her didn't help either, although again, I mostly gambled in binges, constantly trying to fight my urges, but everything around me made it harder to focus on what I needed to do.
I changed my job twice over a two year period, the first of which was in an office at the hospital, it went well for a while, but ironically, it was during my time here that I met Natalie, nobody in the room liked her, and it slowly went pear-shaped, the question is, was it my fault? in one word, probably.
   2011 was the second time I changed my job, I also left Nat and went to work at another hospital with the intention of re-inventing myself, I wanted to get my reputation back again and everything felt like a step up the ladder towards making the necessary positive changes.

You will have noticed that I didn't address my gambling problem straight away after that occasion on Beverley road corner with John, I may have felt ready then, but it somehow turned into a slow process.

The position I was in because of my compulsive gambling meant everything was at the bottom and I had no control over my life, everyone seemed to own me and scope for changes didn't feel available, and every time I took a step towards removing the negativity from my life, I would then binge as my addiction grew stronger and it reset me back to the beginning again.

I knew I had reached the point where I couldn't continue anymore, my choice to gamble had ruined my life financially, emotionally and with lasting damage that I could never undo, this was more prevalent than ever and it had to be now.

It all happened during a hectic June in 2011, finding salvation in a shared house above a shop was epitome to the changes I needed to make, even with little money and only the clothes on my back I was where I needed to be, rock bottom but ready to climb up as a different person.

Having borrowed the deposit and first month's rent from my Dad, I was in such a bad place that I needed further help and initially had to rely on the help of others while I was turning the corner and could get on my feet

It didn't take long for my pride to start coming back from the moment I moved in, and things felt bad when I had to rely on the help of others while I was turning the corner.

Lisa, my own daughter, fetched me a microwave during the first week living there, and my parents also turned up with a big-backed television from a charity shop one evening.

I knew it would take a few months of being paid without gambling and being resourceful with the money I had before I would feel the benefits financially, I didn't know how low I had sunk until I moved into that new abode, but despite being poverty-stricken, I felt like a rich man as I knew I would do anything to stop myself gambling by taking any help that was out there, I was prepared to beg for it if necessary.

It was on the Friday night of that same week that I walked into the doors of Gamblers anonymous for the first time. Soon

I was attending two meetings per week and the twelve steps program on a Monday night.

I never looked back and lived in that room for twenty months while becoming independent again, during that period I learnt to do the things I had forgotten, such as remembering birthdays, buying everyone nice Christmas presents, all the things that I wanted to be part of the new me.

It also made the payments on my voluntary bankruptcy program – the IVA, much easier, paying one monthly transaction to them, and another to my landlord. With the property being inclusive of all bills, my finances were soon in a much better place, but I had lost much more than just money from all the years I gambled, things I would struggle to get back without the help of time.

Once the focus of keeping clean from my gambling addiction had gathered time and momentum, I was able to build myself up as a person, making realistic plans and going forward, till eventually, I accepted an offer in 2013 for a self-contained ground floor flat in the city centre, three doors away from my parents, with my own kitchen and bathroom, it felt like a luxury to no longer have to get dressed to go to a shared toilet in the middle of the night, the benefits were kicking in, rock bottom was a place I enjoyed because I knew I was going to address my problem, I didn't doubt it, but I didn't want to be in that position again, I wanted to grow and flourish.

You will know what happened to this point if you have read the first book, where I itemised this time with more detail, what you won't know is what happened next, and our friend Mr Choc-Ice-John wasn't finished yet, just as I thought he was calming down in his own way too, he was soon going to remind me that where there is gambling, there is insanity.

CHAPTER TWELVE

I was sat peacefully in the town centre library late one evening during the middle of June 2013, it was almost two years since I had my last bet, and everything had improved in all aspects of my life.

My thinking had been clearer in that time, but it was now that I was further down the track that I could see how everything had timed itself to perfection, even without me trying.

I had recently started a new relationship with Debbie, which began by us chatting on a dating site until we eventually met in person in Leeds on the last Friday in May, and although it was still early days, it felt like another turning point.

You can meet a person that is right for you at the wrong time but not in this case as I had been living clean from gambling for a sustained enough period to offer something better from myself, I couldn't have timed it better if I had tried.

I now felt a new wave of happiness, I was like a seventeen-year-old again for two reasons, this was the age that I had my first bet and part of my life paused that day and resumed when I found abstinence from the addiction, and also because you never forget your first girlfriend or boyfriend, usually at that time of being a teenager, and it felt like that all over again as I found myself thinking about her all day long no matter where I was, soppily put, I was falling in love.

Life seemed to be getting better all the time, my new home plus the romance and many other small things meant I was filling in the gaps in my life and feeling like a complete person again for the first time in nearly three decades.

The IVA was still coming out of my account monthly and at this time it was almost as if I had been paying it forever, but it was due to finally end the following April, so I had the thought 'next year at this time' floating around in my head too as I was looking at something that once looked impossible, being debt-free.

The key to sustaining everything was discipline, and as I continued to surf the world wide web that evening, I was about to be visited by Choc-Ice-John.

No surprise, as already mentioned, he found me from time to time after I had applied the brakes on things, and this was one of the first changes in removing areas that were connected to gambling, or things that made me unhappy and left me in the wrong mindset to apply the measures I needed, but I eventually got there and found the help I needed, it had never got that intense with John again since that day I told him to give me space and walked away, but would things stay this way?

You can tell by the hint I've just given there that something was on the horizon again.

The reason John had kept his distance was down to my actions, not his. I refused every gift or treat that he offered when he won, as much as he kept trying, I simply turned them down, even if I was financially struggling.

I should point out that there was one occasion two years earlier when I took a £40 'treat' from him and instantly regretted it, and when he came back the very next day I gave him it back and added a fiver on top, as I handed £45 to him, and by doing what I did, I prevented him gaining leverage over me, even though I had given him a lot more than he had given me, and of course, I said,
"no thanks," on all other occasions.

He did seem calmer of late, and as he was getting older I believed that he might be ready to take things down a couple of notches, he had been gambling longer than I had and he had done the same thing for years and walked all over Hull for money or meals, but he had stated that he was tired of the whole thing and fed up of constantly trekking for miles each day, he gave me the impression enough was enough.

He wore out so many shoes that sometimes he would ask if I had any spare, before getting to the main point of asking to borrow some money.

Here he was, stood above me as I was staring at my screen, and as our friendship or whatever you call it, was on good terms at that time, I was happier to see him than some previous occasions and it would show.

On some occasions, he would see me tightening my face to show a fed-up look when I caught a glance of him, none of that today, I was foreseeing myself giving him a couple of pounds in the minutes that followed, paired with an excuse that it was all I had, believing the bad times with him were a thing of the past, that neither of us said anything, but we both knew how it was to be.

The past couple of years had been a long line of me dishing out chump change and the odd fiver to him, and I was aware that if I added it all together it would probably come to a hefty amount, and just as I logged out of my session and stood up, I instantly noticed that he was clean-shaven and had a neat haircut, I knew there and then this wasn't the John I was used to of late, especially with what he said next,
"don't worry, I'm not after anything, let's go outside," I was intrigued.

We walked down the two flights of stairs and left through the front entrance, he then attempted to hand me a wad of cash, "here Chris, this is £100 and I want you to have it and I don't want it back, I insist," I was very reluctant and explained that I didn't want all of that nonsense starting up again, and that was the reason I had refused everything he had offered for the last two or three years, but I was curious to know why this time would be any different, but he went on to reassure me in one long speech in which he didn't pause for breath,
"Chris, trust me, you have given me more than I could ever possibly give you, I want to get my act together and I won't ask you for money again, but I want to give you something to say thank you, I genuinely don't want one penny of it back."

This was a difficult one, sometimes you can let someone do something for you and you know they get pleasure from it, I hesitated but finally decided to take it despite a large part of

me didn't want to, but he then showed me the rest of his money and there was at least £1,500 in his pocket, I still didn't know if I was doing the right thing, but I showed my gratitude, "thank you so much, you didn't need to give me anything, honestly," but he wasn't finished and reached in his other pocket and pulled out a voucher for Tesco's,
"I want you to have this too, it has £40 credited on it, you deserve it," I didn't know what to say and tried to refuse this, but he pushed it at me, again saying,
"I bought it for someone else, but I gave them something different in the end, it's going spare, so this is an additional thank you."

   I was speechless, I thanked him some more but I also reiterated my current circumstances, that I was two years in abstinence from gambling, running a new place that is better but costs more, and there was still my IVA payments to make and on top of this, I wasn't cured of gambling but in recovery (this is how ex-addicts tend to think and talk to keep a realism on things) and that I didn't have any desire to be in those circles any more, and above all, I didn't want the grief that came with the problem I was trying to leave behind, so, I asked him one more time to make sure he wasn't going to cross the line because I needed to concentrate on my strict regime of staying away from my addiction, he continued to tell me the same thing, that he wouldn't be coming back at me for money.

   As we parted I again told him of my appreciation but emphasised that I couldn't be a free high-interest rate bank for him any longer, I then reminded him that I had probably given him thousands of pounds over the years, just not in one go, but in bits and pieces,
"I know what you have done for me Chris, I never forget, I feel happy that I can finally give you some of it back, I want to treat you and that's all."

   The last part alarmed me a little, if I had given him a lot more than he had given me, how can it be a treat?

For a moment, I considered giving him the card and the money back, but he seemed sincere, and the word 'treat' was just part of his vocabulary or was I being naïve?

We parted company and I went home, the money was welcome as things were tight, but part of me regretted it, whereas another trusted him.

As I arrived home, I looked around the house and noticed I was in short supply of a few items, so I decided to cement my leap of faith that John was true to his word and spent most of the money, so it was too late now.

I thought about John that evening, he seemed a changed man, but I hoped that his past and painful experiences would have taught him that he was on a good run of results, not a road paved with gold.

It wasn't just the extra outlay of residing in my new abode that made it hard to make ends meet, my recovery was a building process, and whereas two years earlier when I first started this journey, I treated my Mums house like a free café and laundry while I lived in the cheaper shared premises above the shop, every day since then, I took a step to grow myself as a person and now I had reached the stage where I didn't want to depend on anyone any more, now I bought and cooked my own food, washed my own clothes and because I wasn't gambling I could budget to the penny with success, I was going forward and I was living independently, I had come on a long way, so with all this in mind, I regretted taking the money from John immediately after I woke up the next morning when everything seemed clear.

I had used resolve when things were tough up to the previous evening, where I felt I had weakened and took an easy way out, a gift.

Rather than beat myself up, I had to accept that I had momentarily taken a step back, and I knew that I needed to put it down to an error in judgement, a weak moment, but at least I hadn't slipped off my road of two years of betting abstinence, and that was the most positive way I could look at it.

It wasn't only the fact that John had a tendency to take advantage of people if he had any leeway, I took my recovery seriously and while I tried to follow every recommendation in the Gamblers Anonymous books, one part of the advice I didn't, and that was to dis-associate from other gamblers, and here I was accepting gifts from one of them, I wasn't inexperienced, so why wasn't alarm bells ringing?

Again it went back to this empathy and infinity with him as well as curiosity as like I had said before, he was a version of me with a different desire, he is what I could have become or perhaps what I still was, but in recovery.

Maybe my desire to stop was the only thing that separated us, as I had the same intensity and insanity as him when I was in full flow.

I left work the next evening and as I stepped off the bus, I nervously looked at my bike that I'd left locked on the railings in the morning, half expecting to see him stood next to it, but he wasn't, and nor was there any sign of him anywhere else either.

I began to think of every permutation, and the most likely one was that John had a lot of experience of blowing large amounts of money quickly, and he was using the experience to his advantage and easing the ship, taking his time and not going gung-ho and hadn't lost the money straight back.

Of course, it did also spring to my mind that he may still have been on a winning run.

As I rode over the bridge I was beginning to have a new bout of confidence for John, it warmed me thinking of the possibility that he had changed and meant what he said, he sounded sincere, and I was starting to believe him more strongly than ever before.

As I turned onto Spring bank, I jumped off my bike and walked with it a few yards to the pedestrian crossing, and as I looked across to the other side, there he was, stood outside the betting shop, not moving, fixated on the corner of the street waiting for me to turn.

I didn't know how long he had been stood there but at first, it looked like William Hills had arranged to have a statue made of their best customer to display outside their shop, but as I crossed the road he waved me to come to him, I couldn't wait to hear what he had to say,
"Chris, I need some money, my fridge is broken, and I need another,"
"how much money do you want John? you said you wouldn't do this, you promised me,"
"I need about a hundred quid for a second hand one, I am skint Chris," at this point, I was wishing I had left all the money in my pocket so I could have handed it back to him, but I dug deep to see what I had, I then counted up,
"I have £42, John, you can have it, it's all I have, is that ok?" I held it back before I was prepared to give it to him and continued with what I had to say,
"John, if you take this, promise me you won't come back again, this is every penny I have on me," he agreed and I handed it to him, although he wasn't finished,
"Chris, I gave you a voucher, you could give me this back," I had forgotten about this, but I quickly responded,
"you mean the other treat you gave me and didn't want back either, John?" I reached in my pocket and found it but I decided I was going to get something from the deal,
"ok I will give you it back, but you're going to buy me a bottle of wine first," I was going to Leeds to see Debbie the following evening, so this seemed fair.

The voucher was still in my hand and there was a small Tesco shop down Spring bank, I locked my bike and proceeded to walk across the road with him, he didn't speak a word and seemed angry, but why was it aimed at me? what had I done?

He had well over a thousand pounds only a day earlier and it was clear that he had lost it all in the betting shop, and not the first time either so why take it out on me?

As I entered the shop, I quickly strolled up to the booze section and bought a bottle of decent looking Sauvignon blanc for £8 to take to Debbie's house, and I then handed him the card, which was met with a look of disdain from him but I didn't care,

"there you go John, there is £32 left on it and you have bought me a bottle of wine, you should feel good, I hope this concludes things."

It felt good to create a little animosity from my end, especially as he seemed full of it towards me.

The next day was Friday, and the last day of the working week, it was Leeds later for the weekend, as I planned a quick change after work before getting the train.

As my bus arrived at the other hospital, Hull Royal Infirmary, I popped inside to the front office to look at what overtime was available and marked myself down for a couple of shifts. I was only in a few minutes and as I was on my way out, Choc-Ice-John was coming into the building, he had been waiting for me and saw where I went.

What I found to be the most dislikeable aspect about him was this air of confidence that was now with him, he had always asked me for money in a nervously sheepish fashion, now it was as if he was a backstreet money lender coming for his dues as if he had a right to be there,

"Chris, I need some money," I very nearly told him where to go, but I remembered the hundred quid, and so did he, so instead I handed him a fiver,

"John, I am going to Leeds so I can't spare any more,"

"you off to see your girlfriend, Chris?"

"John, she will be my ex-girlfriend if you carry on draining me, I regret taking that money off you."

It was clear that I had made a huge mistake, and it was all my fault, I knew I should have refused at the time and it was

also an error in judgement to believe he had changed, but I didn't want to talk about it anymore so I made the conversation more friendly,
"did you spend the Tesco card on anything good John?"
"I spent it wisely Chris," I then pictured him with a shopping trolly full of crisps, sweets and chocolate with a slice of the best beef on top, I would love to have had the receipt for a chuckle, right now I wasn't laughing, and in a friendly but assertive tone, I said,
"please calm this down John, it can't get like it once was, you do understand that don't you?" he nodded his head as I patted him on the shoulder and smiled.

    He took the money and asked if he could walk back with me. As we continued to talk I couldn't get over the difference in him, in a few days, he had gone from acting like he was beneath me to be superior to me, but what he didn't come across as at any point, was being equal.

    Friday evening in Leeds went well but the wine John was forced to buy us went even better, but it was the Saturday that unexpectedly turned out to be the most memorable part of the weekend.

    Debbie and I went for a walk before venturing to our local, the Eldon pub, it was here that we had a conversation with an elderly Scottish chap.

    Somehow we got on the subject of Loch Ness, which was the top of my bucket list of places to visit, but I thought I would need to drive, and as I hadn't been behind the wheel since my failed days as a haulage and forklift driver, the north of Scotland seemed too far to travel, that was until he told me of a local airport near Inverness and a bus that goes directly to the place itself.

    I didn't know flights there even existed. This was slightly before everyone had apps on their phones and most people still popped in travel agents to book holidays, I hadn't even thought of using the internet to organise a plane journey, but I was now keen to experiment with this, as another addition went on my something-to-do list that I'd devised since I had addressed my gambling problem.

Sunday came and as I boarded the train with a white Americano coffee that I bought from Leeds station; I was soon heading back to Hull.

On the journey I was thinking of both a Scottish holiday and Choc-Ice-John, I had more chance of seeing the monster in the loch than I had of getting rid of this man now and cursed my stupidity at allowing him to get leverage over me, and I knew I had to do something.

I stepped off the platform at Paragon station and dashed through the gate that leads to the entrance and who did I see waiting for me? John was stood there, I was stunned!
"What are you doing here John," was the first words that came out of my head, not a polite 'hello' or any form of a warm greeting, he was stood there with that same aura as if he had a right to keep coming to me,
"I'm skint Chris, got no money Chris," and a round of conversation with him saying my name over and over.

I reached in my pocket and pulled out three-pound coins, "can you make it four-pound, Chris?" again the cheek of the guy, and all this wouldn't be happening if I hadn't accepted his gift, and I was still kicking myself because underneath, take away all the pretending, I knew this would happen.

We walked up to Beverley road corner before we parted ways,
"where are you going John," I said as he usually walked further,
"I'm off to a mates, one I treated when I had money," at least this was him admitting the way he really thinks, this was a new friend called Danny, who he had known a couple of years, more of him in a short while, but for now I was just glad that despite having a lasting friendship with John, and I questioned that word, I never gave him my address or allowed him to know where I lived, so I knew that I might have to change my routine soon.

Monday evening came, I arrived home from work via a different route but when I went out in the evening to the internet café, the door opened shortly after I got there and there he was again, he waited for me to finish, looking flustered, and I walked outside with him, waiting for him to start yet another conversation about money,
"do you have anything spare Chris, I've done my balls in," I replied
"I only have a fiver, John," as I went on to tell him once again that this had to stop, he took this then walked away with the money in his pocket, looking disappointed like it wasn't enough, and didn't hear anything I said as if I still owed him.

The following day he was there waiting for me when I got off the bus, as he was every night that week, I didn't have much to give him each time, but it added up to a fair few quid.

There was a time when weekends were Choc-Ice-John free, and on this occasion, I didn't know how he knew I was working on Saturday morning, but he approached me again while I was on the reception desk,
"John, I am sorry, but you shouldn't really come to me here while I am working," I said,
"Chris I have no money and my gas has run out," I was annoyed but I forked out a couple of pounds and told him I didn't have any more.

This couldn't go on, and after he turned up at Paragon station for the second week running when I returned from Leeds, I felt more than ever that I'd had enough, so I gave him an offer,
"you gave me a ton John, I have added it up and you have had three-quarters back in bits and pieces, tell you what I am going to do, I get paid next Thursday, I will give you forty-quid, on the condition, it's a settlement," he then nodded his head, and like most people that make major statements, when you have said what you want to say, you then think of something else,

"one more thing John, it's final, don't take it if you are ever going to ask me for money again, and don't come till Thursday or this final ever transaction between us won't happen,"
"I appreciate it Chris" was his final answer, but not mine,
"and do not say I appreciate it ever again to me, I'm sick of hearing those words that you don't mean coming from your mouth," this could not have left any doubt what-so-ever that I was at the end of my tether with him.

He stuck to it, and I got a three-day break from his nonsense, but what happened in between? remember the friend I mentioned, Danny?

Danny was the latest in a long line of Johns friends who he had met at the same establishment, the betting shop, where else?

On that occasion a few months earlier, John was winning and handed Danny a tenner over, this is how to make a great first impression, just beware of gifts from this guy, but Danny never knew this.

They became friends and unlike me, Danny invited John round to his house, they even had the odd night out, very odd as they were both gamblers, but it only took one of them to have a good day and treat the other.

When John gave me that generous amount of money, he did the same with Danny, but whereas I was in abstinence from gambling and could control my finances for the first time in years, this friend rarely had a bean to his name, and if he did, he wouldn't leave himself short, so what you haven't got means John can't get his hands on it.

It was the Monday night and another seventy-two hours before he could meet me, so even though most trips where fruitless, he decided to try his luck at Danny's and knocked on his door, soon after there was a noise as the locks and chains were taken off and it opened,
"hi, their John, how are you? I don't have any money spare, I'm sorry," he knew John quite well as you can tell,

"Danny, I was hoping you would have something Danny, but I understand Danny," yet another buddy who heard his name over and over, but realised he couldn't help, but offered something else,
"I am going out at 7:30 John, but I can make you something to eat," it was currently 6.40 pm.
"Great Danny, I also could do with a bath," as he came straight to the point, John had no credit on his gas or electric, but why do you need it when you can use someone else's,
"John, err, ok, but you need to be quick, I must be out in less than forty-five minutes," he said with hesitation in his voice.

While the bath was running Danny made a cheese and pickle sandwich, then noticed that John was taking his time eating it,
"I can't stress enough I don't have time for this John, take the sandwich upstairs with you, I have laid clean towels out."

A half-hour passed, it was 7.20 pm and Danny was getting more agitated by the second, he expected John to be downstairs by now, so he went up the carpeted steps quietly, listening for the noise of movement, perhaps the last of the water going down the sink, instead all he could hear was the sound of gentle splashing, he then raised his voice,
"are you still in that bath John?"
"yeah Danny, I'm relaxing," this didn't go down well, as his next move was to bang on the door,
"get dressed now," and he went downstairs, every couple of minutes shouting a few choice words at the direction of the bathroom door till eventually, after fifteen long minutes, John finally came down,
"John, you have a nerve, what part don't you understand when I said don't be long," but John made clear what he thought,
"Danny, I treated you and all I wanted in return was a bath, and I like to soak and relax, I don't like rushing," Danny was as red as a beetroot and shouted at the top of his voice,
"get out John and don't come back, I mean it, you're an idiot," as he slammed the door loudly as John left.

Upon inspecting the bathroom, John had made himself at home, there were bubbles deep in the bath, he had even reached for Danny's best colognes which was left on the side of the basin and shock horror that John had cleaned his teeth with a toothbrush that was on display, as the evidence was there in the sink.
    To John, Danny owed him, as he had accepted a treat, and now he was tootling on, aiming at the other person he viewed as had taken a gift off him, me, only he had to wait as I had him over a barrel, albeit, only temporarily.
    With time still to go to our meeting, John tried to reach Danny over the next two days, but this was not going to be resolved with a few nice words or a convincing sounding apology that he didn't mean, so with no choice, he waited until Thursday and as I stepped off the bus, there he was, large as life as he stood confidently in the middle of the pavement, but I made my feelings clear,
"hello John, nice to see you, I wondered if you were going to turn up, oh, wait a minute, you're getting money from me, of course, you're going to be here on time."
    Although I wasn't very nice to him, it was more than just words, I wanted him to know how much I resented giving him the money, as I walked to the ATM and withdrew forty-quid,
"I can't afford this John and it's going to leave me short by giving it to you, but before you take it, make sure you know that there's a clause, pocket this and you never come for money again, not any other time, no negotiations, we are over in that way, ok? I mean it,"
"I appreciate it, Chris," I laughed when he said this, and not because I found him funny,
"I can get some credit on my gas and buy some food Chris," he said as if he was expecting me to be happy for him, I didn't care about this and he asked if he could walk back with me, I told him I was in a hurry, as I balanced my two wheels and rode off.

I couldn't believe how much he had a selective memory, in fact, a selective everything! I'd given him hundreds, if not thousands of pounds over the years, then he did what I believed to be a nice gesture, while at the same time conning me into thinking he had changed, and now I was in this plight, handing a chunk of cash to him, but it was myself, and not just him that I was mad at for allowing it to happen by handing control over to him and letting him sneak his way back, dragging me into the insanity I wanted to leave behind and rendition from.

But would this work, as far as I was concerned, it was something I wasn't compromising with, but would he listen to the message I made loud and clear?

The week that followed felt weird as I never saw him at all, I was that used to him hunting me down that it left me with a strange feeling of emptiness as if something was missing as it appeared that he was sticking to our deal.

I nervously stepped off the bus each evening and it was bliss when he wasn't there, I didn't see him early into the following week either, but come the Wednesday, there he was, just as I started to think he was complying with the agreement, and as he had a full beard and scruffy hair, I knew he hadn't won, I wouldn't have taken anything from him even if he had, I was never going to allow him to give me any more 'treats, at any time, I had learnt my lesson.

Although I surmised what was coming I decided to let the man speak,

"I'm not after money, you couldn't do me a bit of shopping could you?"

"not right now John" I replied, but then I compromised,

"I really am in a hurry but if you want to meet me tomorrow,"

"I can meet anywhere Chris," he said,

"ha-ha, I bet you can, John, how about outside Ladbrokes at 1.00 pm, I am leaving early tomorrow," which was the truth, "but John, it's a strict one-off."

We often arranged to meet outside betting shops in the past, even now when I didn't bet anymore, it seemed the only place he could relate too.
    The following day arrived, and he was there before me, I only had my bank card with me as I was in the good practice of not carrying too much cash due to my recovery, and he showed me the contempt I expected as if I was a walking ATM giving away free money,
"How much do I have to spend?" making it sound as if my presence was just about the funds, nothing like 'how are you?', or 'how was work?' I didn't bite and I had said I would help him but stressed that it was a one-off, then I gave him the answer to his question,
"£6 how about that? Maybe £7."
    I knew which end of the scale it would end up at, but I had told him I would help and wanted to keep my promise.
    This could have been viewed as part of my twelve-steps to recovery programme, helping others and telling nobody about it, except I had every intention of keeping the receipt and showing Karl on Saturday afternoon so we could laugh about it, John was always material for our afternoon of drunken bantering.
    I took him to Tesco's and he instantly complained that he preferred Asda for some of his shopping, talk about beggars being choosers, he proceeded to buy several packets of Jaffa-cakes in a multi-pack, a dime bar, a small Madeira cake and a can of Coke, followed lastly with a box of cheap cornflakes and a top of the range bread loaf.
    To me, this once again looked like a waste of money shopping basket for a man who was supposed to be desperate, but I didn't care anymore.
"I have a sweet tooth Chris" as he put the sugary products into the basket, it came to a fiver, which he well knew as he said, "I still have two-quid to spend Chris, is it ok to go to another shop," I thought he had a cheek, but I went along with it, "sure John, whatever," again I was numb to him.

He then marched across town to Whitefriargate and went into a bakery where there was a large queue,
"John, if you think for one second that I am waiting outside while you stand queuing then you can think again, how about a bag of chips? I don't have time to shop all afternoon for you,"
"Chris I don't like savoury; I told you I have a sweet tooth," how could I forget?, I was tired of hearing about it.

He then went into the local paper shop and bought three tubes of Smarties, a pint of blue-top milk and some white chocolate mice, I couldn't believe what I was seeing,
"it's come to slightly more than what I have left to spend Chris," he must have been tired of me having a go at him, I know I was fed up of my own voice saying the same things,
"I knew it would John, and I can't do this too often; you know I have debts don't you? You know I have kids don't you? I don't give them as much as I give you, so I am not doing this anymore."

He tried to be nice to me by offering me one of the mice, but I bought them in the first place so where was the logic? As we parted I reiterated the terms of our deal yet again,
"that was a one-off John, you agreed when you accepted that money, we revert back to our agreement, or you owe me that money back, don't come again," but by now I was wondering if I had crossed the line and allowed him some edge in the psychological 'who owes who' battle.

I went away feeling I had wasted yet another precious hour of my life catering for the needs of a man that doesn't try one iota,

I didn't see him on Friday or the whole weekend, but he was there on Monday as I stepped off the bus, I didn't feel shocked anymore, I felt sick as I saw him, he knew I was trying to be firm but I was as passive in my nature as they come, and he could read me like a book.

He came twice that week, only getting two or three pounds each time but being told that it was just that one time only, but by now it was just empty words to him.

Things stayed like this for a few weeks and repeat the last few lines for each seven-day period until it built up, and a month later it started getting silly.

Three, four, six, five and a half, am I back talking about the lottery again? No, change them into pounds and pence and this is what each night of the last week of July meant, as John waited for me each time as I stepped from my bus, always looking as bold as brass, still sporting the aura as if I owed him.

As the weekend came and went, I spent most of it thinking about what I should do, I concluded that I needed to tell him a lot more firmly to leave me alone, and decided that I wasn't going to give him anything and stand firm, but first I had to say a few things.

I did what I planned and made myself clear, but I had done this before and it ended up being the same as I had said previously, but he was trying to play it down,

"I know Chris, I need to get my act together," and this was the best he could come up with.

He couldn't see the wrong in what he was doing, he was in a permanent state of being controlled by the addiction, even when he wasn't imminently gambling.

I relented that evening and felt guilty after the rant and then reached in my pocket and pulled out a five-pound note and said,

"this is the very, very, very last time John, don't come again," then like a broken record, I reminded him what we had agreed for the umpteenth time.

I didn't expect to see him again for a few days, but he was there the next night too, although I flung a quid at him in anger and biked off, that didn't stop him either, every night it was the same, with the opening line usually starting with,

"I won't bother you again Chris," only he did.

It's odd how you get used to things, I stopped getting angry as I got used to the cheek of him, I think a part of me was still looking at him as a case-study or like one of the box sets I used to watch where you just play 'one more', I don't know why as he never changed but the insanity of gambling was very powerful with him, like the Force in Star Wars, and he had so much of it, he was the equivalent of a Jedi Master, but, unfortunately for me, a permanently skint one.

Although he was the only gambler I associated with on the level, I did know others and bumped into them, some of them would tell me they had seen John winning, or walked past him while he had huge amounts in the cash-bank on display, but it was obvious he wasn't going to top his bank of me up any more, yet I still saw him daily, even at the weekends, at the internet cafes, the gym, he even walked into a pub on a Saturday night while I was being served, I still to this day don't know how he figured that one out, was he following me? On that occasion he didn't want a drink when I offered, he wanted money.

I decided to put the amount down I was giving him and plead poverty, but that wasn't the answer long term.

John felt like he had me over a barrel, but I didn't owe him a penny it was just that psychological scale swinging to him because his transactions towards me were larger, whereas mine was smaller but a lot more of them, in his way of doing the maths, the sums didn't add up my way.

I was at the end of my tether with him, but if I could have had my fortune told correctly, it would have revealed something to me that I couldn't have known at the time, the next two weeks were going to see the gambling-insanity bar raised in one of his mad periods where I was going to be embroiled, and he was going to go too far, and push me to the stage where I was finally going to tell him where to go, but that was in 14-days from the point we are currently at in the story, let's start at day one of this new cycle.

Almost two months had passed since I tried to end my associations with him, but I was staring at a brand-new week, and for the first time in a while, I had gone two days without seeing him, I had been away for most of the weekend, but this

Monday began when I generously gave him £3 instead of the usual one or two coins,
"you can't make it £4 can you Chris," he cheekily said before I let loose,
"you are after the last two days lost earnings, aren't you? you really are worse than a loan shark, "your interest rates are ludicrous," I was angry, now it was time for the assertiveness I had previously tried,
"let's get one thing straight John, this is all stopping, full stop, and make no mistake about that as I am warning you, get your act together because I am not going to be there as a cash cow for you when you are skint,"
I then peddled away on my bike in disgust.

   Tuesday was different, he asked me if I had a spare pair of shoes, I couldn't believe he wasn't asking for money. I thought about this and had just the thing,
"ok John, we can walk so far but there is a reason I don't show you where I live, so I will have to bike on in front," in other words I didn't trust him to hang around on my street corner if he knew where it was, we chatted a bit before I got ready to set off as I arranged to meet him outside the Ringside pub on Beverley road, for a change I wasn't meeting him outside a betting shop, but as I was about to leave, he said,
"I couldn't be cheeky and ask for a pair of socks too? my shoes have been letting water in," I laughed and shook my head in disbelief.

   Half an hour later I met him armed with a pair of brown shoes, and I explained as I pointed at these,
"John, these pair were sent by my brother, they are top of the range Ian Boden shoes and they retail at £100, I wore them for 6 months, but I have washed them, great for someone who walks all over Hull as you do."

   I then handed him a pair of socks that had Homer Simpson eating a doughnut on each one, and I must have been naïve thinking that was it, but it wasn't,

"Chris, you couldn't do me a couple of quid, could you? I need some milk,"
"John, Money, shoes, socks, when is it going to end," but I handed him a two-pound coin and rode off, mistakenly towards my street, feeling I should have gone around the block to throw him off any scent, but thinking that at least he didn't know exactly where or which house.

I arrived home wondering what possessed me to give him my Ian Boden shoes, Jeff had got them from a guy in Australia for a present but they didn't fit him, they were tough, durable and if world-war-three broke out and everything blew up, the only thing left would be these shoes, yet another thing that happens when you cross Choc-Ice-John with an idiot like me.

Two days later he was there again as I stepped off the bus and he was looking at me but seemed cocky with it, again I refer to the psychology of the fact he gave me £100 in a single go, he was still living off it and you could tell,
"bet you're not here to give me a Christmas card are you John?" he certainly wasn't,
"I'm looking at myself Chris and I am going to get myself sorted out, don't suppose you could do me anything."

I reached in my pocket and pulled out yet another two-pound, I then noticed he wasn't wearing the shoes I gave him, and I asked him about this,
"they were too big Chris, so I gave them to the charity shop," I was fuming,
"what do you mean John? I would have taken them back, they were Ian Boden shoes not a pair of tenner trainers from Primark, I just tried to do a good turn, don't know why I bother," it was almost as if he did it on purpose, but I gave him the money,
"here, don't come again", I said as we parted ways.

I was tired of the guy and I was going to say no the next time he came and I was going to stick to it, but it was as if he knew, I am not sure if he was telepathic when you see what happens next, but it was part of this crazy two week period I referred to

and it was about to get madder, and as I left work on Friday, he approached me, nothing new there, I rolled my eyes, again same as usual, no different, but then, as I was determined to refuse him any more cash, he said,
"Chris, I am not after money, I need a big favour and I will leave you alone after this," at first I replied,
"hope you're not after shoes after you gave away my Ian Boden ones," but I then listened as I was very curious, this I needed to hear,
"Chris, I owe this guy some money and he is heavy,"
"John, what are you talking about and what do you mean by heavy? overweight? I don't understand," but he further explained,
"I need to meet you and you play-act, I come up to you and give you a package and you walk away with it, and meet me around the corner and give me it back," this was certainly different.

John never seemed into anything dodgy, I knew he lied, cheated, even stole but not the type of thing this suggested, he was a gambler and that's it, so I initially agreed.

The following day he tracked me down at work and I asked him for more details, he wanted me to meet him outside the Hull Daily Mail office on Beverley road corner, and there would be a guy across the road sat in a car watching, presumably someone he owed money too, and he wanted me to pretend I was someone hard and not to be messed with, and I was to take the parcel off him in full view of this other person, and then meet him somewhere later.

I did not know what he had gotten himself into but I didn't want to get involved, I could have ended up running down Beverley road with some mafia hitman chasing after me, or something worse, whatever he was up to he was a liar and if he had got himself into trouble then I was not going to put myself at risk when I didn't know what he was up too, even if he told me the truth I wouldn't believe him, there was no way I was going to pretend to be someone from the mob.

After I told him politely that I couldn't do this for him, he said it was ok and he understood, as we parted.

I never knew what he was up too and never found out, it may have been an empty envelope and a show because he owed someone money, but I wasn't taking any chances, besides if he had a fat parcel full of cash, why did he keep harassing me?

He was there waiting for me the next two evenings after work, again asking if I could spare something, but that changed when on Wednesday night, I was going to my friend's house after work till late, and I didn't tell John.

I caught the bus back at 9.45 pm, it was a quarter of an hour later before I got off at my usual stop, I then walked towards my bike, it was cold and windy, but as I got nearer I saw in the background a familiar shape, and as the silhouette got nearer, I saw that it was John, even late at night I couldn't escape him, as he was waiting for me!

I knew it had already gone beyond the stupid stage, but this was turning into a pantomime,
"I've been visiting someone in the hospital, Chris," he said, I threw £3 at him and as he was picking it up I shouted,
"I don't believe you, John, I only ever tried to help you, because I saw me in you, at this moment you feel like my stalker, leave me alone and don't come again, this is freaking me out."

The following evening, I left work to make the journey home and found the bus at the stop that I usually wait for and got straight on it. Soon I looked at the time and it seemed to be travelling quicker, and it wasn't stopping at scheduled parts of the ride, it was then I realised it was the previous one which had been due twenty minutes earlier that was running behind, and as I eventually got to my destination, I saw John heading down Anlaby road, I got there before him, the driver must have thought I was keen to get home as I ran off the bus, shot towards my bike and peddled over the bridge and out of sight before he got there, he missed me and I felt like punching the air in delight.

This brought to the forefront of my mind the idea that I had contemplated, to drop all my fascination with the guy, I mean, he was interesting, especially as the 'envelope' story was still in my head and made me chuckle, and it would be dull without him but I made the decision that I was going to change my route home, and avoid him, not go to town, lock my bike in different places, anything that would make him think I had disappeared, and then he could go and menace someone else.

Looking on the situation, it was my fault for allowing it to get out of hand, I should have been firm with him instead of needing to know what happens to him next, nothing good because he was a gambling addict and his story was the same as mine, but it was one that I was trying to leave in my past, and it was time to put the whole thing to rest.

I dug out my bicycle pump the next morning and blew my tires hard, I was going to bike to work and stop getting the bus, avoid all my usual haunts and I was determined John wasn't going to find me, I was going to keep out of his way and break my routines and tell-tale signs, and at the end of my five-mile bike ride back home that evening, it felt like a weight was lifted off my shoulder, a huge sense of relief, could I avoid him for six months? I was going to try.

Sitting at home that evening, relaxing, thinking of John missing me the previous evening and no signs of my activities on this day either, I knew that at this moment he was likely to be scouring the city centre, my gym, the places I shop, the library and internet cafes, I wasn't at any of them, I was at home smiling at the thought of him hitting dead end after dead end.

If this didn't teach him a lesson then I doubted that anything would, I didn't want to be vindictive and part of me felt bad, but he had gone too far, if he had come once or twice a week I would have most likely had a much longer tolerance, so it was his fault for taking too much advantage of a good situation, he needed to look up the word sustainability in the dictionary.

I thought about how lucky I was, not just because I felt I had taken measures to stop John, I was heading for a thousand days without gambling, and having my parents down the road was always a good thing, if I left anything at their house they would pop it round, sometimes they would come to tell me it was the bin collections the next day and remind me to leave it out before I set off for work, so when I heard a quiet 'knock-knock', it sounded like my Dad was at the door and I wondered what I had forgotten, I walked down the passageway, still in appreciation for the place I finally had, and I opened the front door, to my amazement, it was Choc-Ice-John stood there!

I opened my mouth, but the words didn't come out, which would have been to ask what he was doing here, but he always had plenty to say and spoke first,
"I was speaking to someone up the road and they told me you lived around here Chris," this was bad enough, till I found out how he discovered which flat I lived in,
"I knocked on all the doors as I didn't know which one to come to," I was appalled, there was a reason I never gave him my address, and now he had humiliated me by bothering my neighbours.

I took a few more seconds of silence to get over the shock and it felt like minutes before I finally spoke, I reached in my pocket and slung all the loose change firmly onto the floor and literally had a meltdown in front of him,
"I bet that cash your picking up isn't enough, you're going to ask me for another quid, quid, quid, quid! aren't you," I was ranting and I did say that word four times, each one getting louder and just as he said,
"no, I'm," I interrupted,
"you had something unique John, you were asking a mug for money who spent week after week asking you to stop, but that was out there and it actually felt like I had some control, you

coming here changes that, this really is it for you, John, now go away and I am through with you."

I was now going to cut all ties with this situation, and I went back into my flat and I was furious, I didn't expect to see him again, but he turned up at work the next night, but my attitude was different to what it was before he violated my trust by coming to my flat door, he didn't know what the word 'no' meant and felt he was invincible, and went far beyond what was acceptable behaviour, and as he began trying to manipulate me, I wasn't letting him apologise, although he started,
"Chris I am sorry I shouldn't have," I jumped straight in with, "damned right you shouldn't have John, but you did," and soon when he tried to talk once more I interrupted him again,
"you coming to my front door is a gamechanger, you have stopped everything because that was going too far and from now on that is it," I then reached into my pocket and got out 40p,
"there you go and don't you dare ask for any more, those days have gone thanks to you coming to my flat, and you won't wear me down because it really has changed things, I don't want to see you here next week or any other week, I will refuse you, soft as I have been I am hard now, thanks to you."

I climbed on my bike and rode off and left him, I knew I should have done this week's earlier, in fact, I will say once again whose fault it was, mine for taking the £100 the day he offered it, it cost me an arm and a leg but something inside me felt good at this moment that I had got shut of him, although I was not confident about this.

He didn't show up the next week, but he paid me the odd visit, I still gave him an odd couple of pounds, but it was less frequent, each time I would say to him,
"don't come again this week," and he did what I said.

He was corrupted with gambling and couldn't see the wood for the trees, this led to him milking any situation for all it was worth until he went too far and the two knocks on my door turned out to be music in my ears after this result.

This takes us to the end of 2013, a year that I was touched by the insanity of gambling when I didn't even have a single bet myself.

When your gambling you don't care of others, he knew what I was going through, he was zombified from the addiction and would do anything to get money, but as they say, give someone enough rope and they will hang themselves, and that's what he did.

Things never got back to what they were, he had never seen me react as I did and over the next few years it remained the way I wanted it, he never offered me any cash gifts again, I never gave him money on a daily basis, just now and again if I felt sorry for him.

My debts were paid in full in the middle of 2014 and I booked a weekend in Loch Ness for Debbie and me to celebrate, remembering the conversation at 'The Eldon' that afternoon

Upon arriving and checking into a lovely hotel called the Lovat inn, we was out that same evening for a purpose, as we had a glass of wine to toast my debt freedom in a nice and friendly little bar called 'the Lock-Inn' that was situated close to the edge of the grade-A water, wondering if they had missed a trick with the spelling of the pub name set on the shores of 'Loch Ness'.

So now we are going to find out what happened to some of the characters we met on this journey, as well as fast-forwarding to the time after the first book to the present day and update a few statuses, and although you have witnessed the Choc-Ice-John story, let's not be too hard on him, remember, it is a mental affliction, and I knew this all too well, as I had been there too, this made me attempt to reach him, and although I failed, I knew that I should have known better, as, for many years, no one could help me either.

CHAPTER THIRTEEN

Before we find out the fate of some of the characters that we have met on this journey, there is a non-living but very prominent influence that itself needs a mention, and that is the fixed-odds-betting-terminals.

With a lot of bad press due to growing debts because of problem gambling since these machines were first introduced into the high street betting shops, while at the same time, the bookmaking industry was thriving as a result, clearing record profits year upon year, mounting pressure was put on the government.

The first steps were posters and adverts intending to warn of the perils of gambling what you can't afford to lose, with the 'stop' and 'stay in control' campaign set up.

In 2017 the bookies were forced to cap the amount the punter could bet on the FOBTs at any given time on a single spin.

This was reduced to a new maximum spin of £50 from the original £100, but with the same ratio of a new number coming in every twenty seconds at full pelt, some believed it didn't go far enough, while others felt that it was a move in the right direction.

Upon researching this, I was alarmed to discover that the limit hadn't been put down for everyone, it was instead meant to help the shops supervise and spot anyone that had a problem, but if they saw fit, the punter was then allowed to bet at the maximum stake of a hundred quid.

Anyone wanting to do this had two options, they could ask the clerk behind the betting shop counter to load this from a remote computer that was situated there and take off the cap, or better still, they could sign up for a card that slots into the machine and simply select to up the limit to the original amount.

A point of interest here, do you remember a while ago when I asked you to earmark the part where Choc-Ice-John was insistent that he would never sign up to any card system or 'anything' that involved giving his name and details? he once even said the words,

"never, never, never" when I asked him about this.

You could even skim back a few more pages and you will see him saying other strong words to this effect, creating the persona that he was a man of principle, you know what I am about to say don't you?

When I asked him about this, you can imagine my surprise when he pulled out a plastic card with his name printed on it, which allowed him to play to the full stake.

It was even more baffling when I asked him how he applied for the card, he replied,

"I opened an email address and took in some identification."

So much for the guy that hates this type of thing, certainly, when we first met him that day on Beverly road, it was now a sure thing that his first love of horse racing was a thing of the past.

Later in 2019, the government took a much firmer stance as problem gambling continued to hit an all-time high, and a change in the law saw the maximum spin allowed at any one time on all games reduced to £2.

This was a hefty drop but too little too late for many punters who had lost homes, relationships, and in some cases, even their lives, sadly.

Despite the new programs being speeded up to cut the time and gap between spins, many betting firms, and William Hills, in particular, closed thousands of their shops around the country, some of which had been there long before the days of machines in the high street bookmakers.

Now bringing us up to 2020, and as promised, the rest of the personalities that I would like to thank for contributing to the story.

Although I worked for Boss John's haulage company for less than a day and a half, he made a lasting impression, I never found out what happened after his yard closed, but a few years later, a sports car, matching the description of the one he owned, same make, the same colour, speeded up while I was crossing a junction on Holderness road as if it was trying to hit me, and it nearly did, I wondered if it was him? Probably not but I had my doubts.

He lost a contract because of me, despite this, the business lasted a year longer, so it couldn't have been my fault that it closed, could it?

Just across the road, John the Barbers became 'Josies haircuts', she still had the spikey blonde hair and dressed to impress, and I'm sure a new batch of lads with jumping hormones replaced her old fans.

Sometimes you can meet old acquaintances when its least expected as in the case when I played pool for Newbridge club on Thursday nights, I'd been in the same team for a few years, and it was during a home fixture in 2004 that this happened.

Our captain, Tom, was a computer programmer who earned megabucks, but he was down to Earth enough to show that he hadn't been brought up with a silver spoon in his mouth.

It was the evening that he brought his Mum and Dad along to play the link-up bingo that I met a blast from the past, his father was JB, the fork-lift driving instructor.

I was shocked at first, but upon talking to him I realised that he didn't remember me, and I didn't approach the subject.

JB looked more subdued and less outspoken but he didn't look a day older, sporting the same greased-back wet-look hair and lopsided grin.

I never told Tom that I'd previously met his Dad, but I was curious what his views were, having been brought up in the same house as a guy who had extreme opinions, hopefully, he had changed in that time.

Tony, the packaging director who employed me as a fork-lift operative, and gave me the break I was looking for after I passed my test under JB, hadn't changed that much when I saw him again five years later, leaving work that day, still dressed immaculate, opening the car door so his wife could get in before him, as much as the place was an awful experience, he remained a real gent with old fashioned values, so it's hard to say anything bad about him despite everything, so I will have to pick on his son Richard instead.

I remembered him vividly for not being able to pronounce the letter 'R' and saying stuff such as "Chwis, you need to wotate the twuck better", he seemed good at what he did although albeit privileged with money and nepotism.

I found out what happened next without trying, by a fluke, it was while speaking to a friend, again while out playing pool, who was talking about his neighbour, when he was described, I knew it was Richard, the same name, couldn't pronounce his R's, had been the sales director at a family business that employed around fifty staff, it had to be him.

I could only use what I was told to fill in the gaps though, he lived on Sutton Park which is a nice estate, but my friend resided in an area where a rich person wouldn't live, had he fallen on hard times?

The business had gone years ago, but unlike Boss-Johns firm, I knew this one wasn't my fault; besides I couldn't imagine Richard or Tony speeding up to hit me from behind the wheel of their posh cars.

I assumed that the business had re-located because it seemed to prosper, but with Richards current situation, it did make me speculate.

Did his father retire to leave Richard in charge, who somehow flushed the business down the toilet?

With an astute guide and mentor like Tony teaching him his trade, it would be hard to imagine this happening.

In another interesting twist, Richard was happily married to a lady from Russia, could she have been a mail-order bride? It did happen back in those days, now you just meet on Tinder for free.

Brian the Alchemist had another adventure because of gambling when he was suspended from his job driving for the pharmaceutical company, not knowing they could track where he was during his working hours, which saw him stuck outside a betting shop for hours on end when he should have been on the road.

Despite the inconvenience, there was a happy ending, upon appeal he won his job back and no long-term damage was done but it's hard to say whether he was a wiser person after the event, as when in the grip of the addiction, does anyone really learn?

Harry the placepot man died a few years ago, he bet for fun but was as likeable as they come. I never wanted to gamble the way he did, but I would have no objections in becoming like him as a person, rest in peace Harry, a true inspiration.

Ron, who worked with my Dad for years, continued to gamble for the rest of his life and sadly died a few years later after developing Parkinson's disease, he did everything the way he wanted right to the end, as he drank a few pints, had a few bets and smoked like a chimney. A quality member of the insanity of gambling club.

The beep-beepers from the Pharmacy both had a similar end to their stories as they relocated in their individual ways, the young lady split with her boyfriend and moved back to London, where she originally came from, whereas the lad did the complete opposite and met a nice young lady from Sweden while on holiday and is now living out there.

Unfortunately, because everything here is based on true events, there are those who I haven't been able to track down, at least with fiction you can invent the closing scene, although if this finished with Choc-Ice-John and me doing a Thelma and Louise ending over a cliff, surrounded by angry bookies, it might be considered a stretch too far with the imagination.

Plus, when you think of the years and effort that it took me to obtain my car licence, I may have needed several more chapters to update the latest on my many driving instructors.

Again, a big thank you to Choc-Ice-John, who sportingly allowed me to write his story, we met up in the Station pub on Beverley road on two occasions, both times my pen was going at a fast pace in my A4 sized notepad while he was jabbering away, in many ways this was probably the first time he had ever spoken about his gambling to this degree and was honest about the effects on his family and where he could have been if he hadn't had that first bet.

In G.A meetings we call this a therapy, it usually helps the compulsive gambler in the same way a counselling session would aid another, everyone's recovery is different but getting it out there can create clarity and realisation, a problem shared is a problem halved, or so they say.

I may have caught a glimpse of the real John while we were doing this project, and this was possibly the person that he would have been without gambling as I couldn't help but notice the difference that I saw in him in the relaxed capacity of the pub, but it was hard listening to his tale, it filled in many gaps and some of it was heart-wrenching, it was like looking in the mirror and even with some of the more selfish actions, I could not judge because I existed in the same void and mindset for many years.

When we left the pub I thought the story was complete and I was ready to tell it, there couldn't possibly be any more?

But, being the legend that he is, he didn't step completely away from the stage and continuing the insanity of gambling theme, there was another twist as he was about to give us an encore.

Two months later, our paths met up again, John explained that since he had last seen me, he had an opportunity and a spur of the moment decision to make, this happened while he was in the William Hill branch on Hessle road.

The incident occurred around lunchtime, which saw him doing what he always did when he had no money, watching punters play on the FOBT, and one smartly dressed chap was playing roulette and doing quite well.

John often knew a few regulars in the shops, but there were none in on this day and he didn't know the guy who he was currently observing.

The guy was playing avidly and enjoying a run of success which was becoming familiar, with the sound of the ball spinning before jumping and cluttering onto some decent numbers, followed by the bank topping up, which was like music to the man's ears, but a different noise was to be heard as Bruno Mars and uptown funk came bellowing from somewhere, it was the man's mobile phone ringing, he reached into his pocket and saw that it was a call he needed to take.

He couldn't hear properly, and it was a private matter, of which he didn't want ear droppers, he then walked outside the shop and onto the main road.

John partially followed him to see what he was doing, the shop didn't have a lot of punters, and most were set about their business, John may have been watching the guy but he was the only one that was, he then looked outside again, weighed up the situation and analysed activities behind the counter to see if the staff were observing him, but as someone came in from lunch and another sat out, it was almost as if the moons and planets were aligning for him, forcing him to spot an opportunity.

John impulsively approached the machine, and looked across and saw that the guy was still pacing around in conversation outside with his jaw going up and down ten to the dozen, he looked at the top right-hand corner of the machine and saw £244 of credit, and without any further thought, he pressed the collect button, the ticket came out and he went to the counter and handed it to the clerk, still looking through the glass door window from where he was stood, the guy was nowhere to be seen.

He was nervous in case the man came back into the shop and it would have been game over,

The Cashier then counted the money out to herself in front of John and would then normally get her colleague to re-count it, but as she was on her own, she proceeded to make sure John could see the amounts as she slowly put each note on top of another,
"twenty, forty, sixty, eighty," until she had a pile of twelve, all twenty-pound notes, she then reached for four - £1 coins, and these were going to come in handy,
"£244 sir," said the cashier,
"thank you Luv," replied John as he then crammed the money into his pocket, followed by a 180-degree turn and the quickening of his steps to leave the shop, in a state of relief.

The guy was still talking but looked like he was going to be finishing soon, and from him leaving the shop to take the call and John coming out with the man's money all happened in the space of around two-minutes, it felt like longer though.

Hessle road is like a concrete maze, lots of passageways and side streets, easy to lose someone if they chase you, and this was on Johns mind as he thought of what to do next, but another stroke of luck, a bus had just pulled up outside with a single elderly lady stepping on, he was straight on it behind her and paid the fare to town, which was £2, I told you those coins would come in handy.

As the bus left, John looked out of the window, the man was pressing the button on his phone to end the call and moved to walk back into the shop, by the time he reached the terminal and realised what had happened, John was well away and heading towards town.

The man's face, when he walked back to the machine and saw his credit had gone would have been a picture, you could criticise him for walking out and leaving the money on display, why didn't he simply press collect and put the ticket in his pocket?

All the same, John stole this money from him, and I am sure the man thought the ticket would be waiting for him behind the counter, that some honest guy or even a member of staff would have acted and collected it for him, he was in for a surprise.

With CCTV and every other person knowing who John was, it wasn't long before the staff worked out exactly what had happened, did the guy get reimbursed by William Hills? your guess is as good as mine.

John had no way to find out and tell me, that is the trouble with true stories, plot-holes, I would love to know what happened though.

Back on the bus, John got off just before the last stop and ventured to a branch of Ladbrokes, still shaking and delighted at the same time, and happy that he had some money, the numb feeling of being in the zone meant he acted on impulse with less than normal regard to what he had just done, which was theft.

So, from having nothing, Choc-Ice-John had some money in his pocket, what did he do with it? he lost the lot, playing the same game the other guy was actively participating in – roulette!

John was struggling prior to receiving that money, hardly any gas or electric credit, and hardly any groceries' in the house, he was on the bare bones of his backside and desperate people do desperate things, but this wasn't even a lifeline to John, he saw it as money to bet with.

The next day (and I have done some stupid things in my time but even I would have thought twice about doing this), John walked into another branch of William Hills, what did he seriously expect?

Straight away the manager came up to John and explained to him that his photo had been sent to every branch of William Hills in the country, he was banned from every shop that bared their logo.

It was also a lifetime exclusion, at no time would he ever be allowed in any of their premises again and was asked to leave.

Although the other shops such as Ladbrokes knew of this, they didn't join the solidarity and he could still bet there.

That is the Choc-Ice-John story up to date, although I am sure more events will follow until he decides he has had enough, and he has kept 'the insanity of gambling' true to the title, compared to me in many of the details, but a man that didn't want to stop and is still betting every opportunity he gets to this day, and with forty-five years on the clock and counting since he first walked into a bookies, it doesn't seem like ending anytime soon.

Although we have had a laugh or two along the way, the seriousness is that this guy has under-achieved, maybe he was happy in his own way and never had any aspirations apart from gambling, which he obviously loves, even though it comes at a cost of more than just money.

Could the real reason William Hills closed thousands of their branches be because Choc-Ice-John is now banned from their shops, causing their profits to nose-dive?

Joking aside, the machines, even with their reduced limits can still do a substantial amount of damage to the compulsive gambler, and with faster games and more addictive software's being developed, it's still a long way from the old high street bookies that once only catered for horse racing enthusiasts, and that's before we even mention that gambling advertising is still allowed everywhere, the problems are still going on and the betting industry may appear to have taken a knock from their point of view, but they are neither down nor out and expect them to be back with a vengeance.

I've mentioned about how the gambler can become two people as they lose the person they once were and become someone else much worse, and families see their loved ones become liars, cheats and thieves acting on selfish impulses to feed the addiction.

This is a poem that I came across, it was almost as if it found me.

One evening an old Cherokee told his grandson
about a battle that goes on inside people.
He said, "My son, the battle is between
two "wolves" inside us all.
One is Evil.
It is anger, envy, jealousy, sorrow, regret, greed,
arrogance, self-pity, guilt, resentment, inferiority, lies,
false pride, superiority, and ego.
The other is Good.
It is joy, peace, love, hope, serenity, humility, kindness,
benevolence, empathy, generosity, truth, compassion and
faith."
The grandson thought about it for a minute
and then asked his grandfather:
"Which wolf wins?"
The old Cherokee simply replied,
"The one you feed."

Printed in Great Britain
by Amazon